Geometry
A Reference Guide

Book Staff and Contributors

Eric Reini   *Content Specialist*

Jill Tunick   *Senior Text Editor*

Kay McCarthy   *Text Editor*

Suzanne Montazer   *Creative Director, Print and ePublishing*

Stephanie Shaw Williams   *Senior Print Visual Designer, Cover Designer*

Julie Jankowski   *Senior Print Visual Designer*

Meredith Condit, Steve Mawyer   *Media Editors*

Susan Raley   *Senior Manager, Writers and Editors*

Dana Flack, Abhilasha Parakh   *Senior Project Managers*

Paul Thomas   *Senior Director, Content and Assessment*

Kelly Engel   *Director, Mathematics Content Specialists*

Michelle Kitt   *Director, Instructional Design*

Jason Golomb   *Senior Director, Program Management Product Development*

Christopher Frescholtz   *Senior Director, Program Management*

Lisa Dimaio Iekel   *Director, Print Production and Manufacturing*

About K12 Inc.

K12 Inc. (NYSE: LRN) drives innovation and advances the quality of education by delivering state-of-the-art digital learning platforms and technology to students and school districts around the world. K12 is a company of educators offering its online and blended curriculum to charter schools, public school districts, private schools, and directly to families. More information can be found at K12.com.

ISBN: 978-1-60153-510-8 (online book)

ISBN: 978-1-60153-504-7 (printed book)

Printed by Walsworth, Marceline, MO October 2019

Contents

K^{12} Summit Curriculum vii

Basic Tools, Transformations, Reasoning, and Proof

Basic Geometric Terms and Definitions 2

Measuring Length 6

Measuring Angles 9

Understanding Transformations 13

Using Algebra to Describe Geometry 16

Polygons and Symmetry 22

Angles in Polygons 26

Dilations 32

Reasoning 35

Styles of Proofs 39

Coordinate Proofs 44

Congruence and Constructions

Bisectors and Line Relationships 47

Congruent Polygons and Their Corresponding Parts 56

Triangle Congruence: SSS, SAS, and ASA 59

Constructions with Polygons 68

Congruence and Rigid Motions 76

Analytic Geometry

Using the Distance Formula 80

Computing Area with Coordinates 86

Slope 91

Proofs and Coordinate Geometry 99

Line and Triangle Relationships

Parallel Lines and Transversals 105

Converses of Parallel Line Properties 112

The Triangle Sum Theorem 117

Bisectors of a Triangle: Circumcenter 124

Midsegments 133

Quadrilaterals and Their Properties 135

Parallelograms 142

Similarity

Dilations and Scale Factors 152

Directed Line Segments 157

Similar Polygons 162

Similar Triangle Relationships

Triangle Similarity 170

Triangle Proportionality Theorem 177

Similarity and the Pythagorean Theorem 184

Area and Volume

Circumferences and Areas of Circles 189

Composite Figures 193

Volumes of Prisms and Cylinders 198

Surface Area of Cones 203

Volumes of Pyramids 207

Volumes of Spheres 211

Volume Ratios 216

Surface Area and Volume 219

Reasoning About Area and Volume 225

Circles

Chords and Arcs 230

Tangents to Circles 235

Inscribed Angles and Intercepted Arcs 241

Angles Formed by Secants and Tangents 250

Similarity in Circles 255

Radian Measure and Sector Areas 257

Right Triangle Trigonometry

Tangents 261

Sines and Cosines 265

Special Right Triangles 271

Using Special Right Triangles 275

Deriving the Formula for Area of a Triangle 280

The Laws of Sines and Cosines 282

Conic Sections

Introduction to Conic Sections 289

Circles 297

Parabolas 303

Deriving Conic Equations. 310

Modeling with Geometry

Geometry in Space. 313

Geometry on Earth 316

Manufacturing: Design and Optimization 319

Density in Two Dimensions 322

Density in Three Dimensions. 324

Fermi Problems 326

Appendices

Pronunciation Guide A-1

Glossary. A-2

Symbols A-18

Properties A-20

Formulary A-23

Postulates and Theorems. A-37

Illustrations Credits A-47

K¹² Summit Curriculum

And remember: The pages in your book are also online!

Go to the online course to look for these digital resources in your lessons:

 **60 – second MATH**

Videos will introduce you to each topic.

 **math CAST**

Visual learning with animations and interaction will help you master key skills.

 **Worked EXAMPLE**

Solve problems with the help of stepped examples.

 **APPLY it!**

Use real-world examples to practice what you've learned.

Basic Tools, Transformations, Reasoning, and Proof

Topic List

- Basic Geometric Terms and Definitions
- Measuring Length
- Measuring Angles
- Understanding Transformations
- Using Algebra to Describe Geometry
- Polygons and Symmetry
- Angles in Polygons
- Dilations
- Reasoning
- Styles of Proofs
- Coordinate Proofs

Frank Gehry is an architect whose innovative building designs are made up of simple geometric shapes put together in interesting ways. Gehry chooses each shape carefully to produce a fascinating yet functional structure.

Basic Geometric Terms and Definitions

Geometry is the study of relationships, characteristics, and measurements of points, lines, angles, surfaces, and solids.

Basic Geometric Terms

The terms *point*, *line*, and *plane* are undefined terms that form the basis of other definitions. You have to start somewhere, so starting by agreeing on what these three terms mean will allow you to write good definitions for other terms.

▶ **Remember** You can imagine a point as a dot on a page or a grain of sand, but a point is simply a location. It has no size.

A **point** references a location in space. It has no length, width, or depth. Represent a point with a dot, and name a point with a capital letter.

point *A*

A **line** is a collection of points arranged in a straight path. A line has no thickness, but it does have direction and infinite length. Use arrows to show that a line continues endlessly in both directions, and name a line by naming any two points on the line in any order. You can also name a line with one lowercase script letter.

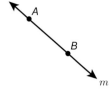

line *AB* or $\overleftrightarrow{AB}$ or line m

A **plane** is a flat surface that has infinite length and width but no thickness. Name a plane with one capital script letter or any three points on the plane that are not on the same line.

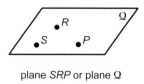

plane *SRP* or plane Ω

More Geometric Terms

A **line segment** is a part of a line that consists of any two points on the line and all the points in between those two points. A line segment has a specific length and can be measured. Name a line segment by naming its endpoints, in either order.

line segment *AB* or $\overline{AB}$
or line segment *BA* or $\overline{BA}$

A **ray** is part of a line that extends infinitely in one direction. Name a ray by naming its endpoint first and then any other point on the ray. The direction of the ray affects the naming of the ray.

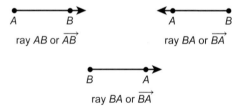

ray *AB* or $\overrightarrow{AB}$ ray *BA* or $\overrightarrow{BA}$

ray *BA* or $\overrightarrow{BA}$

Points that lie on the same line are **collinear**. Points that do not lie on the same line are **noncollinear**. Points that lie on the same plane are **coplanar**.

On the pool table shown, if the balls represent points and the table represents a plane, then

- Any pair of balls is collinear.

- Balls 1, 3, and 13 are noncollinear.

- Balls 1, 2, 3, 8, 10, and 13 are coplanar.

- Balls 2, 4, 6, and 13 are not coplanar.

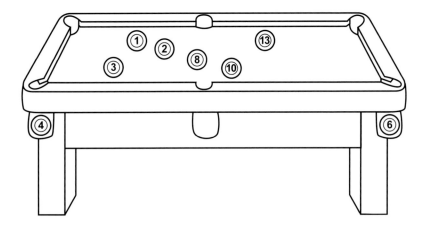

▶ **Think About It** The prefix co– means "together." People who cooperate work together. Points that are collinear are together on the same line, and points that are coplanar are together on the same plane.

Intersections

Line *AB* (another name would be line *BA*) and line *CD* (or line *DC*) share a common point, *X*. That point is where the two lines intersect. The figures show that the intersection of two lines is a point, and the intersection of two planes is a line.

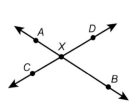

$\overleftrightarrow{AB}$ intersects $\overleftrightarrow{CD}$ at point *X*.

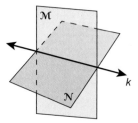

Planes $\mathcal{M}$ and $\mathcal{N}$ intersect in line *k*.

Postulates, Theorems, and Proofs

In mathematics, we accept some statements as true without proof. These statements are called **postulates**.

Postulate GEN-1

Two points determine a line.

Postulate GEN-2

Three noncollinear points determine a plane.

Another kind of mathematical statement, called a **theorem**, is not accepted as true but has to be proven to be true. Each theorem must be proven true by a formal method called a **proof**.

The term *proof* has a specific meaning for mathematicians. In everyday life, proof is evidence that establishes the truth of a claim—for example, in a court of law, a photograph or fingerprints might be used as proof that an accused person committed a crime. In mathematics, however, a proof is a clear, logical structure of reasoning. It begins from accepted ideas, and then proceeds through logic to reach a conclusion.

While proofs can be presented in different ways, all proofs have the same parts and follow the same general order:

- A list of the given information.

- A statement of what is to be proven (in a geometric proof, this statement is often accompanied by a diagram).

- A sequence of statements that leads logically from one to the next.

- The reasons why each statement is true. These reasons can include postulates, previously proven theorems, or accepted definitions.

Measuring Length

You can think of the number line as a "geometry ruler."

Rulers and Number Lines

You can build a number line with a straightedge and compass. Draw a straight line, open your compass to a set width, and mark off segments, keeping the compass open at a constant width throughout. This process will ensure you have an equal space between marks.

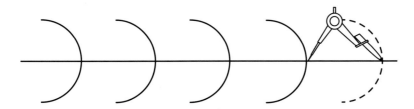

When you make each interval equally spaced and mark each intersection with consecutive numbers, you construct a fair ruler. Now this instrument can be used as a measurement tool.

Measuring Line Segments

A **number line** is like a ruler because it has equally spaced intervals that are labeled with numbers. In addition, it contains equal intervals and numbers to the left or below 0, which represent negative numbers. A ruler begins with 0 and contains only positive numbers, those to the right of 0. On a number line, the numbers are called **coordinates**. A coordinate gives the location of a point.

Postulate MEAS-1

Ruler Postulate The points on a line can be numbered so that positive number differences measure distances.

This postulate means that you can use a number line to measure line segments. The **length of a line segment** is the distance between its endpoints. The length of $\overline{AB}$ is written as AB. When you refer to the length of a segment, you do not include the segment symbol over the two endpoints. When you want to find the length of a line segment by using a number line, subtract the coordinates of the endpoints. If the result is a negative number, make it positive. Distance is always positive.

Look at $\overline{EF}$ on the number line.

To find EF, subtract the coordinate of point E from the coordinate of point F: $5 - 1 = 4$. Notice that if you subtract the coordinate of point F from the coordinate of point E, the result is negative: $1 - 5 = -4$. Either way, the distance between E and F is 4, so $EF = 4$.

The word *between* was used without defining it. You intuitively know what the word means, but in geometry, it has a specific definition.

If point B is between points A and C, then points A, B, and C are collinear, and the length of $\overline{AB}$ plus the length of $\overline{BC}$ equals the length of $\overline{AC}$.

Postulate MEAS-2

Segment Addition Postulate If B is between A and C, then $AB + BC = AC$. Also, if $AB + BC = AC$ and A, B, and C are collinear, then B is between A and C.

Postulate MEAS-3

Segment Congruence Postulate If two segments have the same length as measured by a fair ruler, then the segments are congruent ($\cong$). Also if two segments are congruent, then they have the same length as measured by a fair ruler.

Look at $\overline{EF}$ and $\overline{NM}$ on the number line.

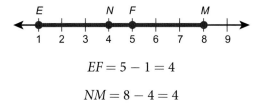

$$EF = 5 - 1 = 4$$

$$NM = 8 - 4 = 4$$

So $EF = NM$ and $\overline{EF} \cong \overline{NM}$.

Congruent line segments are line segments that have equal length. They do not have to lie on the same line, as shown on the number line. In the figures, the tick marks show that $\overline{AB} \cong \overline{BC}$ and $\overline{EF} \cong \overline{GH}$.

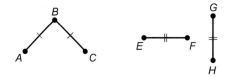

Measuring Angles

You can find angles in many places, including nature, architecture, and sports.

Angles

Definitions

An **angle** is the figure that is formed by two rays, called sides, that share the same endpoint. The common endpoint of the angle is called the **vertex**.

For this angle, $\overrightarrow{BA}$ and $\overrightarrow{BC}$ are the sides, and point B is the vertex. A point that does not lie on the sides of an angle lies in either the interior (shaded region) or exterior (unshaded region) of the angle.

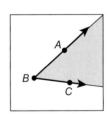

You can name an angle in any of the following ways:

- With the vertex letter, if there is only one angle having the given vertex.

- Using three points—a point on one side of the angle, the vertex, and a point on the other side of the angle.

- Using a small letter or number placed between the sides of the angle and near the vertex.

This angle can be named ∠ABC, ∠CBA, ∠B, or ∠1.

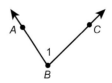

This angle is named ∠a.

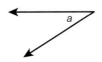

Measuring Angles with a Protractor

The customary measuring unit of an angle is the degree. You can use a protractor to measure angles.

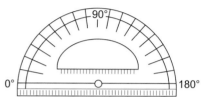

- Place the center point (the small, open circle) of the protractor on the vertex of the angle.

- Align either of the rays with the bottom of the protractor so that one of the rays will cross the 0° mark. The figures show the protractor may be rotated.

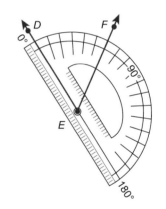

- Look at the ray that is aligned with the bottom of the protractor. If there are two scales, the 0° mark may be either the inside or the outside scale. Whichever scale it is, read that scale where the other ray crosses the protractor's angle marks.

∠*DEF* measures 60°. You can write this statement by using *m* for measure and placing it before the name of the angle: *m*∠*DEF* = 60°.

Postulate MEAS-4

Angle Addition Postulate If point *D* lies in the interior of ∠*ABC*, then *m*∠*ABD* + *m*∠*DBC* = *m*∠*ABC*.

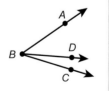

Postulate MEAS-5

Angle Congruence Postulate If two angles have the same measure as measured by a protractor, then the angles are congruent. Also if two angles are congruent, then they have the same measure as measured by a protractor.

Classifying Angles

Angles are classified by their measures.

Definitions

Acute angles measure less than 90°.

Right angles measure exactly 90°.

Obtuse angles measure greater than 90° and less than 180°.

Straight angles measure exactly 180°. A straight angle is a line.

The box symbol indicates that the angle is a right angle.

Angle Pairs

Definitions

Two angles are **adjacent** if they share a common side, have the same vertex, and do not share any interior common points.

Two angles are **complementary** if the sum of their measures is 90°.

Two angles are **supplementary** if the sum of their measures is 180°.

Two angles form a **linear pair** if they have a common side and the same vertex, and their other sides point in opposite directions.

Complementary and supplementary angles may or may not be adjacent.

Pairs of Complementary Angles

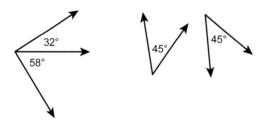

Pairs of Supplementary Angles

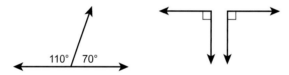

Postulate MEAS-6

Linear Pair Postulate If two angles form a linear pair, then they are
supplementary angles.

Understanding Transformations

There are several ways you can transform a figure.

Transformations

A **transformation** is a change. We can describe sizes, positions, and orientations of shapes under informal transformations such as flips, turns, and slides. In geometry, we describe a transformation as a one-to-one mapping between two sets of points. The original figure is called a **pre-image** and the figure after transformation is called the **image**. Rotations, reflections, and translations preserve the size and shape of the original figure. The image and pre-image are congruent.

Any transformation that results in an image that is congruent to the pre-image is called an isometric transformation or an **isometry**. Reflections, translations, and rotations are isometries. **Dilations** are transformations that result in an image that is a different size from the pre-image. Dilations are not isometries.

Reflections

A **reflection** transforms a figure by flipping it across a line (or line segment) creating a mirror image of the figure. When you look at the figures, you can see the reflection of each image across a line segment or a line. The line segment or line is called the line of reflection.

 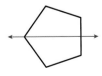

Rotations

A **rotation** turns a figure a certain number of degrees, called the angle of rotation, around a central point, called the center of rotation. The center of rotation can be on the figure, inside the figure, or outside the figure. The centers of rotation in the figures are shown in red.

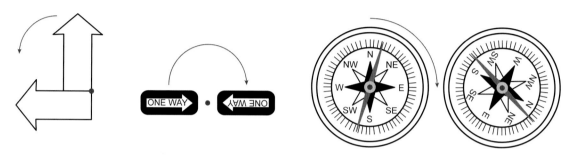

Translations

When you **translate** a figure, you slide it in a straight path without rotating or reflecting it. The straight path the figure takes has a distance and a direction. The path of a bowling ball down a lane and a child going down a playground slide are examples of translations.

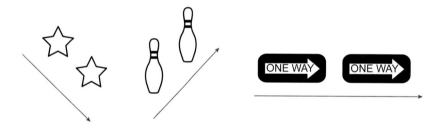

Drawing Transformations with Geometry Software

To construct a mirror image of a figure using geometry software, identify a line, line segment, or ray as the line of reflection (mirror). Select an object and then reflect, or mirror, the object over the line of reflection to create its mirror image. You can further explore these images by changing the shape on either side of the line and watching how the reflection changes.

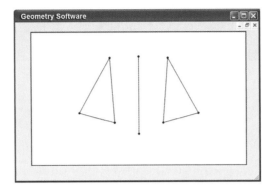

To rotate a figure around a point, you need to identify a point as the center of rotation. You also need to enter an angle of rotation, specifying whether you want to rotate the figure in a clockwise direction or in a counterclockwise direction.

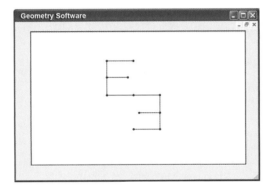

To translate a figure, start by defining a translation vector, which is a line segment that has direction. Once you have your translation vector, you can use it to translate any figure.

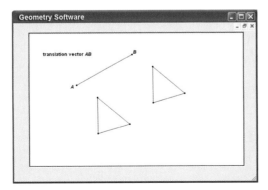

Using Algebra to Describe Geometry

The coordinate plane is an important tool in solving a variety of mathematics problems.

Transformations in the Coordinate Plane

The **coordinate plane** is the intersection of a horizontal number line called the x-axis and a vertical number line called the y-axis. The intersection of the x- and y-axes is called the origin. To find the location of a point on the coordinate plane, you must look at a pair of numbers, one number from each axis. You identify the point's location as an ordered pair where the first number is the x-coordinate and the second number is the y-coordinate.

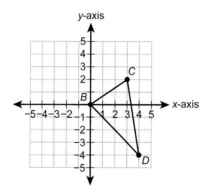

On the coordinate plane shown, point B is located at the origin and is named by the ordered pair $(0, 0)$. Point C is named by the ordered pair $(3, 2)$. The x-coordinate of point D is 4. The y-coordinate of point D is -4.

Reflections

You can reflect a figure in the coordinate plane across either axis, or any line.

Formulas for Reflecting a Figure Across an Axis

To reflect a figure across the x-axis, use the rule $(x, y) \rightarrow (x, -y)$.

To reflect a figure across the y-axis, use the rule $(x, y) \rightarrow (-x, y)$.

The triangle in the diagram is reflected across the x-axis. Determine the coordinates of each point in the image by taking the opposite of each y-coordinate.

$A(-2, 4) \rightarrow A'(-2, -4)$

$B(-3, 1) \rightarrow B'(-3, -1)$

$C(3, 2) \rightarrow C'(3, -2)$

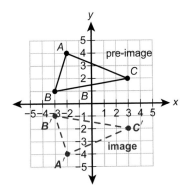

Rotations

Formulas for Rotating a Figure About the Origin

To rotate a figure 180° about the origin, use the rule $(x, y) \rightarrow (-x, -y)$.

To rotate a figure 90° counterclockwise about the origin, use the rule $(x, y) \rightarrow (-y, x)$.

The quadrilateral in the diagram is rotated 180° about the origin. Determine the coordinates of each point in the image by taking the opposite of both the x- and y-coordinates.

$A(-4, 4) \rightarrow A'(4, -4)$

$B(-2, 5) \rightarrow B'(2, -5)$

$C(-1, 4) \rightarrow C'(1, -4)$

$D(-2, 2) \rightarrow D'(2, -2)$

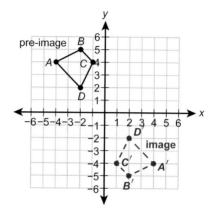

Translations

When you translate a figure, add or subtract to each coordinate a specific amount.

Formulas for Translating a Figure

To translate a figure h units left or right, use the rule $(x \pm h, y)$.

To translate a figure k units up or down, use the rule $(x, y \pm k)$.

The slow sign is translated 4 units to the right and 3 units up, so the rule is $(x, y) \rightarrow (x + 4, y + 3)$.

$A(-2, 0) \rightarrow A'(2, 3)$

$B(0, -2) \rightarrow B'(4, 1)$

$C(-2, -4) \rightarrow C'(2, -1)$

$D(-4, -2) \rightarrow D'(0, 1)$

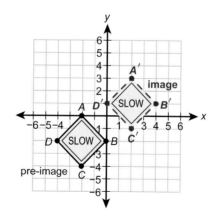

direction	operation
right	add to x
left	subtract from x
up	add to y
down	subtract from y

Transformations can also be used to move or resize the graphs of functions. For example, a quadratic function can be shifted left or right by adding a constant to the x-value.

Functions can be graphed on a coordinate plane and be transformed as well. A quadratic function can be transformed using various mapping rules.

When the constant 4 is added to the x-value of the function $f(x) = x^2$, the function becomes $f(x + 4) = (x + 4)^2$ and the graph shifts 4 units left.

When the constant 4 is subtracted, the function becomes $f(x - 4)$ $= (x - 4)^2$ and the graph shifts 4 units right.

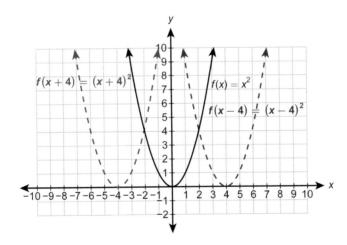

Other transformations to the function shift the graph of the function up or down, reflect the graph of the function horizontally or vertically, or stretch the graph of the function horizontally or vertically.

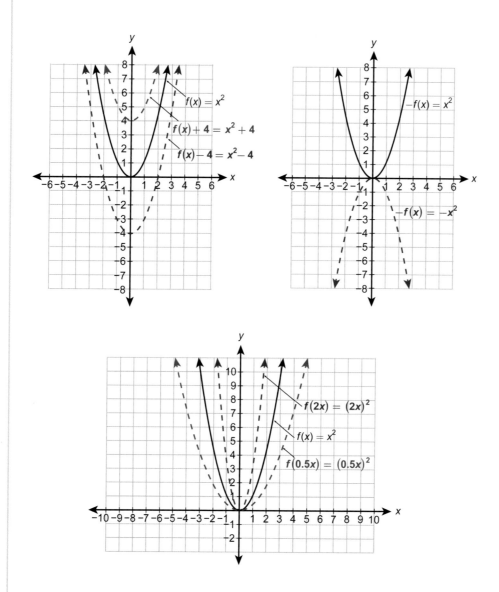

Using Geometry Software

You can mark an axis as a line of reflection (or mirror). You can mark the x-axis as a line of reflection and reflect a triangle over it.

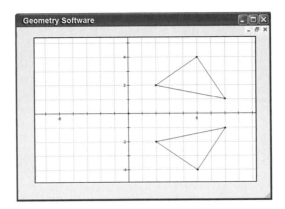

You can rotate a triangle 180° about the origin. Any point, including $(0, 0)$, can be chosen as the center point.

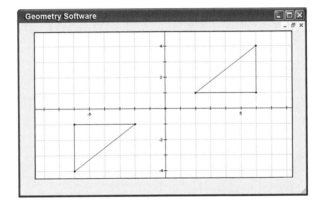

You can translate a figure 2 units up and 4 units right.

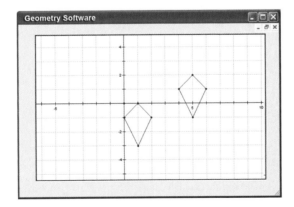

▶ **Remember** Isometric transformations do not change distances, angles, or areas.

Polygons and Symmetry

The prefix *poly–* means "many," and polygons are figures with many sides.

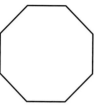
8-sided polygon

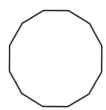
12-sided polygon

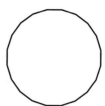
20-sided polygon

Polygons

Definitions

A **polygon** is a closed figure in a plane formed by three or more line segments, such that each line segment intersects exactly two other line segments at their endpoints only.

The line segments form the **sides** of the polygon. A point where the sides intersect is a **vertex.**

▶ **Think About It** Polygons are named for their number of sides.

triangle
three-sided polygon

pentagon
five-sided polygon

octagon
eight-sided polygon

quadrilateral
four-sided polygon

hexagon
six-sided polygon

There is no limit to the number of sides a polygon can have. Here are examples of figures that are, and are not, polygons.

Polygons   Not Polygons

A polygon with all angles congruent is called an **equiangular polygon**.

A polygon with all sides congruent is called an **equilateral polygon**.

A **regular polygon** is both equiangular and equilateral.

Triangles

A triangle is the simplest polygon. You can classify a triangle by its sides.

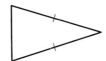

A triangle with no congruent sides is a **scalene triangle**.

A triangle with at least two congruent sides is an **isosceles triangle**.

A triangle with three congruent sides is an **equilateral triangle**. Notice that an equilateral triangle is also an isosceles triangle.

Regular Polygons

Regular polygons have special properties. The **center** is the point inside the polygon that is equidistant from each vertex. An angle formed by line segments drawn from the center to two consecutive vertices is called a **central angle**.

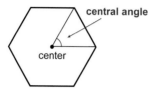

The measure of each central angle of a regular polygon is 360° divided by the number of sides.

Formula for Central Angle of a Regular Polygon

For a regular polygon where m is the measure of the central angle and n is the number of sides,

$$m = \frac{360°}{n}.$$

Symmetry and Regular Polygons

A line drawn through a figure so that one side is a reflection of the image on the opposite side is an **axis of symmetry**, or a line of symmetry.

Definitions

If a figure has **reflection symmetry**, then you can find at least one axis of symmetry in the figure. For figures with reflection symmetry, you can fold the figure along an axis of symmetry and both halves will match up.

If a figure has **rotation symmetry**, then you can rotate it around its center less than one full turn, and the rotated figure looks exactly like the original figure.

All regular polygons have both reflection symmetry and rotation symmetry. The number of axes of symmetry in a regular polygon is equal to its number of sides. The smallest angle by which a regular polygon can be rotated to look exactly like the original polygon is the measure of its central angle.

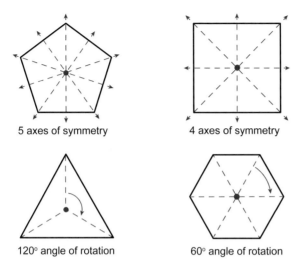

5 axes of symmetry

4 axes of symmetry

120° angle of rotation

60° angle of rotation

Angles in Polygons

A diamond cutter starts with a raw, uncut stone, and carefully chips away at it to create faces that are polygons. Every face has many angles. When the gem cutter creates a face on a gem, it is important that all the angles be just right. Each angle is an important part of a breathtaking piece of jewelry.

diamond cuts

More About Polygons

Just as triangles have both interior and exterior angles, other polygons have interior and exterior angles as well. In this diagram, the interior angles are labeled with odd numbers and the exterior angles are labeled with even numbers.

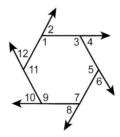

Convex and Concave Polygons

A polygon is **convex** if, for each pair of points inside the polygon, the line segment connecting them lies completely inside the polygon as well.

Convex Polygons

A polygon is **concave** if at least one line segment connecting any two points inside the polygon does not lie completely inside the polygon.

Concave Polygons

▶ **Remember** A concave polygon "caves in" on at least one side.

Interior and Exterior Angles of Polygons

You can use the triangle sum theorem to find the sum of the interior angle measures of any convex polygon.

▶ **Remember** The triangle sum theorem states that the sum of the measures of the angles of a triangle is 180°.

A rectangle can be divided into two triangles. The sum of the angles in each triangle is 180°, so the sum of the angles in the rectangle is 180° + 180°, or 360°.

A pentagon can be divided into three triangles. The sum of the angles in each triangle is 180°, so the sum of the angles in the pentagon is 180° + 180° + 180°, or 540°.

A hexagon can be divided into four triangles. So the sum of the angles in a hexagon is 180° + 180° + 180° + 180°, or 720°.

A heptagon can be divided into five triangles. So the sum of the angles in a heptagon is 180° + 180° + 180° + 180° + 180°, or 900°.

Now put the information into a table and look for a pattern.

Number of sides	Number of triangles	Sum of angle measures
3	1	180°
4	2	$2(180°) = 360°$
5	3	$3(180°) = 540°$
6	4	$4(180°) = 720°$
7	5	$5(180°) = 900°$

Pattern The number of triangles is always the number of sides minus 2. Use the pattern to add a row to the table for a polygon with n sides. The right column shows how to get the angle sum (I).

Number of sides	Number of triangles	Sum of angle measures
n	$n - 2$	$(n - 2)(180°) = I$

This is stated in the following formula.

Formula for the Sum of the Interior Angles of a Polygon

Given I = sum of interior angles and n = number of sides,

$$I = (n - 2)(180°).$$

For a **regular polygon**, you can use the formula for the sum of the interior angle measures to find i, the measure of each interior angle. Because all the angles are congruent, you just divide the sum by the number of angles.

To find the measure of each interior angle of a regular octagon you first find the sum of the angles.

$$I = 6(180°) = 1080°$$

Then, because each angle is the same measure, and there are eight angles, divide by 8.

$$i = \frac{1080°}{8} = 135°$$

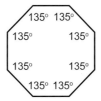

Formula for the Measure of an Interior Angle of a Regular Polygon

Given I = measure of each interior angle and n = number of sides,

$$i = \frac{(n-2)180°}{n}.$$

Now consider the **exterior angles**. Use E for the sum of the exterior angles and e for the measure of each exterior angle.

Each interior angle of a polygon forms a linear pair with an exterior angle, so the sum of each pair is 180°. The number of linear pairs equals the numbers of sides in the polygon, so the sum of all the interior and exterior angles is $n(180°)$.

If you subtract the sum of the interior angles from the sum of all the angles, you will be left with the sum of the exterior angles. You can show that the sum of the exterior angles is 360° with an algebraic proof.

This means the sum of the exterior angles for any convex polygon is always 360°. To find the measure of each exterior angle of a regular polygon, divide 360° by the number of angles (or sides).

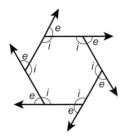

Given a convex polygon

Prove $E = 360°$

Statement	Reason
1. $I = (n-2)(180°)$	Formula for the Sum of the Interior Angles of a Polygon
2. $E = n(180°) - I$	The sum of the exterior angles equals the sum of all the angles minus the sum of the interior angles.
3. $E = n(180°) - [(n-2)180°]$	Substitution Property of Equality
4. $E = 180°n - [180°n - 360°]$	Distributive Property $(180°)$
5. $E = 180°n - 180°n + 360°$	Distributive Property (-1)
6. $E = 360°$	Combine like terms.

Dilations

A dilation changes the size of a figure, but it does not change its shape.

Scale Factor and Center of Dilation

The **scale factor** t of a dilation is the ratio of the length of any side on the image to the length of its corresponding side on the pre-image. In this dilation, $C'B' = 18$ and $CB = 6$, so the scale factor is $\frac{18}{6} = 3$.

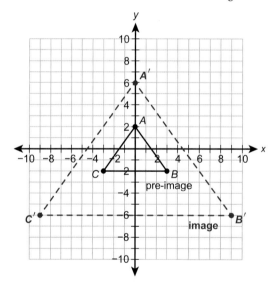

▶ **Think About It** Use the Pythagorean theorem to find that $A'B' = A'C' = 15$ and $AB = AC = 5$.

The lines connecting each point on the pre-image with its corresponding point on the image intersect at the **center of dilation**. Here, the center of dilation is the origin.

To dilate a figure when the center of dilation is the origin and the scale factor is t, use the rule $(x, y) \rightarrow (tx, ty)$.

Compare coordinates of points on the pre-image and image in the dilation.

$$A(0, 2) \rightarrow A'(0, 6)$$
$$B(3, -2) \rightarrow B'(9, -6)$$
$$C(-3, -2) \rightarrow C'(-9, -6)$$

Types of Dilations

Definitions

An **expansion** is a dilation for which the absolute value of the scale factor is greater than 1.

A **contraction** is a dilation for which the absolute value of the scale factor is between 0 and 1.

▶ **Think About It** In an expansion, the image is larger than the pre-image. In a contraction, the image is smaller than the pre-image.

In this dilation, $A'B' = 2$ and $AB = 6$, so the scale factor is $\frac{2}{6} = \frac{1}{3}$. Therefore, the dilation is a contraction.

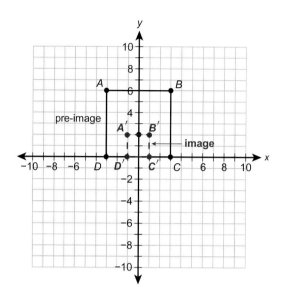

Reasoning

Mathematicians use inductive reasoning to develop conjectures and deductive reasoning to reach conclusions.

Identifying Tools for Reasoning

Definition

Inductive reasoning is a type of reasoning that starts with observation and moves from a specific observation to a general conclusion.

When you look for patterns, you are using inductive reasoning.

EXAMPLE 1

Use inductive reasoning to write a formula for the number of diagonals that can be drawn from one vertex of a polynomial.

SOLUTION
Start by drawing polygons and diagonals from one vertex. As you look from left to right, the number of sides in each polygon increases by one.

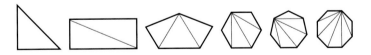

The lines drawn in the polygons are diagonals. Diagonals are segments that connect two vertices of a polygon and do not lie along any side of the polygon. For each polygon, every diagonal that can be drawn from one vertex is shown. The triangle has no diagonals because any line connecting two vertices would lie along a side of the triangle. The numbers of sides and diagonals are listed in the table.

Number of sides of polygon (n)	3	4	5	6	7	8
Number of diagonals	0	1	2	3	4	5

If you study the table for a bit, you will see that there is a relationship between the number of sides of the polygon and the number of diagonals that can be drawn from one vertex of the polygon. You can conclude that the number of diagonals that can be drawn from a single vertex is three less than the number of sides, or $n - 3$. ▪

The conclusion about the number of diagonals was based on observing and studying patterns. You can also derive conclusions on the basis of measurement and experimentation. For example, if you measure both diagonals of any rectangle, you will find that their lengths are always equal.

It is important to note that while observation, measurement, and experimentation can lead you to useful conjectures, those tools are not considered proof. For proof, mathematicians rely on deductive reasoning.

Definition

Deductive reasoning is a type of reasoning that uses previously proven or accepted properties to reach conclusions.

Using Logic and Completing Proofs

Definitions

An **argument** is a set of statements, called **premises**, which are used to reach a **conclusion**. Both the premises and the conclusion are considered to be part of the argument.

Law of Syllogism

The **law of syllogism** is a logical argument that always contains two premises and a conclusion. Syllogisms have the following form:

Premise If a, then b.
Premise If b, then c.
Conclusion Therefore, if a, then c.

Law of Detachment

The **law of detachment** is an argument that has two true premises and a valid conclusion. The premises and conclusion have the following form:

Premise If a, then b.
Premise a is true.
Conclusion Therefore, b is true.

EXAMPLE 2

Use the law of detachment to draw a conclusion.

If a person is taller than 48 in., the person can ride on the roller coaster.
Josh is 52 in. tall.

SOLUTION
This argument is in the form of the law of detachment.

The first premise is the conditional: If **a person is taller than 48 in.**, then **the person can ride on the roller coaster**.

The second premise is **Josh is 52 in. tall.**
Josh is a person who is 52 in. tall, so for him, the **conclusion** is true. Josh can ride the roller coaster. ▪

▶ **Think About It** Deductive reasoning enables you to derive true conclusions from statements accepted as true.

The validity of an argument is based on the structure of the argument. The syllogism in Example 2 is a type of valid argument.

Definition

A **valid argument** is an argument in which, if the premises are all true, then the conclusion must also be true.

EXAMPLE 3

Determine whether the argument is valid or not, and explain your reasoning.

Every member of the Cardinals baseball team wears a red hat. All firemen wear a red hat. Therefore, all members of the Cardinals baseball team are firemen.

SOLUTION

The argument is invalid because the structure of it is faulty. Both premises are true, but the conclusion is false. It doesn't follow from the premises.

A proof is a logical structure of reasoning that begins from accepted ideas and proceeds through logic to reach a conclusion. In other words, a proof uses deductive reasoning. In a proof, only valid arguments are used, so the conclusions must be valid. Forms of valid arguments and different types of formal proofs are the foundation of geometry.

Styles of Proofs

To write a proof, you can use a variety of formats to express the reasoning that leads to your final conclusion.

Definition

A **proof** is a clear, logical structure of reasoning that begins from accepted ideas and proceeds through logic to reach a conclusion.

EXAMPLE 1

Given $\overline{AB} \cong \overline{CB}$

Prove $\angle A \cong \angle C$

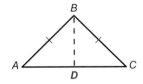

SOLUTION

Statement	Reason
1. $\overline{AB} \cong \overline{CB}$	Given
2. $\overline{BD}$ is the bisector of $\angle ABC$.	As constructed
3. $\angle ABD \cong \angle CBD$	Definition of angle bisector
4. $\overline{BD} \cong \overline{BD}$	Reflexive Property
5. $\triangle ABD \cong \triangle CBD$	SAS Congruence Postulate
6. $\angle A \cong \angle C$	CPCTC

A **two-column proof** is a proof shown in two columns. The first column shows the steps, and the second column shows the justification for each step.

A **paragraph proof** is a proof in the form of a paragraph.

A flowchart proof is another format that can be used to write a proof.

Definition

A **flowchart proof** graphically represents the logical flow of a proof. In a flowchart proof, statements and conclusions are connected with arrows.

How to Write a Flowchart Proof

Step 1 Write each piece of given information in a separate box.

Step 2 Write what is to be proven in a box far below the given information.

Step 3 Use the given information to make a new statement. Write that statement and its corresponding reason in a new box. Draw an arrow connecting the given information to the new box.

Step 4 Continue the process of making and supporting statements. Connect each new box to the box or boxes that directly lead to it.

Step 5 When you have enough information to prove the conjecture, draw an arrow or arrows from that information to the box containing the conjecture. Write the reason the conjecture is true.

EXAMPLE 2

Given $\triangle ABC$

Prove $m\angle 1 + m\angle 2 + m\angle 3 = 180°$

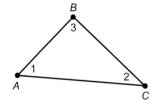

SOLUTION

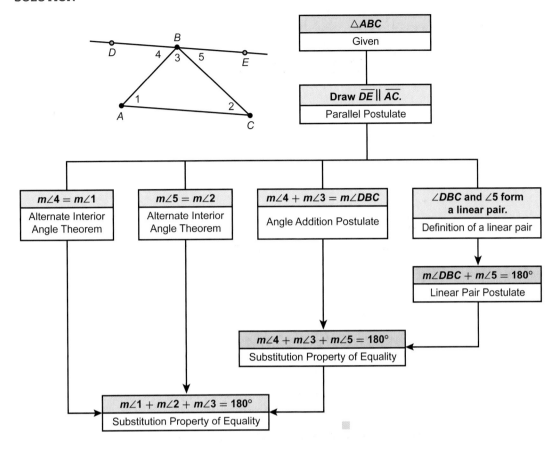

△ABC
Given

Draw $\overline{DE} \parallel \overline{AC}$.
Parallel Postulate

$m\angle 4 = m\angle 1$
Alternate Interior Angle Theorem

$m\angle 5 = m\angle 2$
Alternate Interior Angle Theorem

$m\angle 4 + m\angle 3 = m\angle DBC$
Angle Addition Postulate

$\angle DBC$ and $\angle 5$ form a linear pair.
Definition of a linear pair

$m\angle DBC + m\angle 5 = 180°$
Linear Pair Postulate

$m\angle 4 + m\angle 3 + m\angle 5 = 180°$
Substitution Property of Equality

$m\angle 1 + m\angle 2 + m\angle 3 = 180°$
Substitution Property of Equality

Vertical Angles

Vertical angles are the two nonadjacent angles formed by intersecting lines. The sides of one angle are the opposite rays to the sides of the other angle. In the diagram, $\angle 1$ and $\angle 3$ form a vertical pair, and $\angle 2$ and $\angle 4$ form another vertical pair.

You can prove that vertical angles are congruent by means of a two-column proof.

THEOREM MEAS-1   Vertical Angles Theorem

If two angles form a pair of vertical angles, then they are congruent.

Given ∠1 and ∠3 are vertical angles.

Prove ∠1 ≅ ∠3

Statement	Reason
1. ∠1 and ∠3 are vertical angles.	Given
2. ∠1 and ∠2 form a linear pair. ∠2 and ∠3 form a linear pair.	Definition of linear pair
3. $m\angle1 + m\angle2 = 180°$ $m\angle2 + m\angle3 = 180°$	Linear Pair Postulate
4. $m\angle1 + m\angle2 = m\angle2 + m\angle3$	Substitution Property of Equality
5. $m\angle1 = m\angle3$	Subtraction Property of Equality
6. ∠1 ≅ ∠3	Angle Congruence Postulate

You can also write a proof in the form of a paragraph. This is called a **paragraph proof**. Here is a paragraph proof for the vertical angles theorem. Notice that, similar to the two-column proof, each statement is supported by a reason.

Given ∠1 and ∠3 are vertical angles.

Prove ∠1 ≅ ∠3

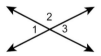

You are given that ∠1 and ∠3 are vertical angles. Because of the definition of linear pair, ∠1 and ∠2 form a linear pair and ∠2 and ∠3 form a linear pair. By the linear pair postulate, $m\angle1 + m\angle2 = 180°$ and $m\angle2 + m\angle3 = 180°$. By using the substitution property of equality and substituting $m\angle2 + m\angle3$ for 180° into the first equation, you get $m\angle1 + m\angle2 = m\angle2 + m\angle3$. By using the subtraction property of equality, you can subtract $m\angle2$ from both sides to get $m\angle1 = m\angle3$. Because of the definition of congruent, ∠1 ≅ ∠3.

Most of the time, you will use the two-column format because it is easier to set up and to understand.

EXAMPLE 3

Find the value of x.

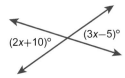

SOLUTION

You can set the values of vertical angles equal to each other because vertical angles are congruent.

$2x + 10 = 3x - 5$

$2x = 3x - 15$	Subtract 10.
$-x = -15$	Subtract $3x$.
$x = 15$	Multiply by -1.

Coordinate Proofs

You can use coordinates to prove and disprove statements about geometric figures.

A Circle Problem

EXAMPLE 1

A circle with a radius of 3 is centered at $(2, 1)$. Use coordinates to prove that the point $(5, 2)$ is not on the circle.

▶ **Remember** A radius is a line segment that connects the center of a circle to a point on the circle.

SOLUTION

If a point is on the circle, then its distance from the center of the circle is 3. So find the distance between $(2, 1)$ and $(5, 2)$.

$$d = \sqrt{(x_2 - x_1)^2 + (y_2 - y_1)^2}$$

$$= \sqrt{(5 - 2)^2 + (2 - 1)^2}$$

$$= \sqrt{9 + 1}$$

$$= \sqrt{10} \approx 3.16$$

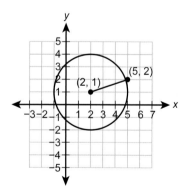

Because the distance is greater than the radius of 3, the point $(5, 2)$ is not on the circle. ▪

A Problem About Triangles

EXAMPLE 2

Use coordinates to prove that $\triangle ABC \cong \triangle DEF$ by the SSS congruence postulate.

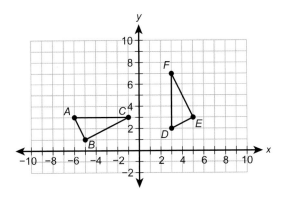

▶ **Remember** You can use the congruence statement to determine which segments are corresponding segments.

SOLUTION

Show that the lengths of all three corresponding sides are equal.

$$AB = \sqrt{\left(-6 - (-5)\right)^2 + (3 - 1)^2} = \sqrt{1 + 4} = \sqrt{5} \text{ and}$$

$$DE = \sqrt{(5 - 3)^2 + (3 - 2)^2} = \sqrt{4 + 1} = \sqrt{5}$$

$$BC = \sqrt{\left(-5 - (-1)\right)^2 + (1 - 3)^2} = \sqrt{16 + 4} = \sqrt{20} \text{ and}$$

$$EF = \sqrt{(5 - 3)^2 + (3 - 7)^2} = \sqrt{4 + 16} = \sqrt{20}$$

$$AC = \sqrt{\left(-6 - (-1)\right)^2 + (3 - 3)^2} = \sqrt{25 + 0} = 5 \text{ and}$$

$$DF = \sqrt{(3 - 3)^2 + (7 - 2)^2} = \sqrt{0 + 25} = 5$$

$\overline{AB} \cong \overline{DE}$, $\overline{BC} \cong \overline{EF}$, and $\overline{AC} \cong \overline{DF}$, so $\triangle ABC \cong \triangle DEF$ by the SSS congruence postulate. ▪

Congruence and Constructions

Topic List

▸ Bisectors and Line Relationships

▸ Congruent Polygons and Their Corresponding Parts

▸ Triangle Congruence: SSS, SAS, and ASA

▸ Constructions with Polygons

▸ Congruence and Rigid Motions

Many sculptors use repeated shapes to create interesting designs. By sliding, flipping, and rotating shapes to different locations, these artists create complex patterns from simple building blocks.

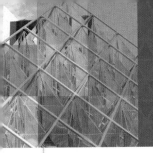

Bisectors and Line Relationships

You can use geometry software to construct, measure, and explore figures.

Special Lines and Bisectors

Parallel lines are coplanar lines that never intersect. **Perpendicular lines** are lines that meet at right angles. The fence's vertical boards are parallel to each other. Each vertical board is perpendicular to the top and bottom horizontal boards.

Parallel and perpendicular lines are everywhere—in your home, in sports, at the mall, and in cities, to name just a few examples.

s parallel to r or $s \parallel r$ k perpendicular to m or $k \perp m$

Bisectors

The **midpoint** of a line segment divides the line segment into two congruent parts. A **segment bisector** is a line, line segment, or ray that passes through the midpoint of a line segment. Although you can draw an infinite number of lines through the midpoint of a segment, you can draw only one line that is perpendicular to the line segment as well. That line is the **perpendicular bisector** of the segment. In the diagram, point M is the midpoint of $\overline{AD}$, **line t** and **line s** are segment bisectors of $\overline{AD}$, and **line n** is the perpendicular bisector of $\overline{AD}$.

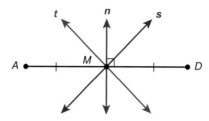

Just as you can bisect lines, you can also bisect angles. An angle bisector is a line, line segment, or ray that divides an angle into two congruent angles. In the diagram, $\overrightarrow{EG}$ bisects $\angle DEF$, which means that $m\angle DEG = m\angle GEF$.

You can use a straightedge and compass to construct an angle congruent to a given angle.

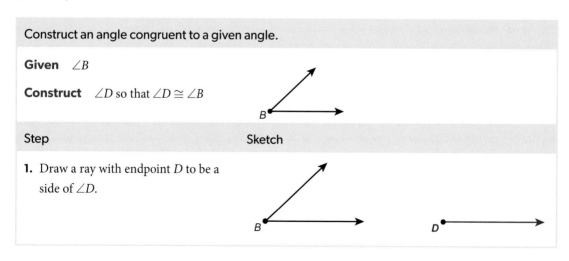

Construct an angle congruent to a given angle.	
Given $\angle B$	
Construct $\angle D$ so that $\angle D \cong \angle B$	
Step	**Sketch**
1. Draw a ray with endpoint D to be a side of $\angle D$.	

Step	Sketch

2. Place the compass on point B at any convenient width. Draw an arc that passes through both sides of the angle. Label the points A and C.

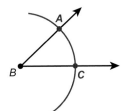 

3. With compass width AB and compass point on D, draw an arc similar to arc AC. Label the intersection point E.

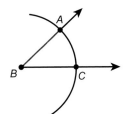 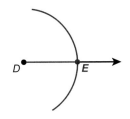

4. Open the compass to width AC. With compass width AC and compass point on E, draw another arc across the first arc as shown. Label the point of intersection of the two arcs as F.

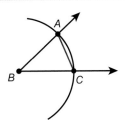 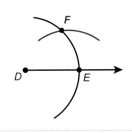

5. Draw ray $\overrightarrow{DF}$.

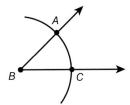 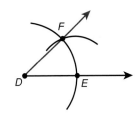

6. $\angle D \cong \angle B$

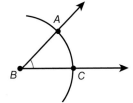 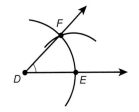

Constructing Bisectors and Lines

Use geometry software to construct a line segment. Draw a point above the original segment, and then construct a line that passes through the point and is parallel to the original segment.

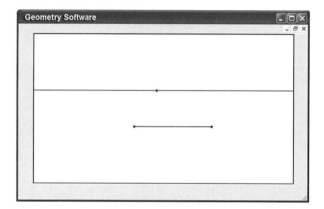

You can use geometry software to construct a line that passes through a point and is perpendicular to a segment.

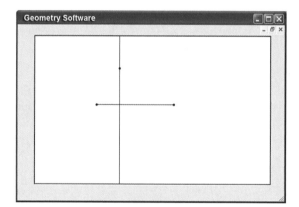

Once you locate the midpoint, you can construct the perpendicular bisector for any segment.

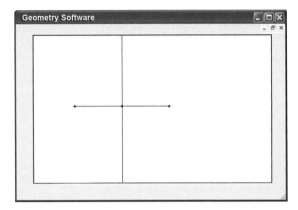

You can use a straightedge and compass to construct a line perpendicular to a given line through a given point not on the line.

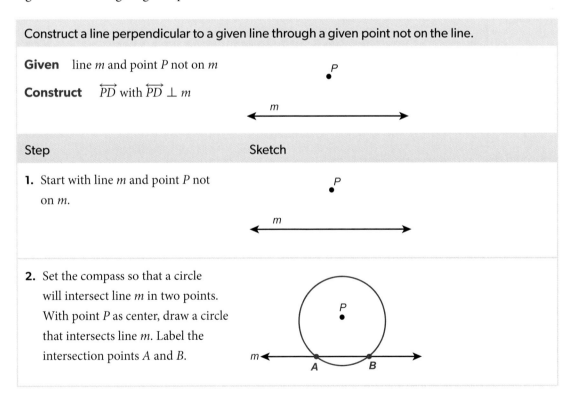

Construct a line perpendicular to a given line through a given point not on the line.

Given line *m* and point *P* not on *m*

Construct $\overleftrightarrow{PD}$ with $\overleftrightarrow{PD} \perp m$

Step	Sketch
1. Start with line *m* and point *P* not on *m*.	
2. Set the compass so that a circle will intersect line *m* in two points. With point *P* as center, draw a circle that intersects line *m*. Label the intersection points *A* and *B*.	

Step	Sketch

3. With points A and B as centers and radius greater than half of the length AB, draw two circles that intersect each other. On the side of the line opposite to point P, label the point of intersection D.

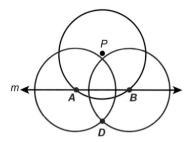

4. Use a straightedge to draw $\overleftrightarrow{PD}$.

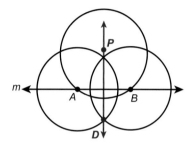

5. $\overleftrightarrow{PD} \perp m$

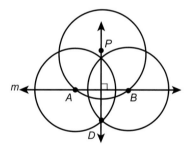

You can use a straightedge and compass to construct a line parallel to a given line through a given point not on the line.

Construct a line parallel to a given line through a given point not on the line.	
Given line PQ and point R not on PQ **Construct** $\overleftrightarrow{RS}$ with $\overleftrightarrow{PQ} \parallel \overleftrightarrow{RS}$	 R $P \qquad\qquad Q$

Step	Sketch
1. Start with line PQ and point R not on $\overleftrightarrow{PQ}$.	R $P \qquad\qquad Q$
2. Use a straightedge to draw a line through point R that intersects line PQ at point J. To draw a parallel line through point R, copy the angle formed at point J onto point R. You will do these procedures in the following steps.	R $P \qquad J \qquad Q$
3. Use the compass to draw an arc with center J and convenient radius.	R $P \qquad J \qquad Q$
4. Without changing the compass setting, draw an arc with center R intersecting $\overleftrightarrow{JR}$. This arc should be about the same length of the first arc.	R $P \qquad J \qquad Q$

Step	Sketch

5. Place the point of the compass on the intersecting point of the first arc as shown. Extend the compass to the other intersecting point on the arc as shown.

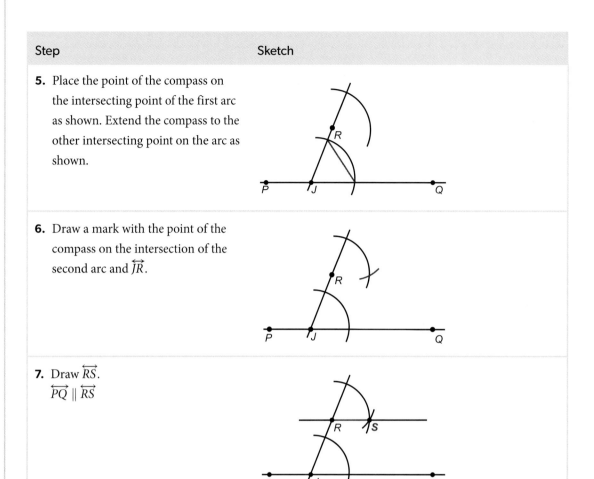

6. Draw a mark with the point of the compass on the intersection of the second arc and $\overleftrightarrow{JR}$.

7. Draw $\overleftrightarrow{RS}$.
$\overleftrightarrow{PQ} \parallel \overleftrightarrow{RS}$

To draw an angle bisector, specify the angle by choosing a point on one side of the angle, the vertex, and a point on the other side. Use geometry software to construct the bisector through the vertex.

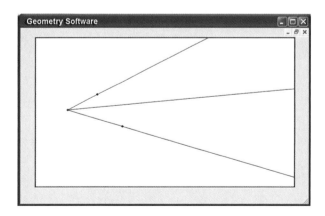

Making Conjectures

A **conjecture** is an educated guess based on observations. For example, in the diagram, you are given that $\overleftrightarrow{AX}$ is the perpendicular bisector of $\overline{CB}$. It certainly looks like $AC = AB$, but that is only a conjecture. It may or may not be true.

Given $\overleftrightarrow{AX}$ is the perpendicular bisector of $\overline{CB}$.

Conjecture $AC = AB$

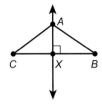

You can use geometry software to investigate the conjecture. Draw the perpendicular bisector of a line segment and a segment from each endpoint to a point on the bisector. Then measure the lengths of the segments. Dragging the point that is point A in this figure up and down the perpendicular bisector, you see that the conjecture appears to be true. You haven't proven anything, but you now have more confidence in your conjecture.

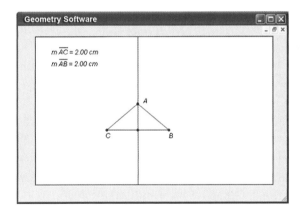

Congruent Polygons and Their Corresponding Parts

Congruent figures may or may not have the same orientation.

Congruence

Congruent polygons are the same size and shape. In the diagram, $ABCD \cong FGHI$. If one is placed on top of the other, they match exactly. $\overline{AB}$ is an exact match with $\overline{FG}$, and $\angle A$ is an exact match with $\angle F$.

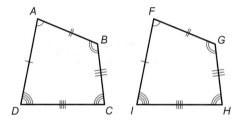

The word **corresponding** refers to angles or sides that lie in the same position in a pair of figures. Congruent polygons have corresponding sides and corresponding angles that are congruent to each other. Mathematicians use tick marks to indicate congruent sides, and multiple arcs or arcs with tick marks to indicate congruent angles.

Postulate CONG-1

Polygon Congruence Postulate Two polygons are congruent if and only if there is a correspondence between their sides and angles so that all pairs of corresponding angles are congruent and all pairs of corresponding sides are congruent.

This postulate lets you make the following statements about polygons *ABCD* and *FGHI*:

$$\angle A \cong \angle F \qquad \angle B \cong \angle G \qquad \angle C \cong \angle H \qquad \angle D \cong \angle I$$

$$\overline{AB} \cong \overline{FG} \qquad \overline{BC} \cong \overline{GH} \qquad \overline{CD} \cong \overline{HI} \qquad \overline{DA} \cong \overline{IF}$$

ABCD $\cong$ *FGHI* is called a **congruence statement**. When you write a congruence statement for a polygon, list the vertices so that corresponding angles match. Doing so allows you to identify corresponding parts of a figure even when one of the figures is rotated.

The two triangles are congruent. They are not positioned the same way, but the congruence statement written beneath the triangles tells you that $\angle R$ corresponds to $\angle X$ because they are both listed first, $\angle S$ corresponds to $\angle Y$ because they are both listed second, and so on. You can also identify corresponding sides. The endpoints will be in the same position in the congruence statement. $\overline{RT}$ corresponds to $\overline{XZ}$ because the endpoints of each one are written in the same order.

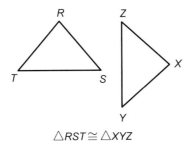

$\triangle RST \cong \triangle XYZ$

Using Geometry Software to Explore Congruent Polygons

The congruent polygons were constructed with geometry software. You can create a copy of a figure by translating it. If you display all the side and angle measures of both polygons, you can see that corresponding angles are congruent and corresponding sides are congruent.

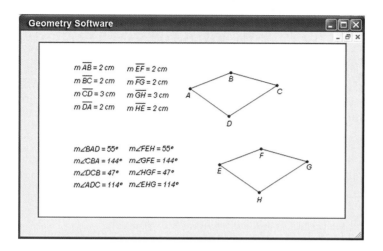

You can translate, reflect, or rotate one of the polygons and see that the orientations of the figures do not change their congruence. The measures of the sides and angles remain the same.

▶ **Remember** Isometric transformations do not change distances, angles, or areas.

Triangle Congruence: SSS, SAS, and ASA

The shape of a triangle cannot change as long as the sides remain the same size.

Congruent Triangles

From the polygon congruence postulate, you know that two polygons are congruent if and only if all corresponding angles and sides are congruent.

Although this postulate is useful for polygons in general, you don't actually need all that information if you want to prove two triangles are congruent. Recall that, by definition, the sides of a polygon must meet only at their endpoints. If you are given three sides of a set length and can join them only at their endpoints, a triangle of only one size can be formed.

Postulate CONG-2

Side-Side-Side (SSS) Congruence Postulate If the three sides of one triangle are congruent to the three sides of another triangle, then the two triangles are congruent.

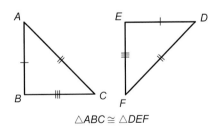

$\triangle ABC \cong \triangle DEF$

The SSS congruence postulate leads into a special theorem for right triangles only. Because of the Pythagorean theorem, if you know the lengths of any two sides of a right triangle, you can find the length of the third side.

Theorem CONG-1

Hypotenuse-Leg (HL) Congruence Theorem If the hypotenuse and a leg of one right triangle are congruent to the hypotenuse and corresponding leg of another right triangle, then the two triangles are congruent.

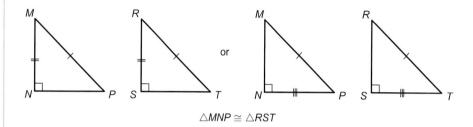

$\triangle MNP \cong \triangle RST$

Included Sides and Angles

Before you look at more ways to show that two triangles are congruent, you must learn two new terms: included angle and included side.

The angle formed by two sides of a triangle is an **included angle**. For example, in $\triangle ABC$, $\angle A$ is the included angle between $\overline{AC}$ and $\overline{AB}$.

An **included side** lies between two specific angles. In $\triangle ABC$, $\overline{AC}$ is the included side between $\angle A$ and $\angle C$.

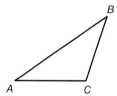

Suppose you are given two segments of a set length and told to connect them at a given angle. Then suppose you must form a triangle with a third piece. There is only one length that will work, which is the basis for the next postulate.

Postulate CONG-3

Side-Angle-Side (SAS) Congruence Postulate If two sides and the included angle in one triangle are congruent to two sides and the included angle in another triangle, then the two triangles are congruent.

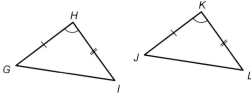

$\triangle GHI \cong \triangle JKL$

Now suppose you are told to form a triangle and are given one segment of a set length. This segment is an included side between two angles whose measures you are also given. To get the endpoints of the other two segments to join at the third vertex, you will find that there is only one pair of segments that will create the triangle. This idea leads to the next postulate.

Postulate CONG-4

Angle-Side-Angle (ASA) Congruence Postulate If two angles and the included side in one triangle are congruent to two angles and the included side in another triangle, then the two triangles are congruent.

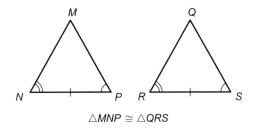

$\triangle MNP \cong \triangle QRS$

Sometimes, congruent sides and angles are not marked as such, but you know they are congruent from previous properties, postulates, theorems, or definitions.

Given $\overline{AD} \perp \overline{BC}$

D is the midpoint of $\overline{BC}$.

Prove $\triangle BDA \cong \triangle CDA$

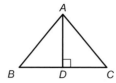

Statement	Reason	Sketch
1. $\overline{AD} \perp \overline{BC}$ D is the midpoint of $\overline{BC}$.	Given	
2. $\overline{BD} \cong \overline{CD}$	Definition of midpoint	
3. $m\angle ADB = 90°$ and $m\angle ADC = 90°$	Definition of perpendicular lines	
4. $m\angle ADB = m\angle ADC$	Substitution Property of Equality	
5. $\angle ADB \cong \angle ADC$	Angle Congruence Postulate	
6. $\overline{AD} \cong \overline{AD}$	Reflexive Property of Congruence	

Statement	Reason	Sketch
7. $\triangle BDA \cong \triangle CDA$	SAS Congruence Postulate	

Given $\overline{AD} \parallel \overline{EC}$ $\overline{DB} \cong \overline{BE}$ **Prove** $\triangle ABD \cong \triangle CBE$	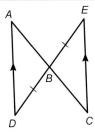	

Statement	Reason	Sketch
1. $\overline{AD} \parallel \overline{EC}$ $\overline{DB} \cong \overline{BE}$	Given	
2. $\angle D \cong \angle E$	Alternate Interior Angles Theorem	

Statement	Reason	Sketch
3. $\angle ABD \cong \angle CBE$	Vertical Angles Theorem	
4. $\triangle ABD \cong \triangle CBE$	ASA Postulate	

CPCTC stands for **c**orresponding **p**arts of **c**ongruent **t**riangles are congruent. Once you prove that two triangles are congruent by using triangle congruence postulates, you can use CPCTC to determine that any corresponding pair of angles or sides is congruent.

Here is a proof of the isosceles triangle theorem, which states that if two sides of a triangle are congruent, then the angles opposite those sides are congruent.

Given $\overline{AB} \cong \overline{BC}$ **Prove** $\angle A \cong \angle C$

Statement	Reason	Sketch
1. $\overline{AB} \cong \overline{BC}$	Given	
2. Draw a median of $\triangle ABC$.	Two points determine a line.	
3. $\overline{AD} \cong \overline{CD}$	Definition of median	
4. $\overline{BD} \cong \overline{BD}$	Reflexive Property of Congruence	
5. $\triangle ABD \cong \triangle CBD$	SSS Congruence Postulate	
6. $\angle A \cong \angle C$	CPCTC	

You can use congruent triangles to determine the measures of sides and angles in triangles.

In the diagram, $\triangle ABC \cong \triangle DEF$.

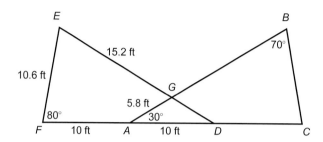

Find the missing values.

You can use CPCTC to find measures of sides and angles in congruent triangles. By the definition of congruence, the corresponding sides and angles have equal measure.

A *AC*

SOLUTION
CPCTC and Segment Addition

$AC = DF$

$DF = FA + AD = 10 + 10 = 20$

$AC = 20$ ft

B *BC*

SOLUTION
CPCTC

$BC = EF$

$EF = 10.6$ ft

$BC = 10.6$ ft

C *GD*

SOLUTION
Sides opposite congruent angles in an isosceles triangle are congruent.

$m\angle BAD = m\angle EDF$

$m\angle BAD = 30°$

$m \angle EDF = 30°$

$\triangle AGD$ is isosceles.

$GA = GD$

$GA = 5.8$ ft

$GD = 5.8$ ft

D BG

SOLUTION
CPCTC and Segment Addition

$DE = AB$

$DE = GD + GE = 5.8 + 15.2 = 21$ ft

$AB = 21$ ft

$BG = AB - GA = 21 - 5.8 = 15.2$ ft

E $m\angle ACB$

SOLUTION
CPCTC

$m\angle ACB = m\angle DFE$

$m\angle DFE = 80°$

$m\angle ACB = 80°$

F $m\angle DEF$

SOLUTION
CPCTC

$m\angle DEF = m\angle ABC$

$m\angle ABC = 70°$

$m\angle DEF = 70°$

G $m\angle AGD$

SOLUTION
CPCTC and the sum of the angles of a triangle is 180°.

$m\angle BAD = m\angle EDF$

$m\angle BAD = 30°$

$m\angle EDF = 30°$

In $\triangle AGD$, $m\angle BAD + m\angle EDF + m\angle AGD = 180°$.

$30° + 30° + m\angle AGD = 180°$

$60° + m\angle AGD = 180°$

$m\angle AGD = 120°$

H $m\angle EDC$

SOLUTION
A linear pair adds to 180°.

$m\angle EDF$ and $m\angle EDC$ form a linear pair and $m\angle EDF = 30°$.

$m\angle EDF + m\angle EDC = 180°$

$30° + m\angle EDC = 180°$

$m\angle EDC = 150°$ ▪

Constructions with Polygons

Many abstract works of art contain geometric shapes, including regular polygons.

You can use a straightedge and compass to construct a square.

Construct a square.	
Given segment with length AB **Construct** a square	

Step	Sketch
1. Draw a segment with length AB.	
2. Set the compass so that the center is A and the radius is AB, and draw circle A.	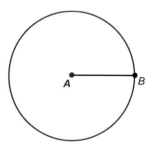
3. Set the compass so that the center is B and the radius is AB, and draw circle B. Label the points of intersections of the two circles C and D.	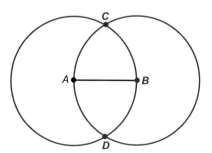

Step	Sketch

4. With a straightedge, draw $\overleftrightarrow{CD}$, the perpendicular bisector of $\overline{AB}$, intersecting the segment at midpoint F.

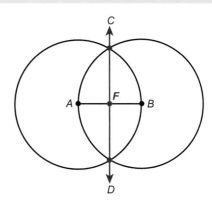

5. Construct a circle with point F as the center and with radius FB.

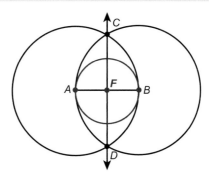

6. Label the points of intersection of circle F and $\overline{CD}$ as G and H.

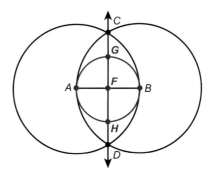

7. Use a straightedge to draw $\overline{AG}$, $\overline{GB}$, $\overline{BH}$, and $\overline{AH}$ to complete square AGBH.

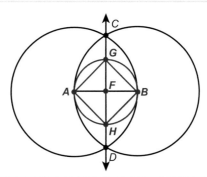

You can use a straightedge and compass to construct an equilateral triangle with a given side length.

Construct an equilateral triangle with a given side length.

Given   segment with length *RS*

Construct   an equilateral triangle with side length *RS*

Step	Sketch
1. Draw a segment with length *RS*.	
2. Draw any point *A*.	
3. Set the compass with center *A* and radius *RS*. Draw circle *A*.	

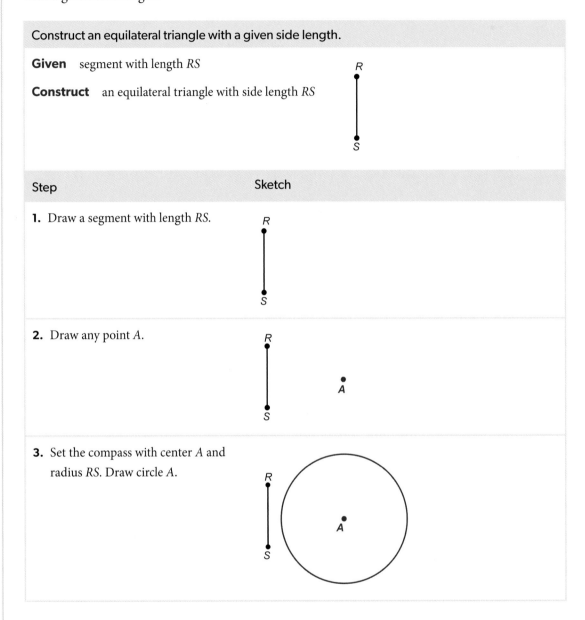

Step	Sketch

4. Draw any point *B* on the circle.

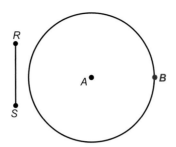

5. Set the compass with center *B* and radius *RS*. Draw circle *B* intersecting circle *A* at point *C*.

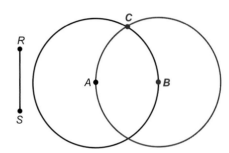

6. Use the straightedge to draw $\overline{AB}$.

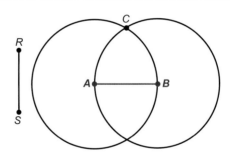

7. Use a straightedge to draw $\overline{BC}$.

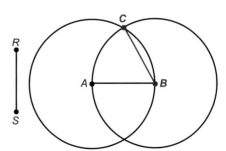

Step	Sketch

8. Use a straightedge to draw $\overline{CA}$.

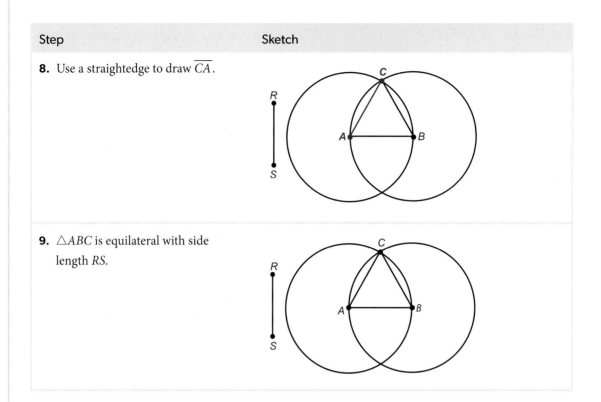

9. $\triangle ABC$ is equilateral with side length RS.

Constructing a Regular Hexagon

A regular hexagon is a six-sided polygon with congruent sides and congruent angles. You can construct a regular hexagon with geometry software using rotations. First you need to determine the measure of each **central angle**. You may recall that the measure of each central angle of a regular polygon is 360° divided by the number of its sides: $360° \div 6 = 60°$.

To start, create a point that will be the center of the hexagon. Then create another point that will be one of its vertices. Since each central angle in a regular hexagon measures 60°, the first vertex should be rotated around the center point by 60° until all the vertices are displayed.

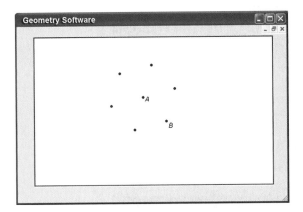

The hexagon is complete once the vertices are joined by segments.

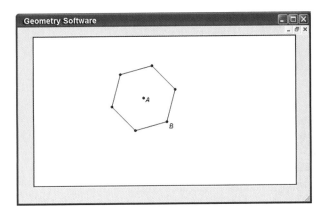

Because it is a regular hexagon, all the sides and angles should be congruent. You can check this by displaying all the measurements. Even if you drag the hexagon and increase the lengths of its sides, the six sides are still congruent and each of the six interior angles measures 120°.

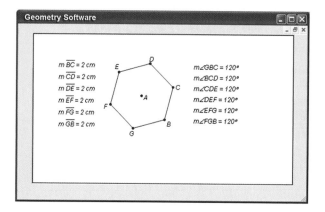

If you construct the angle bisector of each of the interior angles, you will notice that each bisector intersects the center of the hexagon.

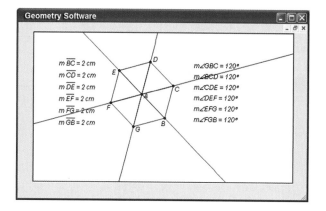

Continue to explore the hexagon by measuring the angles and sides of the triangles formed by the intersection of the angle bisectors. You can make and test conjectures about the congruence of these triangles.

You can also make a regular hexagon by constructing equilateral triangles. One way to make an equilateral triangle is to construct a circle and its radius, and then rotate the radius 60° about the center point. Construct a segment between the two points on the circle. Rotate this triangle 60° until a hexagon is formed. If desired, hide all but the sides of the hexagon.

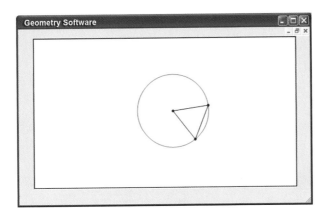

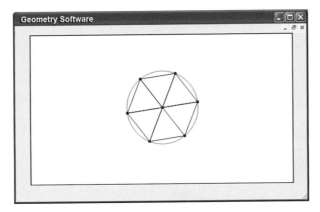

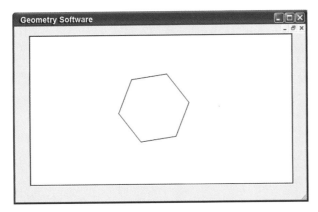

Congruence and Rigid Motions

If you can find a sequence of rigid motions that map one figure onto another, then those two figures are congruent.

Rigid Motion

Definition
A **rigid motion** is a motion that relocates a figure while preserving its shape and size.

Translations, reflections, and rotations are rigid motions. Therefore, any sequence of these motions will result in the pre-image and image being congruent.

▶ **Think About It** A dilation is not a rigid motion because the figure's size is not preserved.

EXAMPLE 1

Use rigid motions to explain whether $\triangle ABC \cong \triangle A'B'C'$.

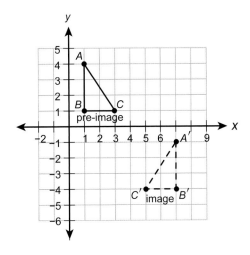

SOLUTION

You can obtain the image by translating the pre-image down 5 units and then reflecting the figure over the line $x = 4$.

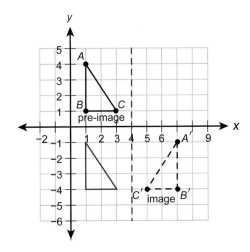

Because both of these transformations are rigid motions, $\triangle ABC \cong \triangle A'B'C'$. ▨

EXAMPLE 2

Use rigid motions to explain whether $\triangle PQR \cong \triangle P'Q'R'$.

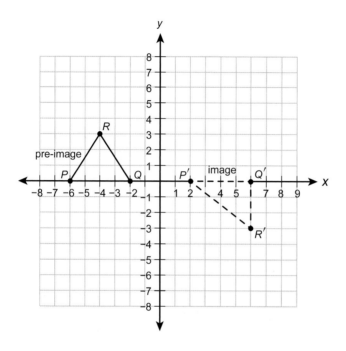

SOLUTION

There is no sequence of rigid motions that would transform the pre-image onto the image. Therefore, the triangles are not congruent. ▪

Analytic Geometry

Topic List

▸ Using the Distance Formula

▸ Computing Area with Coordinates

▸ Slope

▸ Proofs and Coordinate Geometry

NASA's *Curiosity* rover landed on Mars in 2012. Scientists at the Jet Propulsion Laboratory use many tools from analytic geometry to pilot *Curiosity* around the Martian landscape and to analyze data that *Curiosity* sends back.

Using the Distance Formula

You can use the Pythagorean theorem to derive the distance formula.

Distance

Suppose you want to find the distance between the points $(2, 4)$ and $(12, 2)$. The length of the run is the difference between the x-coordinates of the two points, $12 - 2 = \mathbf{10}$. The length of the rise is the difference between the two y-coordinates, $4 - 2 = \mathbf{2}$.

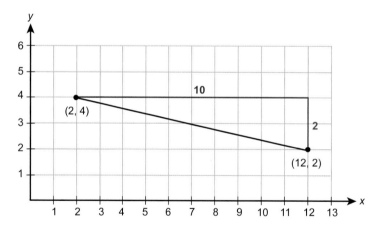

The rise and run are the lengths of the legs of a right triangle. You can find the length of the hypotenuse by using the Pythagorean theorem.

$$c^2 = a^2 + b^2$$
$$c^2 = (\mathbf{10})^2 + (\mathbf{2})^2$$
$$c^2 = 100 + 4$$
$$c^2 = 104$$
$$c \approx 10.2$$

The distance between points $(2, 4)$ and $(12, 2)$ is about 10.2 units.

Calculating Distance

You can use the same steps to find the distance between any two points (x_1, y_1) and (x_2, y_2) on the coordinate plane.

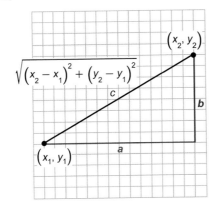

The length of side a is $x_2 - x_1$, and the length of side b is $y_2 - y_1$.

$$c^2 = (x_2 - x_1)^2 + (y_2 - y_1)^2$$
$$\sqrt{c^2} = \sqrt{(x_2 - x_1)^2 + (y_2 - y_1)^2}$$
$$c = \sqrt{(x_2 - x_1)^2 + (y_2 - y_1)^2}$$

This formula is known as the distance formula.

Distance Formula

In a coordinate plane, the distance d between any two points (x_1, y_1) and (x_2, y_2) is

$$d = \sqrt{(x_2 - x_1)^2 + (y_2 - y_1)^2}.$$

EXAMPLE 1

Find the distance between $(3, -1)$ and $(5, 0)$.

SOLUTION

Use the distance formula.

$$d = \sqrt{(x_2 - x_1)^2 + (y_2 - y_1)^2}$$
$$= \sqrt{(5 - 3)^2 + (0 - (-1))^2}$$
$$= \sqrt{(5 - 3)^2 + (0 + 1)^2}$$
$$= \sqrt{2^2 + 1^2}$$
$$= \sqrt{5}$$
$$\approx 2.24$$

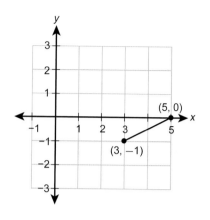

The distance between $(3, -1)$ and $(5, 0)$ is approximately 2.24 units. ▪

▶ **Remember** To subtract a negative number, add the opposite.

$$0 - (-1) = 0 + 1$$
$$= 1$$

EXAMPLE 2

Find the perimeter of rectangle $ABCD$ whose vertices are $A(3, 4)$, $B(4, 2)$, $C(0, 0)$, and $D(-1, 2)$.

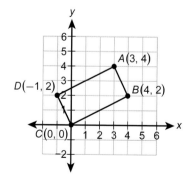

SOLUTION

To determine the perimeter of a rectangle, you need to know its length and width.

> ▶ **Think About It** Rectangles have opposite sides that are congruent. To find the perimeter, you need to find two distances: the length and the width.

Step 1 Use the distance formula to find the length and width of the rectangle. Use $C(0, 0)$ and $B(4, 2)$ for the length and $D(-1, 2)$ and $C(0, 0)$ for the width.

$$CB = \sqrt{(4 - 0)^2 + (2 - 0)^2} = \sqrt{16 + 4} = \sqrt{20} = 2\sqrt{5}$$

$$DC = \sqrt{(0 - (-1))^2 + (0 - 2)^2} = \sqrt{1 + 4} = \sqrt{5}$$

Step 2 Use the formula for the perimeter of a rectangle.

$$P = 2l + 2w$$
$$= 2(2\sqrt{5}) + 2(\sqrt{5})$$
$$= 4\sqrt{5} + 2\sqrt{5}$$
$$= 6\sqrt{5} \approx 13.42$$

The perimeter of rectangle $ABCD$ is approximately 13.42 units. ▪

EXAMPLE 3

Find the perimeter of triangle JKL. Round to the nearest hundredth.

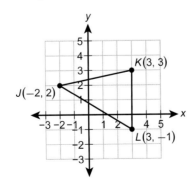

> ▶ **Think About It** When two coordinates have the same *x*- or *y*-values, the distance is the same as the difference between the opposite coordinate values.

SOLUTION

Step 1 Use the distance formula to find the length of each side.

$$JK = \sqrt{(3 - (-2))^2 + (3 - 2)^2} = \sqrt{25 + 1} = \sqrt{26} \approx 5.1$$

$$KL = \sqrt{(3 - 3)^2 + (-1 - 3)^2} = \sqrt{0 + 16} = \sqrt{16} = 4$$

$$LJ = \sqrt{(-2 - 3)^2 + (2 - (-1))^2} = \sqrt{25 + 9} = \sqrt{34} \approx 5.83$$

Step 2 Add the side lengths to find the perimeter.

$$JK + KL + LJ \approx 5.1 + 4 + 5.83 \approx 14.93$$

The perimeter of triangle *JKL* is approximately 14.93 units. ▪

Estimating Area

You can use the distance formula to estimate areas of irregular figures.

> **EXAMPLE 4**

Estimate the area of the lake.

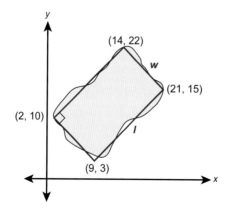

SOLUTION

Draw a rectangle that roughly outlines the perimeter of the lake. Then use the vertices of the rectangle to find its length and width. In this example, each unit on the coordinate plane is 1 mi.

$$\text{length} = \sqrt{(21 - 9)^2 + (15 - 3)^2}$$
$$= \sqrt{12^2 + 12^2}$$
$$= \sqrt{144 + 144}$$
$$= \sqrt{288}$$
$$\approx 17$$

$$\text{width} = \sqrt{(2 - 9)^2 + (10 - 3)^2}$$
$$= \sqrt{(-7)^2 + (7)^2}$$
$$= \sqrt{49 + 49}$$
$$= \sqrt{98}$$
$$\approx 9.9$$

$$A = lw \approx 17 \bullet 9.9 \approx 168$$

The area of the lake is approximately 168 mi^2. ■

Computing Area with Coordinates

The distance formula can be useful for determining areas of polygons in the coordinate plane.

Finding the Area of a Rectangle

To find the area of a rectangle, you need to know its length and its width.

EXAMPLE 1

Find the area of the rectangle.

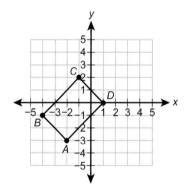

▶ **Remember** $d = \sqrt{(x_2 - x_1)^2 + (y_2 - y_1)^2}$

SOLUTION

Step 1 Find the length of the rectangle. The coordinates of A are $(-2, -3)$, and the coordinates of D are $(1, 0)$.

$$AD = \sqrt{(1-(-2))^2 + (0-(-3))^2} = \sqrt{9+9} = \sqrt{18}$$

Step 2 Find the width of the rectangle. The coordinates of A are $(-2, -3)$, and the coordinates of B are $(-4, -1)$.

$$AB = \sqrt{(-4-(-2))^2 + (-1-(-3))^2} = \sqrt{4+4} = \sqrt{8}$$

Step 3 Use the formula for the area of a rectangle.

$$\begin{aligned} A &= lw \\ &= \sqrt{18} \cdot \sqrt{8} \\ &= \sqrt{144} \\ &= 12 \end{aligned}$$

▶ **Think About It** $\sqrt{a} \cdot \sqrt{b} = \sqrt{ab}$

The area of the rectangle is 12 unit^2. ◼

Finding the Area of a Triangle

To find the area of a triangle, you need to know its base and height.

EXAMPLE 2

Find the area of the triangle whose vertices are $W(-3, 1)$, $X(2, 1)$, and $Y(5, -6)$.

SOLUTION

Step 1 Plot and connect the vertices.

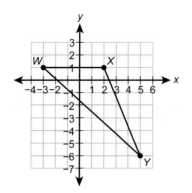

Step 2 Consider $\overline{WX}$ the base. The segment from point Y to the point at $(5, 1)$ is the height. You can count to determine that the base is 5 units and the height is 7 units.

> ▶ **Think About It** While any side could be considered the base, it is best to choose a horizontal or vertical side, if possible.

Step 3 Use the formula for the area of a triangle.

$$A = \frac{1}{2}bh$$

$$= \frac{1}{2} \bullet 5 \bullet 7$$

$$= 17.5$$

The area of the triangle is 17.5 unit^2. ▨

Finding the Area of a Trapezoid

To find the area of a trapezoid, you need to know the length of each base and its height.

EXAMPLE 3

Find the area of the trapezoid whose vertices are $A(0, 4)$, $B(4, 4)$, $C(2, -1)$, and $D(-5, -1)$.

SOLUTION

Step 1 Plot and connect the vertices.

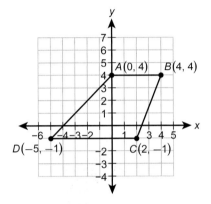

Step 2 Consider $\overline{AB}$ base 1 (b_1) and $\overline{DC}$ base 2 (b_2). The length of base 1 is 4 units and the length of base 2 is 7 units. The segment from $(0, -1)$ to $(0, 4)$ is the height. The height is 5 units.

Step 3 Use the formula for the area of a trapezoid.

$$A = \frac{1}{2}(b_1 + b_2)h$$

$$= \frac{1}{2}(4 + 7)5$$

$$= 27.5$$

The area of trapezoid $ABCD$ is 27.5 units^2. ▪

Finding the Area of a Composite Figure

EXAMPLE 4

Find the area of the polygon.

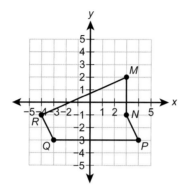

SOLUTION

Draw a segment from point R to point N to create right $\triangle MNR$ and parallelogram $RNPQ$. Find the area of each figure.

$\triangle MNR$

$$A = \frac{1}{2}bh$$

$$= \frac{1}{2} \cdot 7 \cdot 3$$

$$= 10.5$$

parallelogram $RNPQ$

$$A = bh$$

$$= 7 \cdot 2$$

$$= 14$$

Add to find the combined area.

$$10.5 + 14 = 24.5$$

The area of the polygon is 24.5 unit^2. ■

Slope

The steepness of a line is called the slope of the line.

Right Triangles and Slope

The **slope** of a line is a number that describes the steepness of the line. To get from any one point on the line to any other point on the line, you must move a horizontal distance, called the **run**, and a vertical distance, called the **rise**. The slope of the line is equal to the rise divided by the run.

$$\text{slope} = \frac{\textbf{rise}}{\textbf{run}}$$

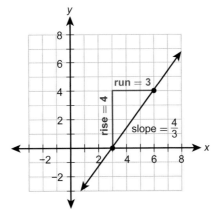

On a coordinate plane, the rise is the difference in the y-coordinates and the run is the difference in the x-coordinates.

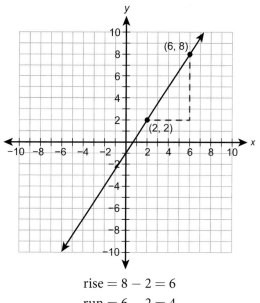

$$\text{rise} = 8 - 2 = 6$$
$$\text{run} = 6 - 2 = 4$$
$$\text{slope} = \frac{6}{4} = \frac{3}{2}$$

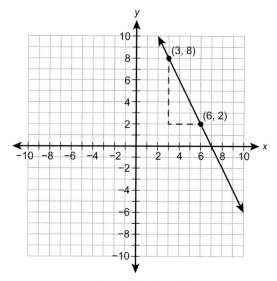

$$\text{rise} = 8 - 2 = 6$$
$$\text{run} = 3 - 6 = -3$$
$$\text{slope} = \frac{6}{-3} = -2$$

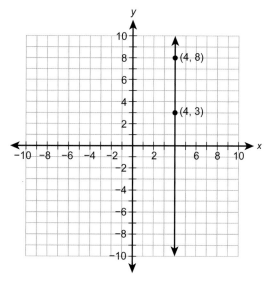

$$\text{rise} = 8 - 3 = 5$$
$$\text{run} = 4 - 4 = 0$$
$$\text{slope} = \frac{5}{0}, \text{ which is undefined}$$

A vertical line has an undefined slope.

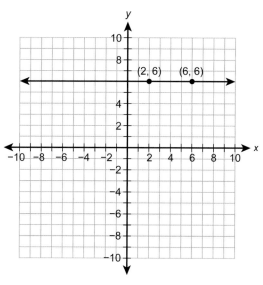

$$\text{rise} = 6 - 6 = 0$$
$$\text{run} = 6 - 2 = 4$$
$$\text{slope} = \frac{0}{4} = 0$$

A horizontal line has a slope of 0.

Between two points (x_1, y_1) and (x_2, y_2), you can write the difference between the y-coordinates as $y_2 - y_1$ and the difference between the x-coordinates as $x_2 - x_1$. Then instead of writing slope as $\dfrac{\text{rise}}{\text{run}}$, you can write the slope formula.

Slope Formula

The slope m of a nonvertical line that contains the points (x_1, y_1) and (x_2, y_2) is

$$m = \frac{y_2 - y_1}{x_2 - x_1}.$$

Parallel and Perpendicular Lines

In the diagram, $p \parallel m$, $s \perp p$, and $s \perp m$.

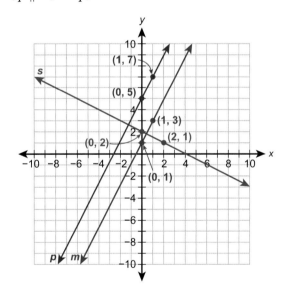

Using the slope formula, find the following:

$$\text{slope of line } p = \frac{7 - 5}{1 - 0} = \frac{2}{1} = 2$$

$$\text{slope of line } m = \frac{3 - 1}{1 - 0} = \frac{2}{1} = 2$$

$$\text{slope of line } s = \frac{1 - 2}{2 - 0} = \frac{-1}{2} = -\frac{1}{2}$$

The slopes of the parallel lines (lines p and m) are equal. The slope of line s is the opposite of the reciprocal of lines p and m. In other words, the product of the slopes of the perpendicular lines is -1.

You can use geometry software to investigate this concept further. Construct two parallel line segments, and then construct a line perpendicular to one of the segments. Use your software to measure the slope of each line and line segment. Although the slopes in the diagram are written in decimal format, remember that $0.25 = \frac{1}{4}$.

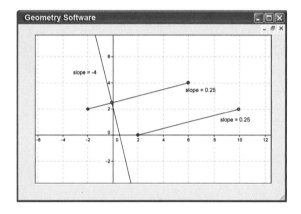

Theorem COORD-1

Parallel Lines Theorem Two coplanar nonvertical lines are parallel if and only if they have the same slope. Any two vertical lines are parallel.

Theorem COORD-2

Perpendicular Lines Theorem Two coplanar nonvertical lines are perpendicular if and only if the product of their slopes equals -1. Any vertical line is perpendicular to any horizontal line.

You can use these theorems to find the equation of a line that is parallel or perpendicular to a given line and that passes through a given point not on the line.

EXAMPLE 1

Write the equation of the line that is parallel to $y = 2x - 6$ and that passes through the point $(2, 1)$.

SOLUTION

Step 1 Find the slope of the line. The slope of the given line is 2. Since parallel lines have the same slope, the slope of the line parallel to this line that goes through the point $(2, 1)$ also has a slope of 2.

Step 2 Use slope-intercept form, where the slope is 2 and the point $(2, 1)$ is on the parallel line, to determine the equation of the parallel line.

$y = mx + b$ Slope-intercept form

$1 = 2(2) + b$ Substitute $x = 2$, $y = 1$, and $m = 2$.

$-3 = b$ Solve for b.

The equation of the line that is parallel to $y = 2x - 6$ and that passes through the point $(2, 1)$ is $y = 2x - 3$. ◼

EXAMPLE 2

Write the equation of the line that is perpendicular to $y = 2x - 6$ and that passes through the point $(2, 1)$.

SOLUTION

Step 1 Find the slope of the line. The slopes of perpendicular lines are opposite reciprocals. The slope of the given line is 2, so the slope of the line perpendicular to this line is $-\dfrac{1}{2}$.

▶ **Think About It** The opposite reciprocal of a number can be found by writing the number as a fraction, and then flipping the numerator and denominator and changing the sign. $\dfrac{3}{4}$ and $-\dfrac{4}{3}$ are opposite reciprocals.

Step 2 Use slope-intercept form, where the slope is $-\frac{1}{2}$ and the

point $(2, 1)$ is on the perpendicular line, to determine the equation of the perpendicular line.

$y = mx + b$ — Slope-intercept form

$1 = -\frac{1}{2}(2) + b$ — Substitute $x = 2$, $y = 1$, and $m = -\frac{1}{2}$.

$2 = b$ — Solve for b.

The equation of the line perpendicular to $y = 2x - 6$ that passes through the

point $(2, 1)$ is $y = -\frac{1}{2}x + 2$. ▪

You can use the parallel lines theorem to show that a quadrilateral drawn in the coordinate plane is a parallelogram. Consider $ABCD$ in the figure. You must show that both pairs of opposite sides are parallel. If $\overline{AB}$ and $\overline{DC}$ have equal slopes, and if $\overline{BC}$ and $\overline{AD}$ have equal slopes, then the opposite sides are parallel.

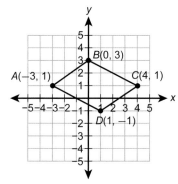

$$\text{slope of } \overline{AB} = \frac{3 - 1}{0 - (-3)} = \frac{2}{3}$$

$$\text{slope of } \overline{DC} = \frac{1 - (-1)}{4 - 1} = \frac{2}{3}$$

$$\text{slope of } \overline{BC} = \frac{3 - 1}{0 - 4} = \frac{2}{-4} = -\frac{1}{2}$$

$$\text{slope of } \overline{AD} = \frac{1 - (-1)}{-3 - 1} = \frac{2}{-4} = -\frac{1}{2}$$

Since the opposite sides have equal slopes, $ABCD$ is a parallelogram.

You can use the perpendicular lines theorem to show that a triangle in a coordinate plane is a right triangle. Consider $\triangle ABC$ in the figure. All you need to do is show that one of the angles of the triangle is a right angle. If two sides have slopes with a product of -1, then the angle formed by those sides is a right angle. Begin by finding the slope of each side.

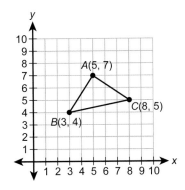

$$\text{slope of } \overline{AB} = \frac{7-4}{5-3} = \frac{3}{2}$$

$$\text{slope of } \overline{AC} = \frac{7-5}{5-8} = \frac{2}{-3} = -\frac{2}{3}$$

$$\text{slope of } \overline{BC} = \frac{5-4}{8-3} = \frac{1}{5}$$

Since the product of the slopes of $\overline{AB}$ and $\overline{AC}$ is -1, $\overline{AB} \perp \overline{AC}$ and $\triangle ABC$ is a right triangle.

Midpoint Formula

Recall that the midpoint of a line segment divides the line segment into two congruent parts. To find the midpoint of a line segment on a number line, you could add the coordinates of the endpoints and then divide by 2. The midpoint of the segment with endpoints 3 and 7 is $\dfrac{3+7}{2} = \dfrac{10}{2} = 5$.

To find the midpoint of a line segment on a coordinate plane, use the midpoint formula.

Midpoint Formula

The coordinates of the midpoint of a line segment with endpoints $\left(x_1, y_1\right)$ and $\left(x_2, y_2\right)$, are

$$\left(\dfrac{x_1 + x_2}{2}, \dfrac{y_1 + y_2}{2}\right).$$

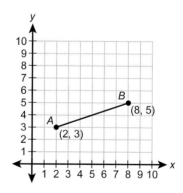

To find the midpoint of $\overline{AB}$, use the midpoint formula.

$$\left(\dfrac{x_1 + x_2}{2}, \dfrac{y_1 + y_2}{2}\right) = \left(\dfrac{2+8}{2}, \dfrac{3+5}{2}\right)$$

$$= \left(\dfrac{10}{2}, \dfrac{8}{2}\right)$$

$$= (5, 4)$$

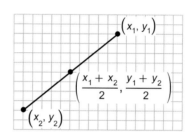

Proofs and Coordinate Geometry

Coordinate proofs combine properties of the coordinate plane, algebra, and geometry.

Placing a Figure for a Coordinate Proof

In a coordinate proof, you start by placing a figure on the coordinate plane. Do not haphazardly place it anywhere. Place it in a way that your calculations will be as simple as possible. The following guidelines can help you do that:

- Place the entire figure in the first quadrant.

- Place at least one side of the polygon on either the *x*- or the *y*-axis.

- Place a center or vertex at the origin.

The examples show wise placement of three figures and how their coordinates are named.

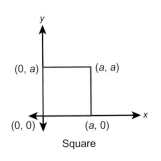

Square

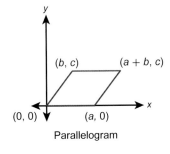

Parallelogram

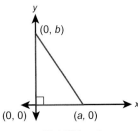

Right Triangle

Examples of Coordinate Proofs

The midsegment of a triangle is a line segment that connects the midpoints of two sides of the triangle. The following proof shows that a midsegment is always parallel to the third side and that it is one-half the length of the third side.

Given G is the midpoint of $\overline{DF}$.
H is the midpoint of $\overline{EF}$.

Prove $\overline{GH} \parallel \overline{DE}$ and $GH = \dfrac{1}{2}DE$

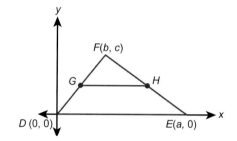

> ▶ **Remember** Midpoint formula
> $$\left(\frac{x_1 + x_2}{2}, \frac{y_1 + y_2}{2} \right)$$

Use the midpoint formula to find the coordinates of G and H.

$$\text{point } G \ \left(\frac{0 + b}{2}, \frac{0 + c}{2} \right) = \left(\frac{b}{2}, \frac{c}{2} \right)$$

$$\text{point } H \ \left(\frac{a + b}{2}, \frac{0 + c}{2} \right) = \left(\frac{a + b}{2}, \frac{c}{2} \right)$$

Prove $\overline{GH} \parallel \overline{DE}$ by showing that the lines have the same slope.

$$\text{slope of } \overline{GH} = \frac{\dfrac{c}{2} - \dfrac{c}{2}}{\dfrac{a + b}{2} - \dfrac{b}{2}} = \frac{0}{\dfrac{a}{2}} = 0$$

$$\text{slope of } \overline{DE} = \frac{0 - 0}{a - 0} = \frac{0}{a} = 0$$

Since both slopes are zero, they are equal and the segments are parallel.
Use the distance formula to find GH and DE.

$$GH = \sqrt{\left(\frac{a+b}{2} - \frac{b}{2}\right)^2 + \left(\frac{c}{2} - \frac{c}{2}\right)^2} = \sqrt{\left(\frac{a}{2}\right)^2 + 0} = \frac{a}{2} = \frac{1}{2}a$$

$$DE = \sqrt{(a-0)^2 + (0-0)^2} = \sqrt{a^2} = a$$

Therefore, $GH = \frac{1}{2}DE$

Q.E.D.

▶ **Think About It** Mathematicians often put Q.E.D. at the end of a proof. It stands for the Latin phrase *quod erat demonstrandum*, which means "which was to be proven."

You can use coordinates to prove that the diagonals of a parallelogram bisect each other.

Given parallelogram $QRST$ with diagonals $\overline{QS}$ and $\overline{RT}$

Prove $\overline{QS}$ and $\overline{RT}$ bisect each other.

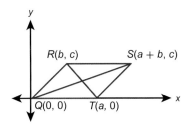

Prove $\overline{QS}$ and $\overline{RT}$ bisect each other by finding the midpoints of $\overline{QS}$ and $\overline{RT}$ and showing the midpoints are the same.

$$\text{midpoint of } \overline{QS} = \left(\frac{a+b+0}{2}, \frac{c+0}{2}\right) = \left(\frac{a+b}{2}, \frac{c}{2}\right)$$

$$\text{midpoint of } \overline{RT} = \left(\frac{a+b}{2}, \frac{0+c}{2}\right) = \left(\frac{a+b}{2}, \frac{c}{2}\right)$$

So $\overline{QS}$ and $\overline{RT}$ bisect each other.

Q.E.D.

Reflecting Over the Line $y = x$

If a point (x, y) is reflected across the line $y = x$, then its image is the point (y, x). For example, if the point whose coordinates are $(3, 4)$ is reflected over $y = x$, its image coordinates will be $(4, 3)$.

With a coordinate proof, you can prove that when a point is reflected over the line $y = x$, the line is the perpendicular bisector of the segment whose endpoints are the pre-image and image points.

Given J is the image of K reflected over $y = x$.

Prove $\overleftrightarrow{LM}$ is the perpendicular bisector of $\overline{JK}$.

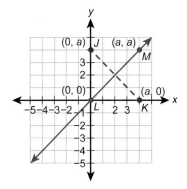

You begin by finding slopes.

$$\text{slope of } \overline{JK} = \frac{a - 0}{0 - a} = \frac{a}{-a} = -1$$

$$\text{slope of } \overleftrightarrow{LM} = \frac{a - 0}{a - 0} = \frac{a}{a} = 1$$

The product of the slopes is -1, so the line and segment are perpendicular. Now you just need to prove that the reflection line bisects the segment. Find the coordinates of the segment's midpoint.

$$\left(\frac{a + 0}{2}, \frac{0 + a}{2} \right) = \left(\frac{a}{2}, \frac{a}{2} \right).$$

This point is on the line $y = x$, so your proof is complete.

Q.E.D.

Connecting the Midpoints of a Rectangle

You can use a coordinate proof to prove that the figure formed by the midpoints of a rectangle is a rhombus.

On a grid, place a rectangle as shown. Label in multiples of 2 to avoid fractions in the midpoints.

Given E, F, G, and H are the midpoints of $\overline{AB}$, $\overline{BC}$, $\overline{CD}$, and $\overline{DA}$, respectively.

Prove $EFGH$ is a rhombus.

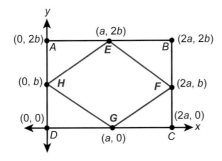

Use the distance formula to find the length of each side formed by the midpoints.

$$GH = \sqrt{(0-a)^2 + (b-0)^2} = \sqrt{a^2 + b^2}$$

$$HE = \sqrt{(a-0)^2 + (2b-b)^2} = \sqrt{a^2 + b^2}$$

$$EF = \sqrt{(a-2a)^2 + (2b-b)^2} = \sqrt{a^2 + b^2}$$

$$FG = \sqrt{(2a-a)^2 + (b-0)^2} = \sqrt{a^2 + b^2}$$

All the sides have the same length. The figure is a rhombus.

Q.E.D.

Line and Triangle Relationships

Topic List

- ▸ Parallel Lines and Transversals
- ▸ Converses of Parallel Line Properties
- ▸ The Triangle Sum Theorem
- ▸ Bisectors of a Triangle: Circumcenter
- ▸ Midsegments
- ▸ Quadrilaterals and Their Properties
- ▸ Parallelograms

Architects use geometric figures to create beautiful, functional buildings. This skylight at the Vatican Museum is composed of clean geometric figures with lots of symmetry that create a stunning contrast with the fluid, ornate spiral staircase leading up to it.

Parallel Lines and Transversals

A line that passes through parallel lines creates special pairs of angles that you can use to solve problems and prove theorems.

Using the Properties of Transversals and Parallel Lines

Definition
A **transversal** is a line that intersects two or more lines in a plane.

In the figure, line *t* is a transversal. Notice that this intersection creates eight different angles. Certain pairs of these angles have special names.

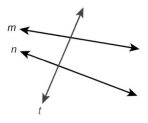

Definition
Corresponding angles are the angles that lie in the same position or match up when a transversal intersects two lines.

If you think of the eight angles as being split into two different groups of four, one group around line *m* and one group around line *n*, then those angles that match up are corresponding angles. The corresponding angles in this figure are the angle pairs ∠1 and ∠5, ∠2 and ∠6, ∠3 and ∠7, and ∠4 and ∠8.

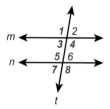

Definition

Alternate interior angles are in between the two lines that are not the transversal, and are on diagonal opposite sides of the transversal.

In this figure, the alternate interior angles are the angle pair ∠3 and ∠6 and the angle pair ∠4 and ∠5.

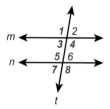

Definition

Alternate exterior angles are outside the two lines that are not the transversal, and are on diagonal opposite sides of the transversal.

In this figure, the alternate exterior angles are the angle pair ∠1 and ∠8 and the angle pair ∠2 and ∠7.

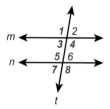

In this figure, the same-side interior angles are the angle pair $\angle 3$ and $\angle 5$ and the angle pair $\angle 4$ and $\angle 6$.

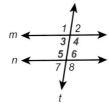

These angle pairs have special relationships. You may have already made some conjectures about them. The following postulates and theorems involve angle pairs formed by two parallel lines intersected by a transversal.

Working with Corresponding Angles

Postulate PAR-1

Corresponding Angles Postulate If two parallel lines are intersected by a transversal, then corresponding angles are congruent.

▶ **Think About It** Euclidean geometry is a system of thinking built on undefined and defined terms, postulates, and theorems.

THEOREM PAR-1   Alternate Interior Angles Theorem

If two parallel lines are intersected by a transversal, then the alternate interior angles are congruent.

Given $m \parallel n$

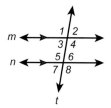

Prove $\angle 3 \cong \angle 6$

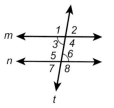

Statement	Reason	Sketch
1. $m \parallel n$	Given	
2. $\angle 3 \cong \angle 2$	Vertical Angles Theorem	
3. $\angle 2 \cong \angle 6$	Corresponding Angles Postulate	
4. $\angle 3 \cong \angle 6$	Transitive Property of Congruence	

THEOREM PAR-2 Alternate Exterior Angles Theorem

If two parallel lines are intersected by a transversal, then the alternate exterior angles are congruent.

Given $m \parallel n$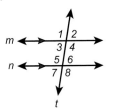

Prove $\angle 1 \cong \angle 8$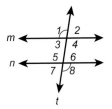

Statement	Reason	Sketch
1. $m \parallel n$	Given	
2. $\angle 1 \cong \angle 4$	Vertical Angles Theorem	
3. $\angle 4 \cong \angle 8$	Corresponding Angles Postulate	
4. $\angle 1 \cong \angle 8$	Transitive Property of Congruence	

THEOREM PAR-3   Same-Side Interior Angles Theorem

If two parallel lines are intersected by a transversal, then the same-side interior angles are supplementary.

Given $m \parallel n$

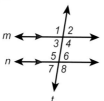

Prove $m\angle 4 + m\angle 6 = 180°$

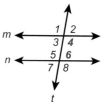

Statement	Reason	Sketch
1. $m \parallel n$	Given	
2. A linear pair is formed from $\angle 6$ and $\angle 8$.	Definition of a linear pair	
3. $m\angle 6 + m\angle 8 = 180°$	Linear Pair Postulate	
4. $m\angle 4 = m\angle 8$	Corresponding Angles Postulate	
5. $m\angle 4 + m\angle 6 = 180°$	Substitution Property of Equality	

You can use the special angles formed by parallel lines and a transversal to find the measurements of missing angles.

EXAMPLE

Given $l \parallel m$ and $m\angle 1 = 37°$, find $m\angle 4$ and $m\angle 7$.

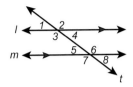

▶ **Remember** Supplementary angles have a sum of 180°. Also, any angles that form a linear pair are supplementary angles.

SOLUTION

Step 1 Find $m\angle 4$.

Since $\angle 1$ and $\angle 4$ are vertical angles, $\angle 1 \cong \angle 4$. Since $m\angle 1 = 37°$, $m\angle 4 = 37°$.

Step 2 Find $m\angle 7$.

You can find $m\angle 7$ in different ways, using the measures of other angles.

Since $\angle 3$ and $\angle 4$ are supplementary angles, their sum is 180°.

$$m\angle 3 + m\angle 4 = 180°$$
$$m\angle 3 + 37° = 180°$$
$$m\angle 3 = 180° - 37°$$
$$m\angle 3 = 143°$$

Since $\angle 3$ and $\angle 7$ are corresponding angles, $\angle 3 \cong \angle 7$. Since $m\angle 3 = 143°$, $m\angle 7 = 143°$. ▪

Converses of Parallel Line Properties

The converses of the postulates and theorems about parallel lines can be used to solve problems and complete proofs.

Using Theorems to Prove Other Theorems

Recall that the converse of a conditional statement switches the hypothesis and the conclusion. If a conditional statement is true, its converse may or may not be true. You have proven theorems about the pairs of angles created when parallel lines are intersected by a transversal. The converses of those theorems, as well as the converse of the corresponding angles postulate, are all true. You now have another postulate and more theorems that you can use to prove that two lines are parallel.

Postulate PAR-2

Converse of the Corresponding Angles Postulate If two coplanar lines are intersected by a transversal and the corresponding angles are congruent, then the lines are parallel.

Theorem PAR-4

Converse of the Alternate Interior Angles Theorem If two coplanar lines are intersected by a transversal and the alternate interior angles are congruent, then the lines are parallel.

Theorem PAR-5

Converse of the Alternate Exterior Angles Theorem If two coplanar lines are intersected by a transversal and the alternate exterior angles are congruent, then the lines are parallel.

Theorem PAR-6

Converse of the Same-Side Interior Angles Theorem If two coplanar lines are intersected by a transversal and the same-side interior angles are supplementary, then the lines are parallel.

You can use the new theorems to prove others.

THEOREM LINES-1

If two coplanar lines are perpendicular to ($\perp$) the same line, then the two lines are parallel.

Given $m \perp t$ and $n \perp t$

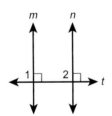

Prove $m \parallel n$

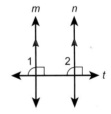

Statement	Reason	Sketch
1. $m \perp t$ and $n \perp t$	Given	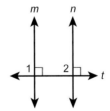
2. $m\angle 1 = 90°$ $\quad m\angle 2 = 90°$	Definition of perpendicular lines	

Statement	Reason	Sketch
3. $m\angle 1 = m\angle 2$	Substitution Property of Equality	
4. $\angle 1 \cong \angle 2$	Angle Congruence Postulate	
5. $m \parallel n$	Converse of the Corresponding Angles Postulate	

THEOREM LINES-2

If two coplanar lines are parallel to the same line, then the two lines are parallel.

Given $m \parallel p$ and $n \parallel p$

Prove $m \parallel n$

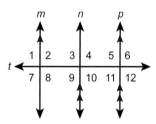

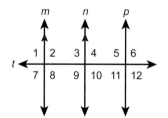

Statement	Reason	Sketch
1. $m \parallel p$ and $n \parallel p$	Given	

Statement	Reason	Sketch
2. $\angle 1 \cong \angle 12$	Alternate Exterior Angles Theorem	
3. $\angle 12 \cong \angle 10$	Corresponding Angles Postulate	
4. $\angle 1 \cong \angle 10$	Transitive Property of Congruence	
5. $m \parallel n$	Converse of Alternate Exterior Angles Theorem	

You can use the measures of pairs of angles to determine whether lines are parallel.

EXAMPLE

Given $m\angle 1 = 53°$ and $m\angle 2 = 53°$, determine whether lines l and m are parallel.

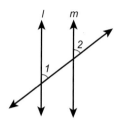

▶ **Remember** Corresponding angles are angles that lie in the same position when a transversal intersects two lines.

SOLUTION

Since $\angle 1$ and $\angle 2$ have the same measure, $\angle 1 \cong \angle 2$.

By the definition of corresponding angles, $\angle 1$ and $\angle 2$ are corresponding angles.

By the converse of the corresponding angles postulate, lines l and m are parallel. ▪

The Triangle Sum Theorem

The sum of the measures of the interior angles of any triangle is always 180°.

More About Triangles

Definition
The **interior angles** of a triangle are the three angles inside the triangle.

You can use geometry software to see if there is a relationship among the interior angles of a triangle.

Start by drawing a triangle and displaying each angle measure. Then find the sum of the angle measures. If you select a point and change the shape of the triangle, the sum is still 180°.

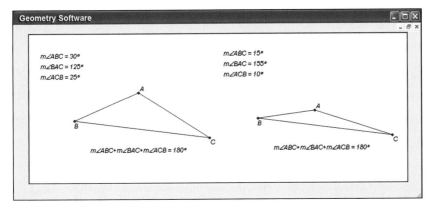

You can prove it. But first you need the following postulate.

Postulate LINES-1

Parallel Postulate Given a line and a point not on the line, there is one and only one line that contains the given point and is parallel to the given line.

The figure shows that an infinite number of lines pass through point *P*, but only one, line *m*, is parallel to line *n*.

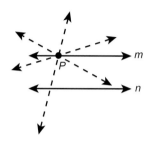

THEOREM TRI-1   Triangle Sum Theorem
The sum of the measures of the interior angles of a triangle is 180°.

Given $\triangle ABC$

Prove $m\angle 1 + m\angle 2 + m\angle 3 = 180°$

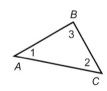

Statement	Reason	Sketch
1. Draw $\overleftrightarrow{DE} \parallel \overleftrightarrow{AC}$.	Parallel Postulate	
2. $m\angle 4 = m\angle 1$ $m\angle 5 = m\angle 2$	Alternate Interior Angles Theorem	

Statement	Reason	Sketch
3. $m\angle 4 + m\angle 3 = m\angle DBC$	Angle Addition Postulate	
4. $\angle DBC$ and $\angle 5$ form a linear pair.	Definition of Linear Pair	
5. $m\angle DBC + m\angle 5 = 180°$	Linear Pair Postulate	
6. $m\angle 4 + m\angle 3 + m\angle 5 = 180°$	Substitution Property of Equality (Steps 3 and 5)	
7. $m\angle 1 + m\angle 3 + m\angle 2 = 180°$	Substitution Property of Equality (Steps 2 and 6)	

Knowing the triangle sum theorem and the definition of different triangles allows you to find the measure of missing angles.

EXAMPLE 1

$\triangle ABC$ is an isosceles triangle. If $m\angle C = 110°$, find $m\angle A$ and $m\angle B$.

SOLUTION

Step 1 To find the measure of the missing angles, first determine how the angles are related. Isosceles triangles have two angles with the same measure. Decide if the given angle could be one of those angles.

▶ **Remember** An isosceles triangle has two congruent sides and two congruent angles.

The sum of the three angles must equal 180°. If $\angle C$ is one of the two congruent angles, is the triangle possible?

$$m\angle C + m\angle C = 110° + 110° = 220°$$

No. Because interior angles are not negative measurements, a triangle with two 110° angles is not possible. Since $\angle C$ is not one of the two congruent angles, $\angle A \cong \angle B$ must be true.

Step 2 Find $m\angle A$ and $m\angle B$.

$m\angle A + m\angle B + m\angle C = 180°$	Triangle Sum Theorem
$m\angle A = m\angle B$	Definition of congruency
$m\angle A + m\angle A + 110° = 180°$	Substitute.
$m\angle A + m\angle A = 70°$	Subtract.
$2(m\angle A) = 70°$	Simplify.
$m\angle A = 35°$	Divide.
$m\angle B = 35°$	Definition of congruency

So $m\angle A$ and $m\angle B$ are each 35°. ▪

To solve a triangle, determine the measurements of all the unknown side and angle measures.

EXAMPLE 2

$\triangle EFG$ is an equilateral triangle, and $EF = 12.5$ cm. Solve $\triangle EFG$.

SOLUTION

Step 1 Find the length of the missing sides.

Because the triangle is equilateral, the sides all have the same length.

$$EF = FG = GE = 12.5 \text{ cm}$$

Step 2 Find the measure of the missing angles.

None of the angle measures are known. But since the three angles all have the same measure, the measure of each angle must be $180° \div 3 = 60°$.

$$m\angle E = m\angle F = m\angle G = 60° \blacksquare$$

Definitions

An **exterior angle** of a triangle is an angle formed by one side of the triangle and another side of the triangle when it is extended.

Remote interior angles are the angles that are inside the triangle and are not adjacent to a given exterior angle.

▶ **Think About It** A remote island is an island faraway. A remote control device allows you to control things that are faraway. The remote interior angles are the two angles farthest from their exterior angle.

In the figure, ∠4 is an exterior angle, and ∠1 and ∠2 are the remote interior angles.

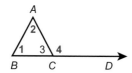

In a triangle, two remote interior angles are related to their exterior angle in a specific way, which is described in the exterior angle theorem.

THEOREM TRI-2 Exterior Angle Theorem

The measure of an exterior angle of a triangle is equal to the sum of the measures of the remote interior angles.

Given ∠4 is an exterior angle of △ABC.

Prove $m\angle 1 + m\angle 2 = m\angle 4$

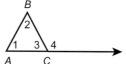

Statement	Reason	Sketch
1. ∠3 and ∠4 form a linear pair.	Definition of a linear pair	
2. $m\angle 3 + m\angle 4 = 180°$	Linear Pair Postulate	
3. $m\angle 1 + m\angle 2 + m\angle 3 = 180°$	Triangle Sum Theorem	
4. $m\angle 1 + m\angle 2 + m\angle 3$ $= m\angle 3 + m\angle 4$	Substitution Property of Equality	
5. $m\angle 1 + m\angle 2 = m\angle 4$	Subtraction Property of Equality	

Use the triangle sum theorem and the exterior angle theorem to find missing angles in figures.

EXAMPLE 3

Find the values of x, y, and z.

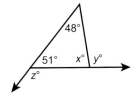

SOLUTION

To find the value of x, add 51 and 48, and subtract from 180.

$$180 - (51 + 48) = 81$$

The value of x is 81.

To find the value of y, add 48 and 51.

$$48 + 51 = 99$$

The value of y is 99.

To find the value of z, add 48 to the value of x.

$$48 + 81 = 129$$

The value of z is 129.

Use the linear pair postulate to check the values.

$$51° + 129° = 180° \text{ and } 81° + 99° = 180°$$

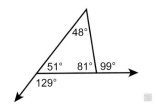

Bisectors of a Triangle: Circumcenter

To understand theorems associated with circles, you need to know the relationships between triangles and circles.

Points of Intersection in Triangles

Definition

The **circumcenter** of a triangle is the point where the perpendicular bisectors on each side of a triangle intersect.

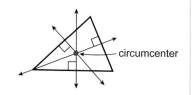

The circumcenter may lie inside, on, or outside the triangle.

If the triangle is acute, the circumcenter lies inside the triangle. If the triangle is a right triangle, the circumcenter lies on the triangle, and if the triangle is obtuse, the circumcenter lies outside the triangle.

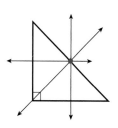 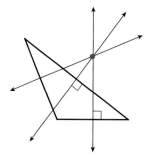

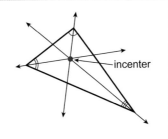
The incenter is always on the inside of a triangle. Just as you can use tick marks to indicate congruent segments, you can use multiple arcs to indicate congruent angles.

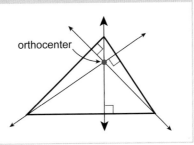
The orthocenter may lie inside, on, or outside the triangle.

If the triangle is acute, the orthocenter lies inside the triangle. If the triangle is a right triangle, the orthocenter lies on the triangle, and if the triangle is an obtuse triangle, the orthocenter lies outside triangle.

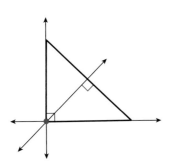

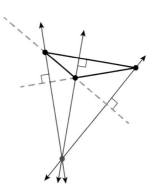

Centroids

Definitions

A **median** of a triangle is a segment from the vertex of a triangle to the midpoint of its opposite side.

The **centroid** of a triangle is the point where all three medians of the triangle intersect.

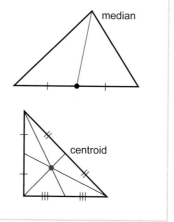

The centroid is especially interesting because it is also known as the center of gravity. You can balance any triangular figure with just your fingertip or pencil tip if you hold it directly under the centroid.

Circumscribed and Inscribed Circles

Definitions

A circle is **circumscribed** about a triangle if each vertex of the triangle lies on the circle. The circumcenter of a triangle is the center of the circumscribed circle.

A circle is **inscribed** in a triangle if the circle touches each side of the triangle at a single point. The incenter is the center of the inscribed circle.

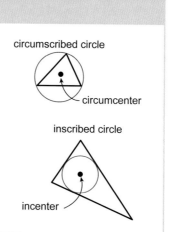

Using Geometry Software

The following diagrams were constructed with geometry software. To construct a circumcenter of a triangle, construct the perpendicular bisectors of each side of a triangle and construct their intersection.

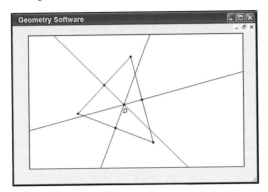

To construct the circumscribed circle, select the circumcenter as the center and one vertex as a point on the circle.

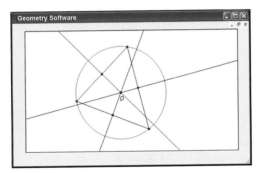

To construct an incenter of a triangle, construct the angle bisectors of each vertex of a triangle and mark their intersection.

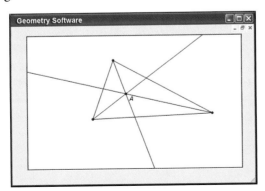

To construct the inscribed circle, first construct a perpendicular line from the incenter to one of the sides. Then construct the circle using the incenter and that intersection. Last hide the perpendicular line.

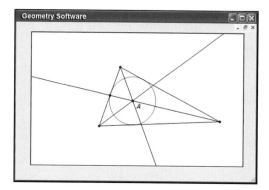

To construct the centroid of a triangle, construct the midpoint of each side of the triangle, draw the segment between each midpoint and its opposite vertex, and then mark their intersection.

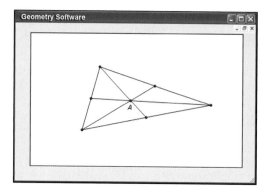

EXAMPLE 1

Find the circumcenter of a triangle whose vertices are $R(3, 3)$, $S(9, 3)$, and $T(3, -1)$.

SOLUTION

The circumcenter is the intersection of the perpendicular bisectors. To find the circumcenter, find the point where the perpendicular bisectors of any two sides meet. The perpendicular bisector goes through the midpoint of the side of the triangle.

Step 1 Draw the triangle on a coordinate plane.

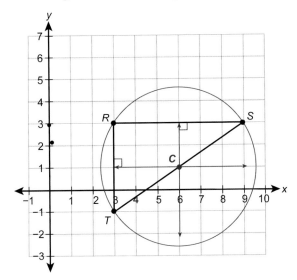

Step 2 Find the perpendicular bisector of $\overline{RS}$ by finding the midpoint.

$$\left(\frac{3+9}{2}, \frac{3+3}{2}\right) = (6, 3)$$

The perpendicular bisector of $\overline{RS}$ is the vertical line $x = 6$.

> ▶ **Think About It** Any two sides of a triangle can be used to determine the circumcenter. If the triangle has horizontal and vertical sides, it is simpler to use them.

Step 3 Find the perpendicular bisector of $\overline{RT}$ by finding the midpoint.

$$\left(\frac{3+3}{2}, \frac{3+(-1)}{2}\right) = (3, 1)$$

The perpendicular bisector of $\overline{RT}$ is the horizontal line $y = 1$.

Step 4 Find the circumcenter. The intersection of the perpendicular bisectors is the circumcenter $C(6, 1)$. ▪

EXAMPLE 2

Point U is the incenter of $\triangle LMN$ and $m\angle MLU = 19°$. What is $m\angle LMN$?

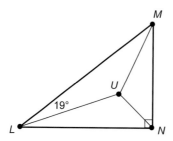

SOLUTION

The incenter is the intersection of the angle bisectors. If $m\angle MLU = 19°$, then $m\angle NLU = 19°$. To find the $m\angle MLN$, add $m\angle MLN = 19° + 19° = 38°$.

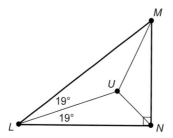

$\triangle LMN$ is a right triangle, so the acute angles of the triangle are complementary.

$$m\angle LMN + m\angle MLN = 90°$$
$$m\angle LMN + 38° = 90°$$
$$m\angle LMN = 52°$$

So $m\angle LMN$ is 52°. ▪

EXAMPLE 3

Find the orthocenter of a triangle whose vertices are $X(-1, 7)$, $Y(1, 3)$, and $Z(-3, 3)$.

SOLUTION

The orthocenter is the intersection of the altitudes. Using geometry software to draw the altitudes from points X, Y, and Z, the intersection of the altitudes is the orthocenter at $K(-1, 4)$.

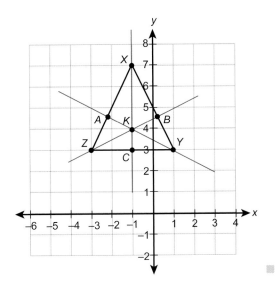

EXAMPLE 4

Find the centroid of a triangle with vertices $D(5, -4)$, $E(1, -4)$, and $F(3, 2)$.

SOLUTION

Find the midpoints of the three sides $G(3, -4)$, $I(2, -1)$, and $H(4, -1)$.

$$EF = \left(\frac{1+3}{2}, \frac{-4+2}{2}\right) = (2, -1) = I$$

$$DF = \left(\frac{5+3}{2}, \frac{-4+2}{2}\right) = (4, -1) = H$$

$$ED = \left(\frac{1+5}{2}, \frac{-4+-4}{2}\right) = (3, -4) = G$$

Construct the medians by connecting the midpoints with their opposite vertices. The intersection of the medians is the centroid $J\ (3, -2)$.

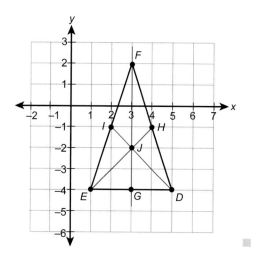

Midsegments

Connecting the midpoints of the sides of a figure creates new segments with helpful properties.

An athlete wants to swim from point A to point B (shown in blue). Her crew can drive to points R and T and she can walk to the lake. The crew can drive the distances marked in red and green. How much farther does the athlete swim than the distance (in red) that the crew drives? Study this topic to find out.

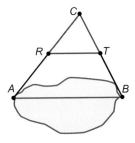

Midsegments of Trapezoids

Recall that a trapezoid has one pair of parallel sides. These sides are called the bases. The nonparallel sides are called the **legs**.

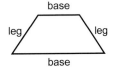

The **midsegment of a trapezoid** is the line segment that connects the midpoints of the legs. The midsegment will always be parallel to the bases. $\overline{EF}$ is a midsegment of $ABDC$.

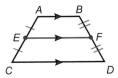

Using Geometry Software to Draw Midsegments

You can use geometry software to draw midsegments of triangles and trapezoids, and to investigate their lengths.

Construct a triangle. Construct the midpoints of any two sides of the triangle. Draw the line segment connecting the two midpoints. Measure and compare the length of the midsegment and the side parallel to it.

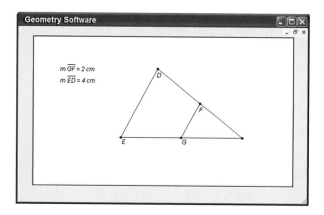

Repeat with a trapezoid. To be certain the bases are truly parallel, either work on a coordinate grid or draw a line parallel to a point not on the line, and then place points on the line. Drag the figures to see that these relationships hold true.

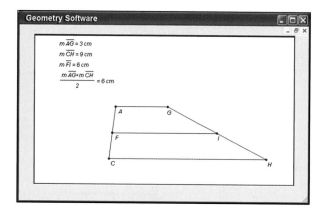

Quadrilaterals and Their Properties

Four-sided shapes can be classified by their unique side and angle relationships.

Identifying Quadrilaterals

A **quadrilateral** is a four-sided polygon. A quadrilateral is named by writing each vertex in consecutive order. The quadrilateral shown could be named *ABCD* or *DABC* or *CBAD*.

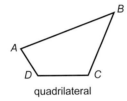

quadrilateral

Some quadrilaterals have special names that are based on their sides and angles. A **parallelogram** is a quadrilateral with two pairs of parallel sides. The arrows in this diagram show which sides are parallel.

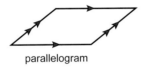

parallelogram

Parallelograms have several properties.

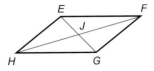

The opposite sides are congruent.

$$\overline{EF} \cong \overline{HG}, \overline{EH} \cong \overline{FG}$$

The opposite angles are congruent.

$$\angle E \cong \angle G, \angle H \cong \angle F$$

The consecutive angles are supplementary.

$$m\angle H + m\angle G = 180°, m\angle G + m\angle F = 180°,$$

$$m\angle F + m\angle E = 180°, m\angle E + m\angle H = 180°$$

The diagonals bisect each other.

$$EJ = JG, HJ = JF$$

▶ **Remember** Diagonals are line segments whose endpoints are on nonconsecutive vertices.

A **rectangle** is a parallelogram with four right angles.

rectangle

All the properties for a parallelogram are true for a rectangle. But there is an additional property just for rectangles.

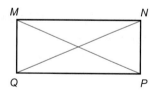

The diagonals are congruent.

$$\overline{MP} \cong \overline{QN}$$

A **rhombus** is a parallelogram with four congruent sides.

rhombus

A rhombus has all the properties of a parallelogram plus the following:

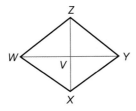

The diagonals are perpendicular.

$$m\angle WVZ = 90°, m\angle ZVY = 90°,$$

$$m\angle YVX = 90°, m\angle XVW = 90°$$

The diagonals bisect the vertices.

$$m\angle WZV = m\angle VZY, m\angle ZYV = m\angle VYX,$$

$$m\angle YXV = m\angle VXW, m\angle XWV = m\angle VWZ$$

EXAMPLE 1

Given rhombus $ABCD$ with diagonals $\overline{AC}$ and $\overline{DB}$, $AD = 5$, $AC = 8$, and $m\angle ADC = 106°$, identify the missing lengths and angle measures.

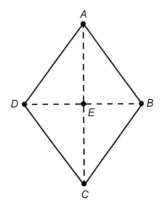

A *BC*

SOLUTION

Since all sides of a rhombus are equal, $BC = 5$.

B *EC*

SOLUTION

The diagonals of a rhombus are perpendicular bisectors of each other, so $EC = \frac{1}{2}AC = \frac{1}{2}(8) = 4$.

C *DB*

SOLUTION

$\triangle BCE$ is a right triangle with $BC = 5$ and $EC = 4$. Use the Pythagorean theorem to find BE.

$$(BE)^2 + (EC)^2 = (BC)^2$$
$$(BE)^2 + 4^2 = 5^2$$
$$(BE)^2 = 9$$
$$BE = 3$$

The diagonals of a rhombus are perpendicular bisectors of each other.

$$DB = 2(EB) = 2(3) = 6$$

D *m∠AEB*

SOLUTION

$m\angle AEB = 90°$ because the diagonals of a rhombus are perpendicular.

E *m∠ADB*

SOLUTION

The diagonals of a rhombus bisect the vertex angles.

$$m\angle ADB = \frac{1}{2}m\angle ADC = \frac{1}{2}(106°) = 53°$$

F *m∠DAB*

SOLUTION

$\triangle ADE$ is a right triangle, $m\angle ADE = 53°$, and the acute angles of a right triangle are complementary.

$$m\angle ADE + m\angle DAE = 90°$$
$$53° + m\angle DAE = 90°$$
$$m\angle DAE = 37°$$

The diagonals of a rhombus bisect the vertex angles.

$$m\angle DAB = 2(m\angle DAE) = 2(37°) = 74°$$

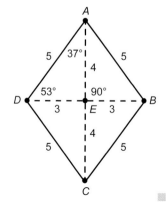

A **square** is a parallelogram with four congruent sides and four right angles. A square is both a rectangle and a rhombus. A square has all the properties of a parallelogram, rectangle, and rhombus.

square

A **trapezoid** is a quadrilateral with exactly one pair of parallel sides. A trapezoid is not a parallelogram, so it doesn't have any of the properties of a parallelogram.

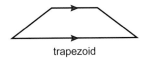

trapezoid

▶ **Think About It** Some people define a trapezoid as having *at least* one pair of parallel sides. This definition would make a parallelogram a type of trapezoid.

EXAMPLE 2

Quadrilateral $ABCD$ has vertices $A(-1, 5)$, $B(3, 1)$, $C(1, -3)$, and $D(-5, 3)$. Prove that $ABCD$ is an isosceles trapezoid.

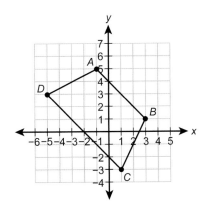

SOLUTION

A trapezoid is a quadrilateral with one pair of opposite sides that are parallel.

$$\text{slope of } \overline{AB}: m = \frac{1-5}{3-(-1)} = \frac{-4}{4} = -1$$

$$\text{slope of } \overline{DC}: m = \frac{-3-3}{1-(-5)} = \frac{-6}{6} = -1$$

$$\text{slope of } \overline{AD}: m = \frac{3-5}{-5-(-1)} = \frac{-2}{-4} = \frac{1}{2}$$

$$\text{slope of } \overline{BC}: m = \frac{-3-1}{1-3} = \frac{-4}{-2} = 2$$

The quadrilateral has exactly one pair of parallel sides, so $ABCD$ is a trapezoid with bases $\overline{AB}$ and $\overline{DC}$.

An isosceles trapezoid has legs with equal measure.

Use the distance formula to determine AD and BC.

$$AD = \sqrt{(-5-(-1))^2 + (3-5)^2} = \sqrt{(-4)^2 + (-2)^2} = \sqrt{16+4} = \sqrt{20} = 2\sqrt{5}$$

$$BC = \sqrt{(1-3)^2 + (-3-1)^2} = \sqrt{(-2)^2 + (-4)^2} = \sqrt{4+16} = \sqrt{20} = 2\sqrt{5}$$

The legs have equal measures.

$ABCD$ is an isosceles trapezoid. ▨

Identifying Relationships Among Special Quadrilaterals

You can use Euler diagrams to show the relationships among special quadrilaterals.

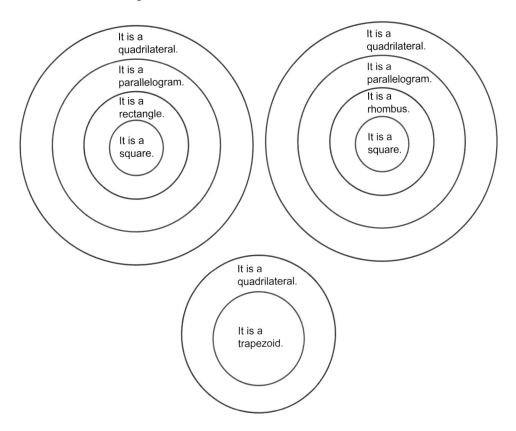

The first diagram allows you to see why it is true to say "If it is a square, then it is a rectangle," but not true to say "If it is a rectangle, then it is a square."

Parallelograms

You can use triangles to prove results about parallelograms.

Properties of Special Quadrilaterals

A parallelogram is a quadrilateral with two sets of parallel sides. You can use a diagonal to divide a parallelogram into two triangles, and then use ASA congruence to prove that opposite sides of a parallelogram are congruent.

THEOREM QUAD-1

In a parallelogram, the opposite sides are congruent.

Given $ABCD$ is a parallelogram.

Prove $\overline{CD} \cong \overline{AB}$ and $\overline{AD} \cong \overline{BC}$

Statement	Reason	Sketch
1. $ABCD$ is a parallelogram.	Given	
2. $\overline{AD} \parallel \overline{BC}$ and $\overline{CD} \parallel \overline{AB}$	Definition of a parallelogram	
3. $\angle DAC \cong \angle BCA$ $\angle DCA \cong \angle BAC$	Alternate Interior Angles Theorem	

Statement	Reason	Sketch
4. $\overline{AC} \cong \overline{CA}$	Reflexive Property of Congruence	
5. $\triangle DAC \cong \triangle BCA$	ASA Congruence Postulate	
6. $\overline{CD} \cong \overline{AB}$ and $\overline{AD} \cong \overline{BC}$	CPCTC	

Using SAS congruence, prove that the diagonals of a rectangle are congruent.

THEOREM QUAD-2
In a rectangle, the diagonals are congruent.

Given $ABCD$ is a rectangle.

Prove $\overline{AC} \cong \overline{BD}$

Statement	Reason	Sketch
1. $\overline{AD} \cong \overline{BC}$	Opposite sides of a parallelogram are congruent.	
2. $\overline{DC} \cong \overline{CD}$	Reflexive Property of Congruence	

Statement	Reason	Sketch
3. $m\angle ADC = 90°$ $m\angle BCD = 90°$	Definition of rectangle	
4. $m\angle ADC = m\angle BCD$	Substitution Property of Equality	
5. $\angle ADC \cong \angle BCD$	Angle Congruence Postulate	
6. $\triangle ADC \cong \triangle BCD$	SAS Congruence Postulate	
7. $\overline{AC} \cong \overline{BD}$	CPCTC	

THEOREM QUAD-3

If two pairs of opposite sides of a quadrilateral are congruent, then the quadrilateral is a parallelogram.

Given $\overline{AB} \cong \overline{DC}$
$\overline{AD} \cong \overline{BC}$

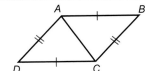

Prove $ABCD$ is a parallelogram.

Statement	Reason	Sketch
1. $\overline{AB} \cong \overline{DC}$ $\overline{AD} \cong \overline{BC}$	Given	
2. $\overline{AC} \cong \overline{CA}$	Reflexive Property of Congruence	
3. $\triangle ADC \cong \triangle CBA$	SSS Congruence Postulate	
4. $\angle DAC \cong \angle BCA$ $\angle ACD \cong \angle CAB$	CPCTC	
5. $\overline{DC} \parallel \overline{AB}$ $\overline{BC} \parallel \overline{AD}$	Converse of Alternate Interior Angles Theorem	
6. $ABCD$ is a parallelogram.	Definition of a parallelogram	

EXAMPLE 1

RSTU is a parallelogram. Find $m\angle 1$, $m\angle 2$, $m\angle 3$, $m\angle 4$, and $m\angle 5$.

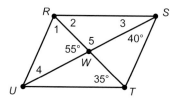

SOLUTION

Use the properties of angles of parallelograms to find the angle measures.

$\overline{RS}$ is parallel to $\overline{UT}$ and $\overline{RU}$ is parallel to $\overline{ST}$. $\angle 2 \cong \angle RTU$ because they are alternate interior angles of parallel lines $\overline{RS}$ and $\overline{UT}$ cut by transversal $\overline{RT}$, so $m\angle 2 = 35°$.

$\angle 4 \cong \angle UST$ because they are alternate interior angles of parallel lines $\overline{RU}$ and $\overline{RT}$ cut by transversal $\overline{SU}$, so $m\angle 4 = 40°$.

$\angle RWU$ and $\angle 5$ form a linear pair and are supplementary.

$$m\angle RWU + m\angle 5 = 180°$$
$$55° + m\angle 5 = 180°$$
$$m\angle 5 = 125°$$

The measures of the three angles of a triangle $\triangle RWU$ have a sum of 180°.

$$m\angle 1 + m\angle 4 + m\angle RWU = 180°$$
$$m\angle 1 + 40° + 55° = 180°$$
$$m\angle 1 + 95° = 180°$$
$$m\angle 1 = 85°$$

The measures of the three angles of a triangle $\triangle RWS$ have a sum of 180°.

$$m\angle 3 + m\angle 2 + m\angle 5 = 180°$$
$$m\angle 3 + 35° + 125° = 180°$$
$$m\angle 3 + 160° = 180°$$
$$m\angle 3 = 20°$$

$m\angle 1 = 85°$, $m\angle 2 = 35°$, $m\angle 3 = 20°$, $m\angle 4 = 40°$, $m\angle 5 = 125°$ ▪

EXAMPLE 2

LMNO is a parallelogram. Fill in the blanks and explain your reasoning.

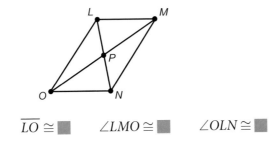

$\overline{LM} \cong$ ▪ $\overline{LO} \cong$ ▪ $\angle LMO \cong$ ▪ $\angle OLN \cong$ ▪

SOLUTION
Use the properties of parallelograms to find the measures.

$\overline{LM} \cong \overline{NO}$ and $\overline{LO} \cong \overline{NM}$ because opposite sides of a parallelogram are congruent.

Opposite sides of a parallelogram are parallel. If two parallel lines are cut by a transversal, the alternate interior angles are congruent. So $\angle LMO \cong \angle NOM$ and $\angle OLN \cong \angle MNL$. ▪

EXAMPLE 3

JKLN is a parallelogram. If $KM = 10$ and $m\angle JMN = 97°$, what is *MN* and what is $m\angle LMN$? Explain.

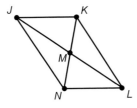

SOLUTION
The diagonals of a parallelogram bisect each other.

$$MN = KM = 10$$

$\angle JMN$ and $\angle LMN$ form a linear pair.

$$m\angle JMN + m\angle LMN = 180°$$
$$97° + m\angle LMN = 180°$$
$$m\angle LMN = 83° ▪$$

Here are the other theorems that describe ways to prove a quadrilateral is a parallelogram.

Theorem QUAD-4

If two opposite sides of a quadrilateral are parallel and congruent, then the quadrilateral is a parallelogram.

Theorem QUAD-5

If the diagonals of a quadrilateral bisect each other, then the quadrilateral is a parallelogram.

What Type of Parallelogram Is It?

There are several theorems that can be used to prove that a parallelogram is a rectangle or rhombus.

▶ **Remember** A **rectangle** is a parallelogram with four right angles.

▶ **Remember** A **rhombus** is a parallelogram with four congruent sides.

The next theorem is another way to prove that a parallelogram is a rectangle.

Theorem QUAD-6

If the diagonals of a parallelogram are congruent, then the parallelogram is a rectangle.

These theorems indicate when a parallelogram is a rhombus.

Theorem QUAD-7

If the diagonals of a parallelogram are perpendicular, then the parallelogram is a rhombus.

Theorem QUAD-8

If two adjacent sides of a parallelogram are congruent, then the parallelogram is a rhombus.

Theorem QUAD-9

If the diagonals of a parallelogram bisect the angles of the parallelogram, then the parallelogram is a rhombus.

EXAMPLE 4

Given rhombus $PQRS$ with diagonals $\overline{PR}$ and $\overline{QS}$, $PQ = 6x + 1$, $QR = 5 - 2x$, and $m\angle PQR = 120°$, determine the missing measurements.

Use properties of sides and angles in a rhombus to find the measures.

A PS

SOLUTION

All sides of a rhombus have equal measures.

$$PQ = QR \qquad PQ = 6x + 1 = 6\left(\frac{1}{2}\right) + 1 = 3 + 1 = 4$$
$$6x + 1 = 5 - 2x$$
$$8x + 1 = 5 \qquad PS = PQ = 4$$
$$8x = 4$$
$$x = \frac{1}{2}$$

B $m\angle PRQ$

SOLUTION

$$m\angle PQR = 120°$$

$\overline{PQ} \parallel \overline{RS}$ because opposite sides of a rhombus are parallel. $\angle PQR$ and $\angle QRS$ are same-side interior angles of parallel lines, so they are supplementary.

$$m\angle PQR + m\angle QRS = 180°$$
$$120° + m\angle QRS = 180°$$
$$m\angle QRS = 60°$$

The diagonals of a rhombus bisect the vertex angles.

$$m\angle PRQ = \frac{1}{2}\left(m\angle QRS\right)$$

$$m\angle PRQ = \frac{1}{2}\left(60°\right) = 30°$$

Similarity

Topic List

▸ Dilations and Scale Factors

▸ Directed Line Segments

▸ Similar Polygons

To make a model railroad scene look accurate, every object must have the same scale factor. That is, if the model train is one hundredth the length of the original train, then each model building should be one hundredth the height of the original building.

Dilations and Scale Factors

Dilations transform the size but not the shape of an image.

Dilations

Definition
A **dilation** is a transformation that changes the size but not the shape of a figure. A dilation is not a rigid transformation, which preserves both size and shape.

In a dilation, the lines connecting each point on the pre-image with its corresponding point on the image intersect at a point called the center of dilation. The center of dilation can lie on, inside, or outside the figure. In the illustrations of this topic, the pre-image will always be shown with solid segments and the image with dashed segments.

The figures show a dilation about a center point that lies on each figure.

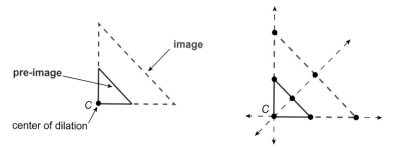

▶ **Think About It** Think of the pupils of your eyes dilating. The shape stays the same (a circle), but the size changes.

The figure shows a dilation about a center point that lies outside the figure.

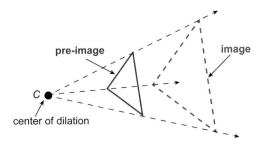

Definition

The **scale factor** t of a dilation is the ratio of the length of a side on the image to the length of its corresponding side on the pre-image.

In the diagram, $\overline{CA}$ is the pre-image and $\overline{CT}$ is the image. For this dilation, the scale factor is 3.

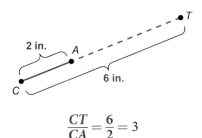

$$\frac{CT}{CA} = \frac{6}{2} = 3$$

The figures show the pre-image $\overline{AB}$ and the image $\overline{RT}$. $\overline{AB}$ is first enlarged by a scale factor of 2 and then by a scale factor of -2. In both cases, the length of the image $\overline{RT}$ is twice the length of $\overline{AB}$, but the images appear on opposite rays.

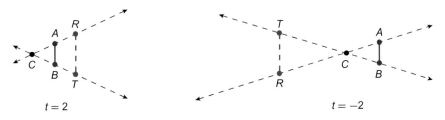

$t = 2$ $\qquad$ $t = -2$

In the next set of illustrations, the pre-image $\overline{AB}$ is reduced by a scale factor of $\frac{1}{2}$ and then by a scale factor of $-\frac{1}{2}$. In both figures, the length of the image $\overline{RT}$ is one-half the length of $\overline{AB}$, but again, the image points that result from applying a positive scale factor are on rays opposite the image points that result from applying a negative scale factor.

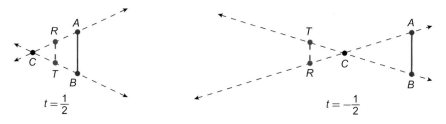

If the image is larger than the pre-image, then the dilation is an expansion. If the image is smaller than the pre-image, then the dilation is a contraction.

Definitions

An **expansion** is a dilation for which the absolute value of the scale factor, as related to the pre-image, is greater than 1.

A **contraction** is a dilation for which the absolute value of the scale factor, as related to the pre-image, is between 0 and 1.

Dilations on the Coordinate Plane

You can perform dilations on the coordinate plane just as you can perform other transformations on the plane. To determine image points when the center of dilation is the origin, multiply both coordinates of the pre-image points by a scale factor. That is, each point (x, y) dilated with a scale factor of t becomes (tx, ty).

▶ **Think About It** A transformation is a rule that maps one set of points to another set of points.

To dilate trapezoid $ABCD$ with a scale factor of $-\dfrac{1}{2}$, multiply the x- and y-coordinates by $-\dfrac{1}{2}$.

▶ **Think About It**

NOTATION The result of a transformation is often shown with a prime symbol. For instance, A' is read as "A prime" and usually means the result of transforming point A.

$$A\left(2, 2\right) \to A'\left(-1, -1\right)$$
$$B\left(4, 6\right) \to B'\left(-2, -3\right)$$
$$C\left(8, 6\right) \to C'\left(-4, -3\right)$$
$$D\left(10, 2\right) \to D'\left(-5, -1\right)$$

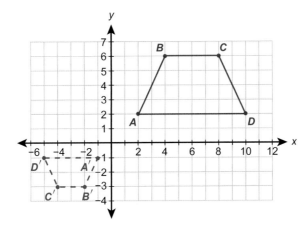

You can also perform dilations on a grid using geometry software. In this sketch, the origin is the center of dilation.

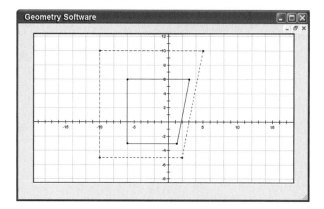

To determine the scale factor used in the dilation, find the lengths of corresponding sides. Use the lengths to form the ratio $\dfrac{\textbf{image length}}{\textbf{pre-image length}}$. If possible, choose a pair of sides whose lengths can be determined easily. Here, the left side of each figure is $\dfrac{9}{15}$, which reduces to a scale factor of $\dfrac{3}{5}$.

Directed Line Segments

A directed line segment can be portioned into segments based upon a given ratio.

Partitioning Directed Line Segments

Definition

A **directed line segment** is a segment between two points A and B with a specified direction from A to B or from B to A and a standard distance between the two points.

The directed line segment $\overline{AB}$ signifies that you start at point A and go to point B.

Definition

To **partition a directed line segment** is to divide it into segments based upon a given ratio.

To partition a directed line segment, identify both the direction and the ratio. If the ratio is a $1 : 4$ partition of the directed line segment $\overline{AB}$, start at point A and mark 1 part followed by 4 parts to give a total of 5 equal parts. The line segment would be partitioned at point P.

EXAMPLE 1

Use the given endpoints to find the coordinates of the point that partitions the directed line segment into the identified ratio.

A endpoints: $A(-6, 2)$ and $B(4, 2)$

Partition directed line segment $\overline{BA}$ into a 7 : 3 ratio.

SOLUTION

The graph of the line segment with endpoints at A and B is horizontal. Partitioning the segment into a 7 : 3 ratio results in 10 equal parts. Since the line segment is horizontal, you only need to consider the change in the x-values. Between -6 and 4, there are exactly 10 parts. Each part is 1 unit in length. Since the directed line segment starts at point B, 7 of the 10 parts must be closer to point B. The point that partitions the directed line segment $\overline{BA}$ into a 7 : 3 ratio is located at $(-3, 2)$.

B endpoints: $C(-2, 2)$ and $D(-2, 5)$

Partition directed line segment $\overline{CD}$ into a 1 : 5 ratio.

SOLUTION

The graph of the line segment with endpoints at C and D is vertical. Partitioning the segment into a 1 : 5 ratio results in 6 equal parts. Since the line segment is vertical, you only need to consider the change in the y-values. Between 2 and 5, there are exactly 6 parts. Each part is a half-unit in length. Since the directed line segment starts at point C, 1 of the 6 parts must be closer to point C. The point that partitions the directed line segment $\overline{CD}$ into a 1 : 5 ratio is located at $\left(-2, 2\frac{1}{2}\right)$. ∎

Using the Midpoint Formula to Partition Directed Line Segments

When a directed line segment is neither vertical nor horizontal, you need to calculate changes in both the x- and y-values to determine the point that will partition the segment according to the given ratio. The midpoint formula can be used when the total number of parts required equals a power of 2.

> ▶ **Remember** The coordinates of the midpoint of a line segment with endpoints (x_1, y_1) and (x_2, y_2) are
> $$\left(\frac{x_1 + x_2}{2}, \frac{y_1 + y_2}{2} \right).$$

EXAMPLE 2

Use the midpoint formula and the given endpoints to find the coordinates of the point that partitions the directed line segment into the identified ratio.

A endpoints: $A(-5, 1)$ and $B(3, 7)$

Partition directed line segment $\overline{AB}$ into a $1 : 3$ ratio.

SOLUTION
The ratio of $1 : 3$ requires the line segment be divided into 4 parts. Because 4 is a power of 2, the midpoint formula can be used. The midpoint of line segment $\overline{AB}$ is $\left(\frac{-5 + 3}{2}, \frac{1 + 7}{2} \right)$, or $(-1, 4)$. This point divides line segment $\overline{AB}$ into 2 equal parts. Since the desired ratio is $1 : 3$, find the midpoint between $(-5, 1)$ and $(-1, 4)$. It is $\left(\frac{-5 + (-1)}{2}, \frac{1 + 4}{2} \right)$, or $\left(-3, 2\frac{1}{2} \right)$. This point divides the first of the 2 equal parts in half. The section closest to point A is 1 of the 4 equal parts. The point that partitions the directed line segment $\overline{BA}$ into a $1 : 3$ ratio is located at $\left(-3, 2\frac{1}{2} \right)$.

B endpoints: $C(-20, 3)$ and $D(-4, 15)$

Partition directed line segment $\overline{DC}$ into a $3 : 5$ ratio.

SOLUTION

The ratio of 3 : 5 requires the line segment be divided into 8 parts. Because 8 is a power of 2, the midpoint formula can be used. The midpoint of line segment $\overline{DC}$ is $\left(\dfrac{-4+(-20)}{2}, \dfrac{15+3}{2}\right)$, or $(-12, 9)$. This point divides line segment $\overline{DC}$ into 2 equal parts. Since the desired ratio is 3 : 5, find the midpoint between $(-12, 9)$ and $(-4, 15)$. It is $\left(\dfrac{-12+(-4)}{2}, \dfrac{9+15}{2}\right)$, or $(-8, 12)$. Then find the midpoint between $(-12, 9)$ and $(-8, 12)$. It is $\left(\dfrac{-12+(-8)}{2}, \dfrac{9+12}{2}\right)$, or $\left(-10, 10\frac{1}{2}\right)$. This point divides the segment into 8 equal parts. The section closest to point D represents 3 of the 8 equal parts. The point that partitions the directed line segment $\overline{DC}$ into a 3 : 5 ratio is located at $\left(-10, 10\frac{1}{2}\right)$. ∎

Using the Section Formula to Partition Directed Line Segments

When a directed line segment is neither vertical nor horizontal or when the use of the midpoint formula is not feasible, you can use the section formula to determine the point that will partition the segment according to the given ratio.

Section Formula

If a directed line segment has endpoints at $A(x_1, y_1)$ and $B(x_2, y_2)$, the coordinates of the point that separates the directed line segment into a ratio of $m : n$ are

$$\left(\dfrac{mx_2 + nx_1}{m+n}, \dfrac{my_2 + ny_1}{m+n}\right).$$

EXAMPLE 3

Use the section formula and the given endpoints to find the coordinates of the point that partitions the directed line segment into the identified ratio.

A endpoints: $A(-25, 15)$ and $B(30, 70)$

Partition directed line segment $\overline{AB}$ into a $2 : 5$ ratio.

SOLUTION

Since the directed line segment starts at point A, the ordered pair $(-25, 15)$ represents (x_1, y_1) and $(30, 70)$ represents (x_2, y_2). The value of m is 2 and the value of n is 5. Use the section formula.

$$\left(\frac{mx_2 + nx_1}{m + n}, \frac{my_2 + ny_1}{m + n} \right) = \left(\frac{2(30) + 5(-25)}{2 + 5}, \frac{2(70) + 5(15)}{2 + 5} \right)$$

$$= \left(\frac{60 + (-125)}{7}, \frac{140 + 75}{7} \right)$$

$$= \left(-\frac{65}{7}, \frac{215}{7} \right)$$

$$= \left(-9\frac{2}{7}, 30\frac{5}{7} \right)$$

The point that partitions the directed line segment $\overline{AB}$ into a $2 : 5$ ratio is located at $\left(-9\frac{2}{7}, 30\frac{5}{7} \right)$.

B endpoints: $C(-10, 6)$ and $D(-2, 18)$

Partition directed line segment $\overline{DC}$ into a $1 : 3$ ratio.

SOLUTION

Since the directed line segment starts at point D, the ordered pair $(-2, 18)$ represents (x_1, y_1) and $(-10, 6)$ represents (x_2, y_2). The value of m is 1 and the value of n is 3. Use the section formula.

$$\left(\frac{mx_2 + nx_1}{m + n}, \frac{my_2 + ny_1}{m + n} \right) = \left(\frac{1(-10) + 3(-2)}{1 + 3}, \frac{1(6) + 3(18)}{1 + 3} \right)$$

$$= \left(\frac{-10 + (-6)}{4}, \frac{6 + 54}{4} \right)$$

$$= \left(-\frac{16}{4}, \frac{60}{4} \right)$$

$$= (-4, 15)$$

The point that partitions the directed line segment $\overline{DC}$ into a $1 : 3$ ratio is located at $(-4, 15)$. ◼

Similar Polygons

Properties of similarity and proportions are used to create figures that have the same shape.

Solving Proportions

A ratio compares two quantities by division. That's why people often write the ratio of two quantities—for example, a and b—as the fraction $\frac{a}{b}$, although the ratio can also be written as $a : b$.

Definition
A **proportion** is an equation that states that two ratios are equal. It is often written as $a : b = c : d$ or $\frac{a}{b} = \frac{c}{d}$.

In the proportion $\frac{a}{b} = \frac{c}{d}$, b and c are called the **means** and a and d are called the **extremes**. These definitions are easier to remember when you write the proportion with colons, because the **extremes** are on the **exterior** and the **means** are in the **middle**.

$$a : b = c : d$$

▶ **Remember** Division by 0 is undefined. In the ratio $\frac{a}{b}$, b cannot be 0.

When you clear the fractions of a proportion by multiplying both sides by the product of the denominators, you find that the product of the means equals the product of the extremes.

$$\frac{a}{b} = \frac{c}{d}$$

$$bd \cdot \frac{a}{b} = \frac{c}{d} \cdot bd$$

$$da = cb$$

This property is known as the means-extremes product property. It is one of the most useful properties of proportions.

Properties of Proportions

Means-Extremes Product Property If $\frac{a}{b} = \frac{c}{d}$, then $ad = bc$, given that b and d are not 0.

Reciprocal Property If $\frac{a}{b} = \frac{c}{d}$, then $\frac{b}{a} = \frac{d}{c}$, given that a, b, c, and d are not 0.

Exchange Property If $\frac{a}{c} = \frac{b}{d}$, given that a, b, c, and d are not 0.

Add-One Property If $\frac{a}{b} = \frac{c}{d}$, then $\frac{a+b}{b} = \frac{c+d}{d}$, given that b and d are not 0.

You can solve proportions by using these properties.

EXAMPLE 1

Solve the proportion.

$$\frac{3}{2.25} = \frac{4}{x}$$

▶ **Think About It** Using the means-extremes product property is sometimes called cross multiplying.

SOLUTION

Use the means-extremes product property.

$$\frac{3}{2.25} = \frac{4}{x}$$

$$3x = 2.25 \cdot 4$$

$$3x = 9$$

$$x = 3 \ \blacksquare$$

The corresponding sides of figures are said to be proportional if every pair of sides has the same ratio. The corresponding sides of these two rectangles are proportional because the ratio of the widths is equal to the ratio of the lengths.

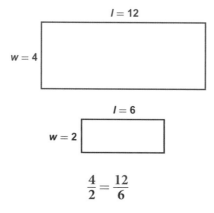

$$\frac{4}{2} = \frac{12}{6}$$

You can tell the ratios are equal because the product of the means equals the product of the extremes (both are 24). Also, both ratios reduce to 2.

You may have noticed that the large rectangle can be thought of as the image of the small rectangle after a dilation with a scale factor of 2. That is no coincidence. The corresponding sides of dilated figures are always proportional, and their ratios are always equal to the scale factor that was used in creating them.

Determining Whether Polygons Are Similar

The triangles shown are similar. In similarity statements, write the corresponding vertices in the same order, just as you do for congruence statements.

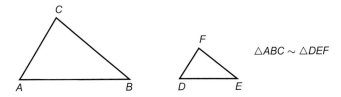

$\triangle ABC \sim \triangle DEF$

Because images created by dilations are proportional to their pre-images, two polygons are similar if and only if one is congruent to the image of the other by a dilation. If the ratios of the corresponding sides of these triangles equal 2, then $\triangle ABC$ is congruent to the image of $\triangle DEF$ after a dilation with a scale factor of 2.

The following postulate gives another definition of similar polygons.

Postulate SIM-1

Polygon Similarity Postulate Two polygons are similar if and only if there is a correspondence between their angles and their sides so that all corresponding angles are congruent and all corresponding sides are proportional.

This diagram shows two trapezoids, *DEFG* ~ *QRST*. Because it is given that the two polygons are similar, the polygon similarity postulate lets you write the following statements.

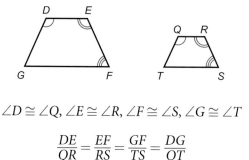

$$\angle D \cong \angle Q, \angle E \cong \angle R, \angle F \cong \angle S, \angle G \cong \angle T$$

$$\frac{DE}{QR} = \frac{EF}{RS} = \frac{GF}{TS} = \frac{DG}{QT}$$

EXAMPLE 2

Use the polygon similarity postulate to determine whether these two triangles are similar.

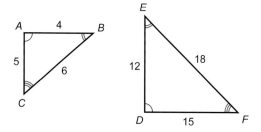

SOLUTION

The corresponding angles are congruent, and you are given the side lengths. You can check to see whether the corresponding sides are proportional.

$$\frac{AB}{DE} = \frac{4}{12} = \frac{1}{3} \qquad \frac{AC}{DF} = \frac{5}{15} = \frac{1}{3} \qquad \frac{BC}{EF} = \frac{6}{18} = \frac{1}{3}$$

The sides are proportional; therefore, △*ABC* ~ △*DEF*. ▪

You can also use the polygon similarity postulate to find unknown lengths in similar figures.

EXAMPLE 3

Solve for x given that $ABCD \sim EFGH$.

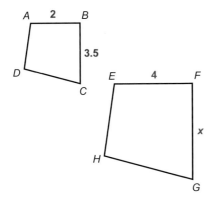

SOLUTION

Set up a proportion with corresponding sides and solve for x.

$$\frac{2}{4} = \frac{3.5}{x}$$
$$2x = 14$$
$$x = 7$$

EXAMPLE 4

A student 5 ft tall casts a 7.5 ft shadow at the same time that a flagpole casts a 48 ft shadow. What is the height of the flagpole?

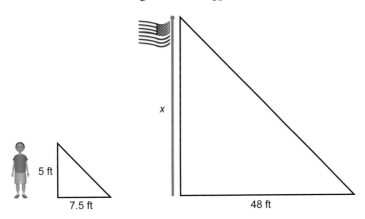

SOLUTION

The triangles formed are similar. Since the sides of the triangles are proportional, set up a proportion with corresponding sides and solve for x.

$$\frac{5}{x} = \frac{7.5}{48}$$
$$7.5x = 240$$
$$x = 32$$

The height of the flagpole is 32 ft. ■

Similar Triangle Relationships

Topic List

▶ Triangle Similarity

▶ Triangle Proportionality Theorem

▶ Similarity and the Pythagorean Theorem

Civil engineers use triangles that have the same shape but different sizes to design incredibly strong bridges that span long distances. The Navajo Bridge uses triangular trusses to span 221 m across the Colorado River.

Triangle Similarity

To determine whether triangles are similar, you can use the angle-angle similarity postulate, the side-side-side similarity theorem, or the side-angle-side similarity theorem.

Proving Triangles Are Similar

You can prove that two triangles are similar by using the polygon similarity postulate, which means proving that the three pairs of corresponding angles are congruent and the three pairs of corresponding sides are proportional. But sometimes you don't have all six measures, so you need to use one of the postulates or theorems for triangle similarity, which require fewer comparisons.

Suppose you were told to draw a triangle with an angle with a measure of 60° and another angle with a measure of 70°. By the triangle sum theorem, you would have no choice but to make the third angle measure 50°. You can make many different triangles with those angle measurements—some small, some large—but they will all have the same shape, which is the idea behind the next postulate.

Postulate SIM-2

Angle-Angle (AA) Similarity Postulate If two angles of a triangle are congruent to two angles of another triangle, then the triangles are similar.

▶ **Think About It** The sum of the measures of the angles of a triangle is always 180°.

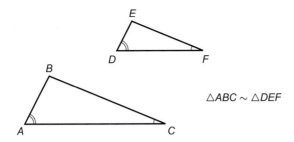

$\triangle ABC \sim \triangle DEF$

When you draw two triangles whose corresponding sides are proportional, the corresponding angles are automatically congruent. The next theorem states that another way to prove triangles similar is to check the ratios of the sides.

Theorem SIM-1

Side-Side-Side (SSS) Similarity Theorem If the three sides of a triangle are proportional to the three sides of another triangle, then the triangles are similar.

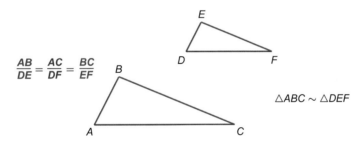

$$\frac{AB}{DE} = \frac{AC}{DF} = \frac{BC}{EF}$$

$\triangle ABC \sim \triangle DEF$

Recall that once two sides and the included angle of a triangle are drawn, there is only one way to complete the triangle. Once you know that the corresponding sides of two triangles are proportional and the included angles are congruent, the lengths of the third side cannot vary, which leads to the last combination that proves triangles similar.

Theorem SIM-2

Side-Angle-Side (SAS) Similarity Theorem If two sides of a triangle are proportional to two sides of another triangle and if their included angles are congruent, then the triangles are similar.

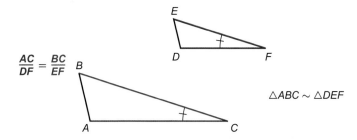

$$\frac{AC}{DF} = \frac{BC}{EF}$$

$\triangle ABC \sim \triangle DEF$

You can use the triangle similarity postulate and the two similarity theorems in two-column proofs.

Given $\angle C \cong \angle E$

Prove $\triangle ABC \sim \triangle DBE$

Statement	Reason	Sketch
1. $\angle C \cong \angle E$	Given	
2. $\angle ABC \cong \angle DBE$	Vertical Angles Theorem	
3. $\triangle ABC \sim \triangle DBE$	AA Similarity Postulate	

You can also use the postulate and the two theorems to determine whether two triangles are similar.

EXAMPLE 1

Determine whether $\triangle DEF \sim \triangle DYZ$.

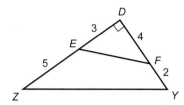

SOLUTION

Start by separating and reflecting the triangles so they have the same orientation.

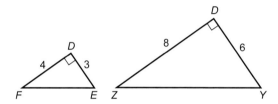

You have measurements for two sides and for the included angle. The included angles are congruent, so check to see if the corresponding sides are proportional.

$$\frac{DF}{DZ} = \frac{4}{8} = \frac{1}{2} \text{ and } \frac{DE}{DY} = \frac{3}{6} = \frac{1}{2}$$

The ratios are equal. The sides are proportional. $\triangle DEF \sim \triangle DYZ$ by the SAS similarity theorem. ■

▶ **Think About It** Proportional reasoning is the key to similarity.

Perimeter, Area, and Volume Ratios

Similar plane figures and similar solids have the same shape and all the corresponding dimensions are proportional by a certain ratio called the scale factor. When two similar figures are changed by a scale factor, the effect on the perimeter, area, and volume of the resulting figure can be expressed using the scale factor.

Ratios of Measures of Similar Figures

If the dimensions of similar figures are changed by a factor of t, then

- The perimeter or circumference changes by a factor of t.
- The area changes by a factor of t^2.
- The volume changes by a factor of t^3.

EXAMPLE 2

If $\triangle DEF \sim \triangle ABC$ and the scale factor is 3, determine the perimeter and area of $\triangle DEF$.

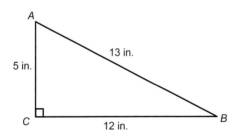

▶ **Think About It** You could check the answers by multiplying each dimension of the triangle by 3 and then calculating the perimeter and area.

SOLUTION

Find the perimeter of $\triangle ABC$ by adding the lengths of the sides. Then use the scale factor to find the perimeter of $\triangle DEF$.

$$\text{perimeter of } \triangle ABC = 5 + 12 + 13$$
$$= 30$$

The perimeter of $\triangle ABC$ is 30 in.

$$\text{perimeter of } \triangle DEF = (3) \cdot (\text{perimeter of } \triangle ABC)$$
$$= 3 \cdot 30$$
$$= 90$$

The perimeter of $\triangle DEF$ is 90 in.

Find the area of $\triangle ABC$ by using the formula for area of a triangle. Then use the scale factor to find the area of $\triangle DEF$.

▶ **Remember** For area, the scale factor is squared when determining the area of the similar figure.

$$\text{area of } \triangle ABC = \frac{1}{2} bh$$
$$= \frac{1}{2} \cdot 12 \cdot 5$$
$$= 30$$

The area of $\triangle ABC$ is 30 in^2.

$$\text{area of } \triangle DEF = (3^2) \cdot (\text{area of } \triangle ABC)$$
$$= 9 \cdot 30$$
$$= 270$$

The perimeter of $\triangle DEF$ is 90 in. and the area is 270 in^2. ▪

EXAMPLE 3

A triangular prism has volume 96 cm^3 and surface area 144 cm^2. If its dimensions are decreased by a factor of $\frac{1}{2}$, what are the volume and surface area of the resulting prism?

▶ **Remember** The surface area of a solid is the sum of the areas of the faces.

SOLUTION

To find the volume of the new prism, multiply the volume of the original prism by the cube of the scale factor.

$$\text{volume of new prism} = (\text{scale factor})^3 \cdot (\text{volume of original prism})$$
$$= \left(\frac{1}{2}\right)^3 \cdot 96$$
$$= 12$$

The volume of the new prism is 12 cm^3.

To find the surface area of the new prism, multiply the surface area of the original prism by the square of the scale factor.

$$\text{area of new prism} = (\text{scale factor})^2 \cdot (\text{surface area of original prism})$$
$$= \left(\frac{1}{2}\right)^2 \cdot 144$$
$$= 36$$

The volume of the new prism is 12 cm^3 and the surface area is 36 cm^2. ■

Triangle Proportionality Theorem

To find the distance between parallel lines cut by a transversal, you can use the triangle proportionality theorem and the two-transversal proportionality corollary.

Proving the Triangle Proportionality Theorem

The triangle proportionality theorem is an often-used theorem that describes the relationships created when a line is drawn through a triangle such that it is parallel to one side of the triangle. Before proving the theorem, recall the add-one property of proportions.

Add-One Property of Proportions
If $\dfrac{a}{b} = \dfrac{c}{d}$, then $\dfrac{a+b}{b} = \dfrac{c+d}{d}$, given that b and d are not 0.

The converse of the add-one property of proportions is if $\dfrac{a+b}{b} = \dfrac{c+d}{d}$, and b and d are not 0, then $\dfrac{a}{b} = \dfrac{c}{d}$.

You can show algebraically why the converse is true.

$$\frac{a+b}{b} = \frac{c+d}{d}$$

$$\frac{a}{b} + \frac{b}{b} = \frac{c}{d} + \frac{d}{d}$$

$$\frac{a}{b} + 1 = \frac{c}{d} + 1$$

$$\frac{a}{b} = \frac{c}{d}$$

This property can help prove the triangle proportionality theorem.

THEOREM SIM-3 Triangle Proportionality Theorem

A line parallel to one side of a triangle divides the other two sides proportionally.

Given $\overline{CD} \parallel \overline{AB}$

Prove $\dfrac{AC}{CE} = \dfrac{BD}{DE}$

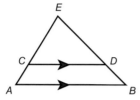

Statement	Reason	Sketch
1. $\overline{CD} \parallel \overline{AB}$	Given	
2. $\angle ECD \cong \angle EAB$ $\angle EDC \cong \angle EBA$	Corresponding Angles Postulate	
3. $\triangle AEB \cong \triangle CED$	AA Similarity Postulate	
4. $\dfrac{AE}{CE} = \dfrac{BE}{DE}$	Polygon Similarity Postulate	
5. $AE = AC + CE$ $BE = BD + DE$	Segment Addition Postulate	
6. $\dfrac{AC + CE}{CE} = \dfrac{BD + DE}{DE}$	Substitution (Steps 4 and 5)	
7. $\dfrac{AC}{CE} = \dfrac{BD}{DE}$	Converse of the Add-One Property of Proportions	

EXAMPLE 1

Find the value of x.

SOLUTION

Use the triangle proportionality theorem.

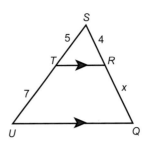

$$\frac{5}{7} = \frac{4}{x}$$

$$5x = 28$$

$$x = 5.6 \; \blacksquare$$

THEOREM SIM-4 Angle Bisector Theorem

An angle bisector of an angle of a triangle divides the opposite side in two segments that are proportional to the other two sides of the triangle.

Given $\triangle ABC$ with $\overline{BD}$ the bisector of $\angle B$

Prove $\dfrac{AB}{BC} = \dfrac{AD}{DC}$

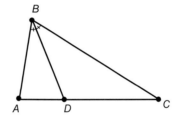

Statement	Reason	Sketch
1. $\triangle ABC$ with $\overline{BD}$ the bisector of $\angle B$	Given	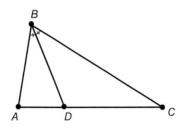
2. Draw an auxiliary line through point A parallel to $\overline{BD}$. Extend $\overline{CB}$ through B to intersect the parallel line at point E.	There is exactly one line that can be drawn that is parallel to the given line and goes through a given point not on the line.	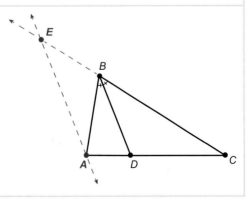

Statement	Reason	Sketch
3. $\angle E \cong \angle DBC$	Corresponding Angles Postulate	
4. $\angle DBA \cong \angle BAE$	Alternate InteriorAngle Theorem	
5. $\angle DBA \cong \angle DBC$	Definition of angle bisector	
6. $\angle E \cong \angle BAE$	Angles congruent to congruent angles are congruent.	

Statement	Reason	Sketch
7. $\overline{AB} \cong \overline{EB}$	Isosceles Triangle Theorem	
8. $\triangle BCD \sim \triangle ECA$	AA Similarity Postulate	
9. $\dfrac{EB}{BC} = \dfrac{AD}{DC}$	Triangle Proportionality Theorem	
10. $\dfrac{AB}{BC} = \dfrac{AD}{DC}$	Substitution	

EXAMPLE 2

Given $\overline{CD}$ is the angle bisector of $\angle ACB$,
$AB = 10$, $m\angle ACD = 2x + 8°$,
and $m\angle BCD = 3x - 2°$, find the
missing measures.

AD   BD $m\angle ACB$

SOLUTION

Let $y = AD$ and $10 - y = BD$.

Use the angle bisector theorem to write a proportion.

$$\frac{AC}{BC} = \frac{AD}{BD}$$

$$\frac{8}{12} = \frac{y}{10 - y}$$

$$8(10 - y) = 12y$$

$$80 - 8y = 12y$$

$$80 = 20y$$

$$y = 4$$

$AD = 4$

$BD = 10 - y = 10 - 4 = 6$

Use the definition of angle bisectors to write an equation relating the angle
measures. Then substitute the expressions into the equation to solve for x.

$$m\angle ACD = m\angle BCD$$
$$2x + 8° = 3x - 2°$$
$$8° = x - 2°$$
$$10° = x$$

Substitute the value for x into the expressions. Then add the angle measures
to find the $m\angle ACB$.

$$m\angle ACD = 2x + 8° = 2(10°) + 8° = 20° + 8° = 28°$$

$$m\angle BCD = 3x - 2° = 3(10°) - 2° = 30° - 2° = 28°$$

$$m\angle ACB = m\angle ACD + m\angle BCD = 28° + 28° = 56°$$

Definition

A **corollary** is a proposition that follows directly from a postulate or theorem and can be easily proven.

The two-transversal proportionality corollary follows from the triangle proportionality theorem.

Corollary SIM-1

Two-Transversal Proportionality Corollary Three or more parallel lines divide two intersecting transversals proportionally.

The two-transversal proportionality corollary follows directly from the triangle proportionality theorem because intersecting transversals across several lines form several triangles. This diagram has $\triangle CXD$, $\triangle BXE$, and $\triangle AXF$.

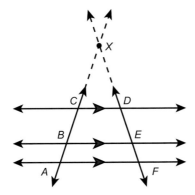

Two of the proportions you can write are $\dfrac{CB}{CA} = \dfrac{DE}{DF}$ and $\dfrac{AC}{FD} = \dfrac{AB}{FE}$.

Similarity and the Pythagorean Theorem

You can use similarity to understand the Pythagorean theorem, which is the most famous and useful mathematical property.

Pythagorean Theorem

The Pythagorean theorem is a mathematical rule that relates the lengths of the sides of a right triangle to each other.

Theorem RIGHT-1

Pythagorean Theorem For all right triangles, the square of the length of the hypotenuse c equals the sum of the squares of the lengths of the legs a and b.

$$c^2 = a^2 + b^2$$

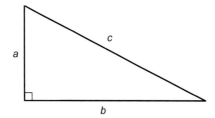

A soccer field is a rectangle with a length of 120 m and a width of 90 m. Before practice, the players have to run from one corner to the corner diagonally across the field. How many meters do the players run?

SOLUTION

Let d equal the distance diagonally across the field. The diagonal divides the field into two congruent right triangles. To find d, use the Pythagorean theorem equation.

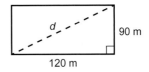

$$c^2 = a^2 + b^2$$
$$d^2 = 120^2 + 90^2$$
$$d = \sqrt{120^2 + 90^2}$$
$$d = \sqrt{14,400 + 8100}$$
$$d = \sqrt{22,500}$$
$$d = 150$$

The players run 150 m. ▪

Foundations for Proving the Pythagorean Theorem

The Pythagorean theorem is often proven using principles and properties of algebra. However, the theorem can also be proven using principles of geometry. One of the principles of geometry that is used to prove the Pythagorean theorem is the angle-angle (AA) similarity postulate.

The AA similarity postulate says that if two angles of a triangle are congruent to two angles of another triangle, then the triangles are similar.

To develop a geometric proof for the Pythagorean theorem, review the definition of an altitude.

Creating Three Similar Right Triangles

To begin this proof of the Pythagorean theorem, look at the relationship of the resulting triangles when an altitude is constructed to the hypotenuse of a right triangle.

Statement	Sketch
1. Given $\triangle ABC$ is a right triangle, you know that $m\angle A = 90°$.	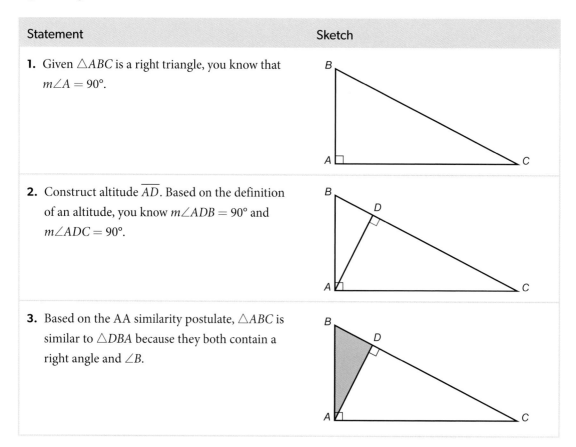
2. Construct altitude $\overline{AD}$. Based on the definition of an altitude, you know $m\angle ADB = 90°$ and $m\angle ADC = 90°$.	
3. Based on the AA similarity postulate, $\triangle ABC$ is similar to $\triangle DBA$ because they both contain a right angle and $\angle B$.	

Statement	Sketch
4. Based on the AA similarity postulate, $\triangle ABC$ is similar to $\triangle DAC$ because they both contain a right angle and $\angle C$.	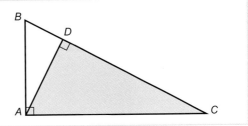

This reasoning about the similar triangles formed when an altitude is constructed from the right angle in a right triangle can help you prove the Pythagorean theorem.

Area and Volume

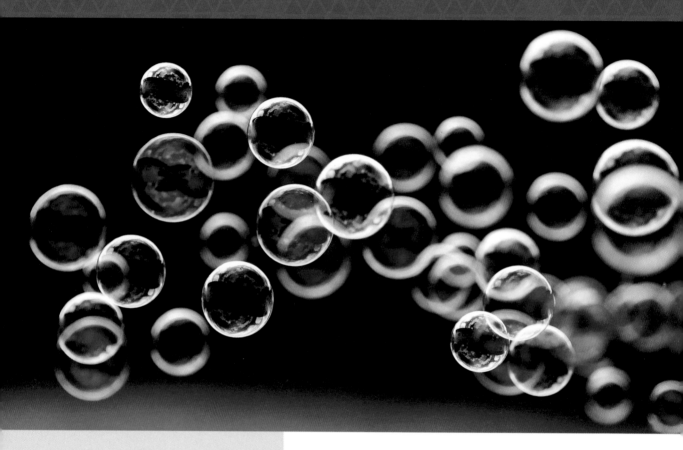

Topic List

▸ Circumferences and Areas of Circles

▸ Composite Figures

▸ Volumes of Prisms and Cylinders

▸ Surface Area of Cones

▸ Volumes of Pyramids

▸ Volumes of Spheres

▸ Volume Ratios

▸ Surface Area and Volume

▸ Reasoning About Area and Volume

Why are soap bubbles round? Nature wants to surround any volume of air with the minimal surface area, and a sphere has the least surface area for any given volume.

Circumferences and Areas of Circles

To find the circumference and area of a circle, you need to know some important terms and formulas.

Circles

Definitions

A **circle** is the set of all points on a plane that are the same distance from a given point in the plane known as the **center** of the circle.

A circle is named by its center, so circle O is the circle shown.

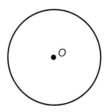

Definition

A **radius** of a circle is a line segment that connects the center of the circle to a point on the circle. Every radius of a given circle has the same length, so the term *radius* can also refer to the length of any radius of a circle.

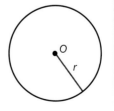

The plural form of the word *radius* is *radii*.

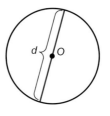

In a given circle, the length of any diameter is twice the length of the radius, $d = 2r$.

Definition

A **sector** of a circle is a region whose boundaries are two radii and part of the circle.

The shaded region in the diagram is a sector.

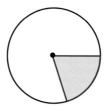

Circumference of a Circle

Recall that circumference is the perimeter of a circle. The circumference C of any circle, divided by its diameter, always equals pi, which is represented by the Greek letter π. In other words, $\pi = \dfrac{C}{d}$. You can multiply both sides of this equation by d to write a formula for the circumference of a circle: $C = \pi d$. Since $d = 2r$, the formula can also be written in terms of the radius.

Formula for the Circumference of a Circle

The circumference C of a circle with radius r is

$$C = 2\pi r.$$

The number π is an irrational number, which means that when you write it out as a decimal, it never repeats and never ends. If you do not have a π button on your calculator, you can approximate pi as 3.14. Calculations with pi are approximate unless you leave the pi symbol as part of the calculation.

EXAMPLE 1

Find the circumference of the circle. Use 3.14 for π.

SOLUTION

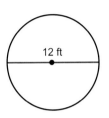
12 ft

$C = \pi d$
$ = \pi \cdot 12$
$ \approx 3.14 \cdot 12 \approx 37.7$

The circumference is exactly 12π ft, which is about 37.7 ft. ■

▶ **Think About It** The ≈ symbol means "is approximately equal to."

Area of a Circle

Suppose a circle is divided into eight equal sectors—you might think of a pizza divided into eight equal slices. If you arrange the sectors as shown, you see that they almost form a parallelogram. The two bases of the figure came from the pizza's circumference, so the length of each base is one-half of the circumference, or one-half of πd, which is the same as πr. The height is the radius of the pizza, r. The area of a parallelogram is base times height, so the area of the pizza is close to πr^2.

As the number of sectors increases, the bases become straighter and come closer to forming a parallelogram.

Formula for the Area of a Circle

The area A of a circle with radius r is

$$A = \pi r^2.$$

EXAMPLE 2

Find the area of the circle. Use 3.14 for π.

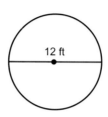

SOLUTION

$$A = \pi r^2$$
$$= \pi \cdot (6)^2$$
$$= \pi \cdot 36$$
$$\approx 3.14 \cdot 36 \approx 113$$

The area is exactly 36π ft^2, which is about 113 ft^2. ▨

Approximating Circles with Polygons

You can approximate the area and circumference of a circle with regular polygons inscribed in a circle. The greater the number of sides, the better the approximations because there is less space in the interior of the circle not covered by the polygon. The diagrams, from left to right, show an inscribed triangle, square, and hexagon.

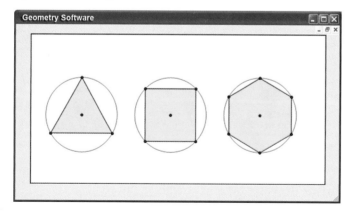

Composite Figures

Putting two or more figures together makes a new, more complicated shape. You can use what you know about the simple shapes to answer questions about the more complicated one.

Perimeter of Composite Figures

The perimeter of a figure is the distance around the two-dimensional shape, or the sum of the lengths of its sides.

EXAMPLE 1

Find the perimeter of the composite figure. A rectangle and an equilateral triangle compose the figure.

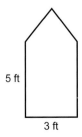

5 ft

3 ft

▶ **Remember** An equilateral triangle has sides that are all the same length.

SOLUTION

Because the triangle is an equilateral triangle, all sides have the same length.

Label the missing side lengths and then add to find the perimeter.

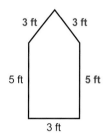

$$3 + 5 + 3 + 3 + 5 = 19$$

The perimeter of the figure is 19 ft. ▨

Figures in the Coordinate Plane

For figures in the coordinate plane, you can use the distance formula to find the lengths of each side.

▶ **Remember** The distance between points (x_1, y_1) and (x_2, y_2) is $d = \sqrt{(x_2 - x_1)^2 + (y_2 - y_1)^2}$.

EXAMPLE 2

Find the perimeter of the figure in the coordinate plane.

A

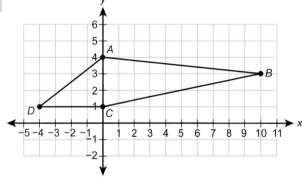

SOLUTION

Use the distance formula to find the length of each side.

$$AB = \sqrt{(10-0)^2 + (3-4)^2} = \sqrt{100+1} = \sqrt{101}$$

$$BC = \sqrt{(10-0)^2 + (3-1)^2} = \sqrt{100+4} = \sqrt{104} = 2\sqrt{26}$$

$$CD = \sqrt{(0-(-4))^2 + (1-1)^2} = \sqrt{16} = 4$$

$$AD = \sqrt{(-4-0)^2 + (1-4)^2} = \sqrt{16+9} = \sqrt{25} = 5$$

The perimeter of the figure is $\sqrt{101} + 2\sqrt{26} + 4 + 5 \approx 29.25$ units.

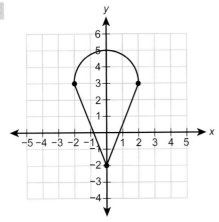

SOLUTION

The top part of the figure is a semicircle. Find half the circumference of a circle with radius 2.

$$\frac{1}{2}C = \frac{1}{2} \cdot 2\pi r = \pi(2) = 2\pi$$

Use the distance formula to find the length of the remaining sides.

$$d\left[(-2,3), (0,-2)\right] = \sqrt{(-2-0)^2 + (3-(-2))^2} = \sqrt{4+25} = \sqrt{29}$$

$$d\left[(2,3), (0,-2)\right] = \sqrt{(2-0)^2 + (3-(-2))^2} = \sqrt{4+25} = \sqrt{29}$$

The perimeter of the figure is $2\pi + 2\sqrt{29} \approx 17$ units. ■

Area of Composite Figures

To find the area of a composite figure, break it down into recognizable pieces.

Area of Basic Shapes

Area of a rectangle or parallelogram: $b \times h$

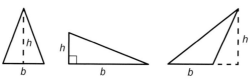

Area of a triangle: $\frac{1}{2}bh$

Area of a circle: πr^2

EXAMPLE 3

Find the area of the figure.

A

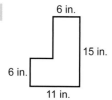

SOLUTION

Divide the figure into basic shapes.

This figure can be represented as the combination of two rectangles.

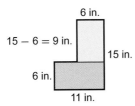

area of vertical part: $6 \times 9 = 54$ in^2

area of horizontal part: $6 \times 11 = 66$ in^2

The area of the figure is $54 + 66 = 120$ in^2.

B

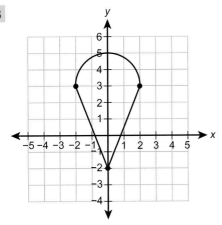

SOLUTION

Divide the figure into basic shapes.

The semicircle has radius $r = 2$, so the area of the semicircle is $\frac{1}{2}\pi r^2 = \frac{1}{2}\pi(2^2) = 2\pi \approx 6.28$ units^2.

The base of the triangle is 4 units, and the height is 5 units. The area of the triangle is $\frac{1}{2}bh = \frac{1}{2}(4)(5) = 10$ units^2.

The area of the composite figure is approximately $6.28 + 10$, or 16.28, units^2.

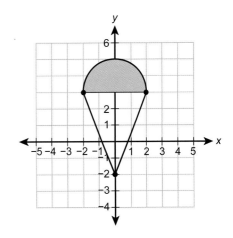

Volumes of Prisms and Cylinders

For solids, surface area is the number of squares it would take to cover the surfaces of the solid. Volume is the number of cubes it would take to fill the inside of the solid.

Surface Area and Volume

The **surface area** of a figure is the amount of space that covers the figure. To find the surface area of a solid, find the sum of the areas of its outer surfaces.

Compare the area calculations with the three-dimensional figure.

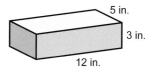

top	$12 \times 5 = 60$
bottom	$12 \times 5 = 60$
left side	$3 \times 5 = 15$
right side	$3 \times 5 = 15$
front	$12 \times 3 = 36$
+ back	$12 \times 3 = 36$
	222

The surface area of the three-dimensional figure is 222 in^2.

The **volume** of a solid is the amount of space inside the figure, measured in cubic units. If it's a small rectangular figure, you may be able to count the cubes. This is normally not possible, however, because of either the size or the shape of the figure.

▶ **Remember** Measurement is the process of using a unit to determine how much of something you have.

In a three-dimensional figure like this prism, you can multiply or count to find the area of one "layer" of cubes and multiply by the number of layers. Because each layer in this figure is a rectangle, you can find its volume by multiplying its dimensions.

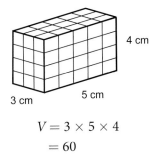

4 cm

3 cm   5 cm

$$V = 3 \times 5 \times 4$$
$$= 60$$

The volume of the figure is 60 cm^3.

Cylinders

A **cylinder** is a solid with two parallel, congruent, circular bases joined by a curved surface. The curved surface of a cylinder is called the **lateral surface**. An altitude of a cylinder is a perpendicular line segment that joins the planes of the bases. An altitude may lie inside, on, or outside the cylinder. The height of a cylinder is the length of an altitude. The line connecting the centers of the bases is the **axis of the cylinder**. If the axis is an altitude, then the cylinder is a **right cylinder**. Otherwise it is an **oblique cylinder**.

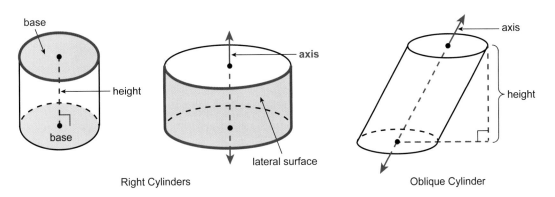

Right Cylinders   Oblique Cylinder

Surface Area of a Right Cylinder

The base area of a cylinder is the area of its base and the lateral area is the area of the lateral surface. The surface area of a right cylinder is the sum of the lateral area and 2 times the base area.

Take a closer look at the lateral surface. As shown, the lateral surface can be unrolled to form a rectangle. The length of the rectangle is the circumference of the circle, πd, or $2\pi r$. The height of the rectangle is the height of the cylinder. Therefore, the lateral area can be written as $2\pi rh$.

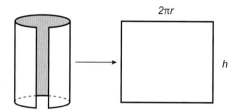

In the geometry software sketch, the radius of the base is 1 cm, and the rectangle has a length of $2\pi r$, which is approximately 6.28 cm.

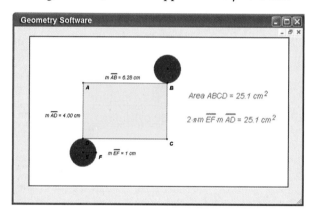

Now that you know that the area of the lateral surface is $2\pi rh$, all you have to do to find the surface area is to add the base areas. Each base is a circle, so the area of one base is πr^2 and the area of both bases is $2\pi r^2$.

Formula for the Surface Area of a Right Cylinder

The surface area S of a right cylinder with lateral area L and base area B is
$$S = L + 2B.$$

By replacing L with $2\pi rh$, and B with πr^2, you can write the formula as
$$S = 2\pi rh + 2\pi r^2.$$

Use the formula to find the surface area of the cylinder.

$$\begin{aligned}
S &= 2\pi rh + 2\pi r^2 \\
&= 2\pi(4)(8) + 2\pi(4)^2 \\
&= 64\pi + 32\pi \\
&= 96\pi \approx 302
\end{aligned}$$

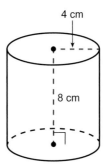

4 cm

8 cm

The surface area of the cylinder is approximately 302 cm^2.

Most calculators have a key for π, although you may need to press another key first. The answer is still an estimate because it has been rounded to fit on the display, but it is a better estimate than using 3.14. Using a precise approximation for π allows you to round your answers to the tenths, hundredths, and even thousandths place with confidence. As shown in the previous problem, always wait until the last possible step before rounding.

```
2*π*4*8
           201.0619298
Ans+2*π*4²
           301.5928947
```

Volume of a Cylinder

Cavalieri's Principle

If two solids have equal heights and the cross sections formed by every plane parallel to the bases of both solids have equal areas, then the two solids have equal volume.

You can use Cavalieri's principle to find the volume of a cylinder because the principle refers to solids, not just to prisms. A cylinder with the same height and cross-sectional areas at every level as a prism will have the same volume as the prism, which can be found using $V = Bh$.

Formula for the Volume of a Cylinder

The formula for the volume V of a cylinder with base area B and height h is

$$V = Bh.$$

By replacing B with πr^2, you can write the formula as

$$V = \pi r^2 h.$$

Cavalieri's principle tells you that the formula for the volume of a cylinder can be used to find the volume of any cylinder, including oblique cylinders.

To find the volume of this cylinder, substitute 10 for r and 12 for h.

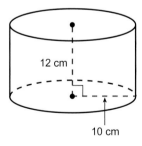

12 cm

10 cm

$$V = \pi r^2 h$$
$$= \pi(10)^2(12)$$
$$= 1200\pi$$
$$\approx 3770$$

The volume of the cylinder is approximately 3770 cm^3.

Surface Area of Cones

How much batter does it take to make an ice-cream cone? How much ice cream does a cone hold? You can answer such questions once you understand how to calculate surface area and volume of cones.

Cones

A **cone** is a solid with a circular base, a **vertex**, and a curved surface. The curved surface of a cone is called the lateral surface. The altitude of a cone is a perpendicular line segment that joins the vertex to the plane of the base. An altitude may lie inside, on, or outside a cone. The height of a cone is the length of the altitude. The **slant height** of a cone is the distance from the vertex to a point on the edge of the base. The line connecting the vertex of a cone to the center of the base is the axis of the cone. If the axis is an altitude, then the cone is a **right cone**. Otherwise it is an **oblique cone**.

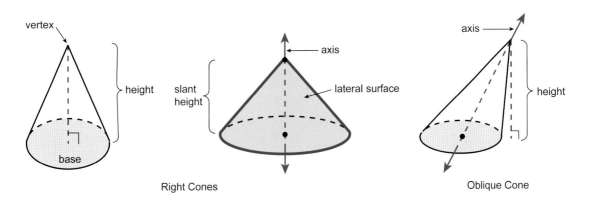

Right Cones

Oblique Cone

Surface Area of a Right Cone

The surface area of a right cone is the sum of the lateral area and the base area. The lateral surface of a right cone can be unrolled to form the fanlike shape shown as the shaded area of the figure.

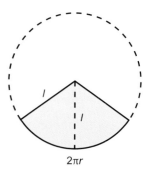

The length of the arc is the circumference, or perimeter, of the base of the cone. The formula for circumference is $2\pi r$. The sides are the slant height l of the cone. Notice that the fanlike shape resembles a triangle. The lateral surface area of a cone is similar to the area of a triangle $\frac{1}{2}bh$, or $\frac{1}{2}(2\pi r)(l)$, which simplifies to $\pi r l$.

You can check this conjecture algebraically. The figure shows that the lateral surface is a sector of a circle where the slant height is the radius. Recall that a sector is the region bounded by two radii and part of the circle. The area of a sector is proportional to the area of its circle. You can write and solve the following proportion to find the area of the sector.

$$\frac{\textbf{area of sector}}{\text{area of circle}} = \frac{\text{length of arc}}{\text{circumference of circle}}$$

$$\frac{x}{\pi l^2} = \frac{2\pi r}{2\pi l}$$

$$2\pi l x = 2\pi^2 r l^2$$

$$x = \frac{2\pi^2 r l^2}{2\pi l} = \pi r l$$

▶ **Remember** You can solve a proportion by cross multiplying.

Now that you know that the lateral area of a right cone is $\pi r l$, all you need to do to find the surface area is add the area of the base. The base is a circle, so the base area is πr^2.

Formula for the Surface Area of a Right Cone

The surface area S of a right cone with lateral area L and base area B is

$$S = L + B.$$

By replacing L with πrl, and B with πr^2, the formula can also be written as

$$S = \pi rl + \pi r^2.$$

Use the formula to find the surface area of the right cone.

$$
\begin{aligned}
S &= \pi rl + \pi r^2 \\
&= \pi(5)(10) + \pi(5)^2 \\
&= 50\pi + 25\pi \\
&= 75\pi \approx 236
\end{aligned}
$$

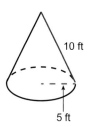

10 ft

5 ft

The surface area of the cone is approximately 236 ft^2.

Volume of a Cone

You can use Cavalieri's principle to find the volume of a cone. A cone with the same height and cross-sectional areas at every level as a pyramid will have the same volume as the pyramid, which is found by using $V = \frac{1}{3}Bh$.

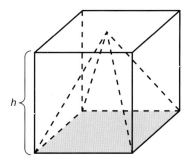

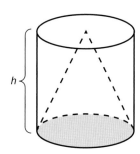

Formula for the Volume of a Cone

The formula for the volume V of a cone with base area B and height h is

$$V = \frac{1}{3}Bh.$$

When B is replaced with πr^2, the formula can also be written as

$$V = \frac{1}{3}\pi r^2 h.$$

Cavalieri's principle tells you that the formula for the volume of a cone can be used to find the volume of any cone, including oblique cones.

Find the volume of the cone shown.

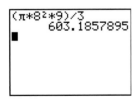

$$V = \frac{1}{3}\pi r^2 h$$

$$= \frac{1}{3}\pi(8)^2(9)$$

$$= 192\pi$$

$$\approx 603$$

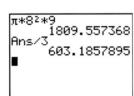

9 in.

8 in.

The volume of the cone is approximately 603 in^3.

On a calculator, you can divide by three instead of multiplying by one-third, which can be done in one step or two.

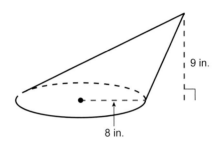

```
(π*8²*9)/3
        603.1857895
■
```

or

```
π*8²*9
        1809.557368
Ans/3
        603.1857895
■
```

Volumes of Pyramids

To determine the volume of a pyramid, you need to find one-third the product of the area of its base and its height.

Pyramids

Definitions

A **pyramid** is a polyhedron with a polygonal base and lateral faces. The faces are triangles that meet at a common vertex.

The common vertex is called the **vertex of the pyramid**.

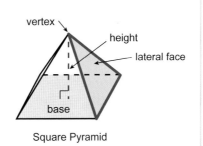

Square Pyramid

Pyramids are classified by the shapes of their bases. So if the base of a pyramid is a square, the pyramid is called a square pyramid.

Definitions

A **regular pyramid** has a base that is a regular polygon and lateral faces that are congruent isosceles triangles.

The edges that form the base of a pyramid are called **base edges**.

The remaining edges are **lateral edges**.

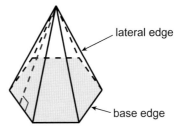

Regular Hexagonal Pyramid

An **altitude** of a pyramid is a perpendicular line segment that joins the vertex to the plane of the base. An altitude may lie inside, on, or outside a pyramid. The height of a pyramid is the length of the altitude. A right pyramid's altitude intersects the center of its base; an oblique pyramid's altitude does not.

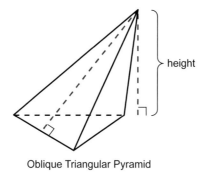

Oblique Triangular Pyramid

Volume of a Pyramid

This figure shows a square pyramid and a cube. The areas of the bases of each figure, and their heights, are equal. The ratio of the volume of the pyramid to the volume of the cube is $\frac{1}{3}$. Because the volume of the prism can be found using $V = Bh$, the volume of the pyramid can be found by taking one-third of that product.

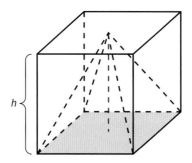

Formula for the Volume of a Pyramid

The formula for the volume of a pyramid V with base area B and height h is

$$V = \frac{1}{3}Bh.$$

EXAMPLE 1

Determine the volume of the oblique pyramid.

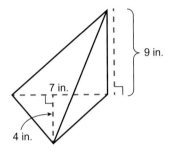

9 in.

7 in.

4 in.

SOLUTION

Find the area of the triangular base, and then use the value for the area in the volume formula.

$$B = \frac{1}{2}bh$$

$$= \frac{1}{2}(7)(4)$$

$$= \frac{1}{2}(28)$$

$$= 14$$

Use the volume formula.

$$V = \frac{1}{3}Bh$$

$$= \frac{1}{3}(14)(9)$$

$$= \frac{1}{3}(126)$$

$$= 42$$

The volume of the pyramid is 42 in^3. ■

EXAMPLE 2

The Great Pyramid of Giza is the largest pyramid ever built. It has a square base with sides that are 230 m long. The height of the pyramid is 146 m. What is the volume of the Great Pyramid?

SOLUTION

To find the volume of a pyramid, you need to know the area of the base, B, and the height, h.

The base is a square with side lengths $s = 230$ m, so $B = s^2 = 230^2 = 52{,}900 \text{ m}^2$.

Substitute 146 for h.

$$V = \frac{1}{3}Bh$$

$$= \frac{1}{3} \cdot 52{,}900 \cdot 146$$

$$= \frac{7{,}723{,}400}{3}$$

$$\approx 2{,}574{,}467$$

The volume of the Great Pyramid is approximately $2{,}574{,}467 \text{ m}^3$. ▪

Volumes of Spheres

To determine the volume of a sphere, you need to find four-thirds of the product of its radius cubed and pi.

Spheres

Definitions
A **sphere** is the set of all points in space that are a given distance from a point called the **center**.

The radius of a sphere is a line segment joining the center of the sphere and a point on the surface of the sphere.

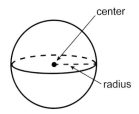

The diameter is a line segment passing through the center that joins two points on the sphere.

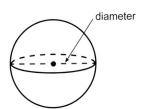

Volume of a Sphere

When a plane and a sphere intersect at more than one point, their intersection creates a circle. This figure shows a plane intersecting a sphere at perpendicular distance x from the center of the sphere. The radius of the sphere is r. The shaded circle created by the intersection has radius y. You know from the Pythagorean theorem that $x^2 + y^2 = r^2$.

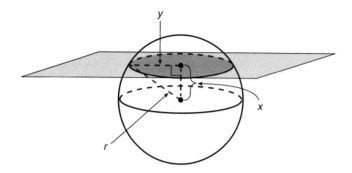

You can solve this equation for y^2.

$$y^2 = r^2 - x^2$$

The formula for the area of the purple shaded circle is $A = \pi y^2$. Substitute $r^2 - x^2$ for y^2 and distribute.

$$
\begin{aligned}
A &= \pi y^2 \\
&= \pi\left(r^2 - x^2\right) \\
&= \pi r^2 - \pi x^2
\end{aligned}
$$

The expression $\pi r^2 - \pi x^2$ can be viewed as the difference between the areas of two circles, one with radius r and one with radius x. In the diagram, there are two concentric circles. The difference is the darker area, which is called the annulus.

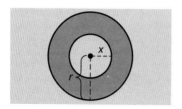

Definition

The **annulus** is the region between two concentric circles.

The area of the circle in the sphere has the same area as the annulus. To use Cavalieri's principle, you will need to find a solid that has cross sections like the concentric circles in the diagram—and it needs to work for every cross section of the sphere.

You can use part of a cylinder. The cylinder in the diagram has two identical cones inside it. The bases of the cones are the bases of the cylinder, and the vertices meet in the center of the cylinder. The part of the cylinder you want is the part that remains when the two cones are removed.

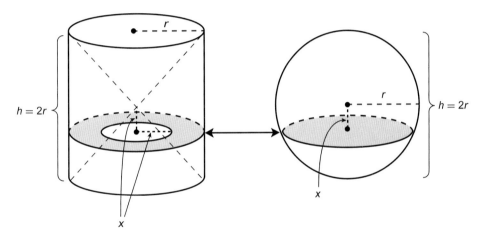

Both the cylinder and the sphere have a height of $2r$. The area of every cross section of the cylinder is equal to every area of the cross section of the sphere at that height. In the diagram, visualize moving the cross sections up and down the figures, and match the size of the annulus on the left with the corresponding circle on the right—it's larger near the center of the sphere, and smaller near the top and bottom of the sphere.

By Cavalieri's principle, the two solids have equal volume. To find the volume of the sphere, subtract two cones from the cylinder.

volume of a sphere = volume of a cylinder − 2(volume of a cone)

$$= \pi r^2 h - 2\left(\frac{1}{3}\pi r^2 h\right)$$

$$= \pi r^2 (2r) - 2\left(\frac{1}{3}\pi r^2 r\right)$$

$$= 2\pi r^3 - \frac{2}{3}\pi r^3$$

$$= \frac{4}{3}\pi r^3$$

Formula for the Volume of a Sphere

The formula for the volume V of a sphere with radius r is

$$V = \frac{4}{3}\pi r^3.$$

EXAMPLE 1

Find the volume of the sphere. Use 3.14 for π.

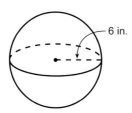

6 in.

SOLUTION
Substitute 6 for r.

$$V = \frac{4}{3}\pi r^3$$

$$= \frac{4}{3}\pi (6)^3$$

$$= 288\pi$$

$$\approx 904$$

The volume of the sphere is exactly 288π in^3, which is about 904 in^3. ∎

EXAMPLE 2

The diameter of a regulation-size soccer ball is approximately 22 cm. What is the volume of air contained inside the soccer ball? Use 3.14 for π.

SOLUTION

The diameter is 22 cm, so the radius is $\frac{22}{2} = 11$ cm. Substitute 11 for r.

$$V = \frac{4}{3}\pi r^3$$

$$= \frac{4}{3}\pi (11)^3$$

$$= \frac{5324}{3}\pi$$

$$\approx 5570$$

The volume of the soccer ball is approximately 5570 cm^3.

Volume Ratios

The ratio of the volumes of similar solids is the cube of the ratio of their corresponding dimensions.

Volumes of Similar Solids

Like similar plane figures, **similar solids** have the same shape, and all the corresponding dimensions are proportional.

These rectangular prisms are similar. The ratios of the corresponding dimensions are $\frac{6}{2} = \frac{6}{2} = \frac{9}{3} = 3$.

$V = 12$ unit^3

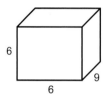

$V = 324$ unit^3

The ratio of their volumes is $\frac{324}{12} = 27$, which is the cube of the ratio of the corresponding dimensions, 3. This principle is true for the volumes of all similar solids.

Ratios of Volumes of Similar Solids

If two similar solids have corresponding dimensions in the ratio of t, then the ratio of their volumes is t^3.

EXAMPLE 1

These two cylinders are similar. The volume of the smaller cylinder is 4.5π in^3. Find the volume of the larger cylinder.

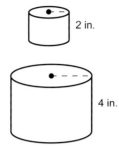

2 in.

4 in.

SOLUTION

First find the ratio of the heights.

$$\frac{4}{2} = \frac{1}{2}$$

Cube this ratio to get the ratio of the volumes.

$$\left(\frac{1}{2}\right)^3 = \frac{1}{8}$$

Write and solve a proportion.

$$\frac{1}{8} = \frac{4.5\pi}{x} \quad \longrightarrow \text{smaller cylinder}$$
$$\longrightarrow \text{larger cylinder}$$
$$x = 36\pi$$

The volume of the larger cylinder is 36π in^3. ▪

EXAMPLE 2

The volume of a cone is 200π m^3 and the volume of a similar cone is $25{,}000\pi$ m^3. Find the ratio of the corresponding dimensions.

SOLUTION

Divide to find the ratio of the volumes.

$$\frac{25{,}000}{200} = 125$$

Then take the cube root.

$$\sqrt[3]{125} = 5$$

The ratio of the corresponding dimensions is 5. ▪

Relationships also exist between the height of a solid and its volume, area, and cross-sectional area; between the height of a solid and its volume; and between the volume of a solid and the pressure inside the solid. These relationships play critical roles in the sciences.

EXAMPLE 3

A block weighs 20 lb. A second block, made of the same material, is similar to the first block, and its length is 3 times the length of the first block. How much does the second block weigh?

SOLUTION

Similar to volume, the ratio of the weights is t^3. Because the second block is 3 times as long as the first, the ratio of the lengths is $\frac{1}{3}$. Cube it to get the ratio of the weights.

$$\left(\frac{1}{3}\right)^3 = \frac{1}{27}$$

Then set up and solve a proportion.

$$\frac{1}{27} = \frac{20}{x} \quad \begin{array}{l} \longrightarrow \text{smaller block} \\ \longrightarrow \text{larger block} \end{array}$$

$$x = 540$$

The second block weighs 540 lb. ▪

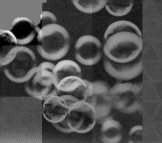

Surface Area and Volume

An understanding of surface area and volume can help you maximize and be more efficient in the use of space and the materials available.

Right Rectangular Prisms

Recall that the **surface area** of a solid is the sum of the areas of the outer surfaces of the figure. You can use the net of a right rectangular prism to develop a formula for finding its surface area. In the geometry software sketch, the area of each face is written as a product of its dimensions (length, width, and height), with the sum written to the right. Notice that there are three pairs of congruent faces.

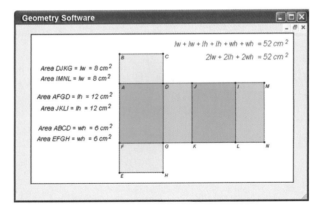

Formula for the Surface Area of a Right Rectangular Prism

The formula for the surface area S of a right rectangular prism of length l, width w, and height h is

$$S = 2lw + 2lh + 2wh.$$

The calculator screen shows how to find the surface area of the prism displayed in the previous sketch.

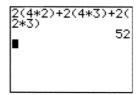

Recall that the **volume** of a solid is the number of unit cubes inside the figure. You can use transformations or isometric dots to draw the prism of the net in the previous sketch. The number of unit cubes that fills the figure is equal to the product of the length, width, and height of the prism.

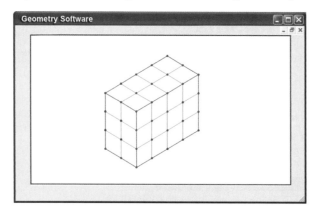

Formula for the Volume of a Right Rectangular Prism

The formula for the volume V of a right rectangular prism of length l, width w, and height h is

$$V = lwh.$$

The volume of the prism in the diagram above is $4 \cdot 2 \cdot 3$, or 24 cm^3.

Surface Area and Volume of Cubes

When every face of a right rectangular prism is a square, the prism is called a cube. Because a square has sides of equal length, each side is *s*.

The area of every face of a cube is the same. That means it is possible to find a cube's surface area by multiplying the area of just one face by 6.

Formula for the Surface Area of a Cube

The formula for the surface area *S* of a cube of side *s* is
$$S = 6s^2.$$

The calculator screen shows how to use this formula to find the surface area of a cube with a side length of 2 units.

```
6(2²)
              24
```

By substituting *s* for *l*, *w*, and *h* in the formula for the volume of a right rectangular prism, you can derive the formula for the volume of a cube.

Formula for the Volume of a Cube

The formula for the volume *V* of a cube of side *s* is
$$V = s^3.$$

To cube a number on a graphing calculator, use the caret key (^). The display shows that a cube with a side length of 2 units has a volume of 8 units^3.

```
2^3
              8
```

Changing Attributes of Figures

The length of the rectangle on the left is doubled. Notice that when one dimension is doubled, the area doubles.

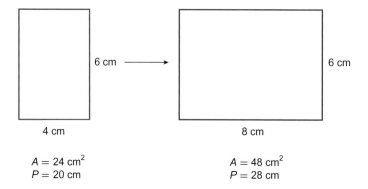

$A = 24$ cm^2
$P = 20$ cm

$A = 48$ cm^2
$P = 28$ cm

If you tripled one dimension, the area would also triple. Now what if both dimensions were doubled?

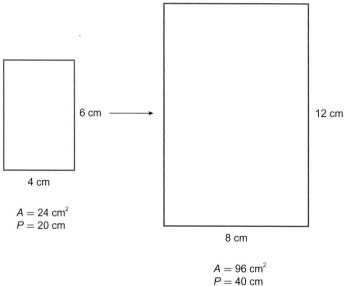

$A = 24$ cm^2
$P = 20$ cm

$A = 96$ cm^2
$P = 40$ cm

When both dimensions were doubled, the area quadrupled. In other words, it was doubled twice. The perimeter doubled as well.

The length of the cube on the left is doubled. The figure becomes a rectangular prism, and the volume doubles as well.

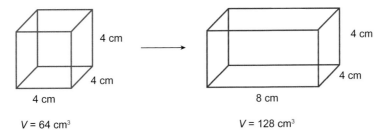

$V = 64$ cm³ $V = 128$ cm³

If you tripled one dimension, the volume would triple as well. Consider what happens when two dimensions and three dimensions are doubled.

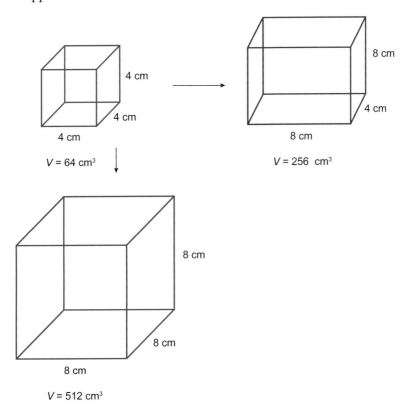

When two dimensions were doubled, the volume quadrupled, or doubled twice. When three dimensions were doubled, the volume became 8 times greater, which is the same as being doubled 3 times.

Surface Area to Volume Ratio

The **surface area to volume ratio** of a figure plays a large role in the sciences, such as in studying the cooling rates of animals. An animal with a greater surface area to volume ratio will lose heat more quickly than an animal with a smaller surface area to volume ratio.

The ratio is found by simply dividing the surface area of a figure by its volume. The surface area to volume ratio of a cube is

$$\frac{\text{surface area of a cube}}{\text{volume of a cube}} = \frac{6s^2}{s^3} = \frac{6}{s}.$$

▶ **Remember** A ratio is a comparison of two quantities by division.

Compare the ratios for cubes with side lengths of 2, 3, and 6.

Side length of cube, s	2	3	6
Surface area to volume ratio of a cube, $\dfrac{6}{s}$	$\dfrac{6}{(2)} = 3$	$\dfrac{6}{(3)} = 2$	$\dfrac{6}{(6)} = 1$

Notice that as the side length *increased*, the surface area to volume ratio *decreased*. This is true for any solid: The surface area to volume ratio is *inversely proportional* to the size of the solid.

Maximizing Volume and Minimizing Surface Area

A common dilemma in manufacturing is determining how to maximize the volume of a box while minimizing its surface area. In this sketch, the yellow area is a net of a box without a top. You can increase or decrease the length of the sides of the squares in white to change the volume and surface area of the yellow box until you are content with the measurements.

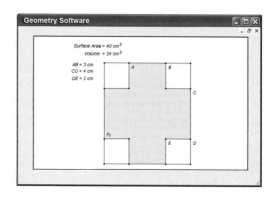

Reasoning About Area and Volume

You can use the concept of dilation to understand the area and volume ratios for similar figures.

Dilations

Definitions

A **dilation** is a transformation that changes the size of a shape, either by enlarging it or shrinking it.

The **scale factor** for a dilation is the ratio of the side length of the image to the corresponding side length of the pre-image.

Here are dilations of a triangle and a prism.

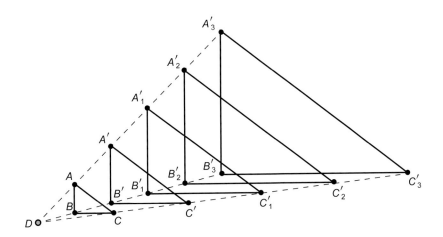

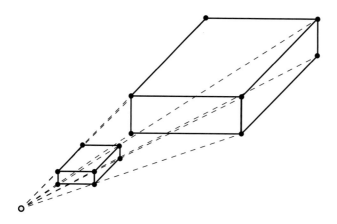

A dilation is an **expansion** if the absolute value of the scale factor is greater than 1 and a dilation is a **contraction** if the absolute value of the scale factor is between 0 and 1.

Dialating with a Scale Factor

If a point (x, y) is dilated with a scale factor of t and the center of dilation is at the origin, then the image of the point is (tx, ty).

Area Ratios

Ratios of Areas of Similar Polygons

If two similar polygons have the lengths of their corresponding sides in the ratio of t, then the ratio of their areas is t^2.

EXAMPLE 1

Given that $\triangle ABC \sim \triangle DEF$ and that points D, E, and F are corresponding dilations of points A, B, and C with a scale factor of 2, show that the ratio of the area of $\triangle DEF$ to the area of $\triangle ABC$ is 4 : 1.

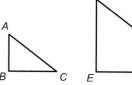
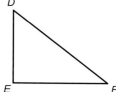

SOLUTION

Points H, I, and J are midpoints of sides DE, EF, and FD.

$$\triangle ABC \cong \triangle HEI \cong \triangle DHJ \cong \triangle JIF \cong \triangle IJH$$

area of $\triangle DEF =$ area of $\triangle HEI +$ area of $\triangle DHJ +$ area of $\triangle JIF +$ area of $\triangle IJH$

$$\text{area of } \triangle DEF = 4 \cdot \left(\text{area of } \triangle ABC\right)$$

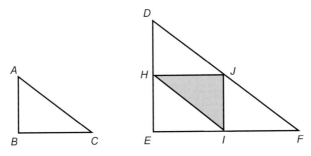

The ratio of the area of $\triangle DEF$ to the area of $\triangle ABC$ is $4:1$. ▪

Volume Ratios

Ratios of Volumes of Similar Polygons

If two similar solids have the lengths of their corresponding sides in the ratio of t, then the ratio of their volumes is t^3.

EXAMPLE 2

Given that Prism 1 is similar to Prism 2 and that points I, J, K, L, M, O, and P are corresponding dilations of points A, B, C, D, E, G, and H with a scale factor of 3, show that the ratio of the volume of Prism 1 to the volume of Prism 2 is $27:1$.

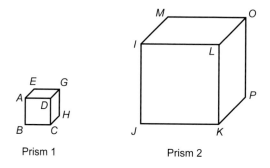

Prism 1   Prism 2

SOLUTION

Line segment *IJ* and line segment *LK* have been cut into three sections. Each section is congruent to line segment *AB*.

Line segment *IL* and line segment *JK* have been cut into three sections. Each section is congruent to line segment *BC*.

Line segment *LK* and line segment *OP* have been cut into three sections. Each section is congruent to line segment *DC*.

The cutting of the line segments in Prism 2 results in prisms that have the same dimensions as Prism 1.

Prism 2 is made up of 27 prisms that have the same dimensions and volume as Prism 1.

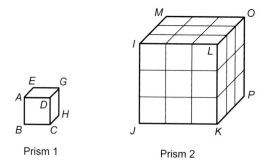

Prism 1   Prism 2

The ratio of the volume of Prism 2 to the volume of Prism 1 is 27 : 1. ▪

Circles

Topic List

▸ Chords and Arcs

▸ Tangents to Circles

▸ Inscribed Angles and Intercepted Arcs

▸ Angles Formed by Secants and Tangents

▸ Similarity in Circles

▸ Radian Measure and Sector Areas

When lines intersect a circle, the angles and arcs that are created are related to each other. These lengths and angles can help you solve many problems.

Chords and Arcs

To use theorems associated with circles, you need to understand chords and arcs.

Parts of Circles

Definition
A **chord** connects any two points on a circle.

In circle T, $\overline{TX}$, $\overline{TW}$, $\overline{TZ}$, and $\overline{TV}$ are radii; $\overline{XV}$ is a diameter; and $\overline{XY}$ and $\overline{XV}$ are chords. Notice that $\overline{XV}$ is a chord and a diameter. A **diameter** is a chord that passes through the center of a circle.

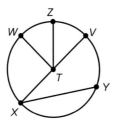

Definitions
An **arc** is the set of points on a circle between two points on the circle.
A **semicircle** is an arc with endpoints that are also the endpoints of a diameter.
Minor arcs are arcs smaller than a semicircle.
Major arcs are arcs larger than a semicircle.

In circle C, $\overset{\frown}{AB}$ is a minor arc, which also could be named $\overset{\frown}{BA}$. To describe the longer arc that has endpoints A and B (the major arc that goes around the other way), write $\overset{\frown}{ADB}$ or $\overset{\frown}{BEA}$. Two semicircles in circle C are $\overset{\frown}{DAB}$ and $\overset{\frown}{DEB}$.

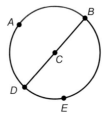

Definitions

A **central angle** is an angle that has its vertex at the center of a circle and its sides as radii of the circle.

An **inscribed angle** is an angle that has its vertex on a circle and its sides as chords of the circle.

In circle T, $\angle XTW$, $\angle WTZ$, and $\angle ZTV$ are central angles, and $\angle VXY$ is an inscribed angle.

Angle and Arc Measures

Arc Measures

The degree measure of a minor arc is the measure of its central angle.

The degree measure of a major arc is 360° minus the degree measure of its acute central angle.

The degree measure of a semicircle is 180°.

EXAMPLE 1

Find $m\overset{\frown}{AXB}$.

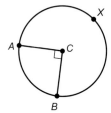

SOLUTION

$m\angle ACB = 90°$, so $m\overset{\frown}{AB} = 90°$.

Since a complete rotation measures 360°,

$$
\begin{aligned}
m\overset{\frown}{AXB} &= 360° - m\overset{\frown}{AB} \\
&= 360° - 90° \\
&= 270° \; \blacksquare
\end{aligned}
$$

Two circles are congruent if they have the same radius. Two arcs are congruent if they are on congruent circles and have the same angle measure.

The circumference of a complete circle is $2\pi r$. Because an arc is part of a circle, **arc length** is a part of the circumference of a circle. It can be found by writing the part as a fraction over 360° and multiplying by the circumference.

Formula for Arc Length

The length L of an arc, where m is the degree measure of the arc and r is the radius, is

$$
L = \left(\frac{m}{360°} \right) 2\pi r.
$$

EXAMPLE 2

Find the length of $\overset{\frown}{AB}$.
Use 3.14 for π.

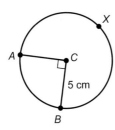

SOLUTION

$$L = \left(\frac{90°}{360°}\right)2\pi\left(5\right)$$

$$= \left(\frac{1}{4}\right)10\pi$$

$$= 2.5\pi \approx 7.85$$

The arc length of $\overset{\frown}{AB}$ is about 7.85 cm. ▪

Chords and Arcs Theorem and Its Inverse

Chords and arcs have the following relationship.

THEOREM CIRC-1   Chords and Arcs Theorem

In a circle or in congruent circles, the arcs of congruent chords are congruent.

Given   circle C with $\overline{RS} \cong \overline{DF}$

Prove $\overset{\frown}{RS} \cong \overset{\frown}{DF}$

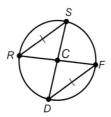

Statement	Reason	Sketch
1. circle C with $\overline{RS} \cong \overline{DF}$	Given	

Statement	Reason	Sketch
2. $\overline{CR} \cong \overline{CS} \cong \overline{CD} \cong \overline{CF}$	All radii of a circle are congruent.	
3. $\triangle CRS \cong \triangle CDF$	SSS Congruence Postulate	
4. $\angle RCS \cong \angle DCF$	CPCTC	
5. $\overparen{RS} \cong \overparen{DF}$	The measure of a minor arc is the measure of its central angle.	

The converse of the chords and arcs theorem is also true.

Theorem CIRC-2

Converse of the Chords and Arcs Theorem In a circle or in congruent circles, the chords of congruent arcs are congruent.

Tangents to Circles

Understanding tangents will help you apply theorems associated with circles to real-world situations.

Tangents and Secants

Definitions

A **tangent** to a circle is a line in the plane of the circle that intersects the circle in exactly one point.

A **point of tangency** is a point where a circle and one of its tangents intersect.

A **secant** is a line that intersects a circle in two points.

In the diagram, $\overleftrightarrow{BD}$ is a tangent to circle C. You can also say $\overleftrightarrow{BD}$ is a tangent of circle C. Point B is the point of tangency. $\overleftrightarrow{EF}$ is a secant of circle C.

Notice that secant $\overleftrightarrow{EF}$ contains the chord $\overline{EF}$.

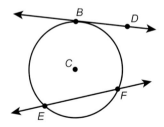

Tangent Theorems

Theorem CIRC-3

Tangent Theorem A line that is tangent to a circle is perpendicular to a radius of the circle at the point of tangency.

You can use the tangent theorem to find angle measures.

EXAMPLE 1

Solve for x.

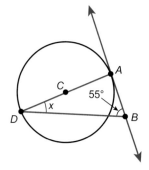

SOLUTION

In the diagram, $\overleftrightarrow{AB}$ is tangent to circle C and $m\angle ABD = 55°$.

The tangent theorem tells you that $m\angle DAB = 90°$. The sum of the measures of the angles of a triangle is $180°$.

$$m\angle DAB + m\angle ABD + m\angle BDA = 180°$$
$$90° + 55° + x = 180°$$
$$145° + x = 180°$$
$$x = 35° \ \blacksquare$$

The converse of the tangent theorem is also true.

Theorem CIRC-4

Converse of the Tangent Theorem A line that is perpendicular to a radius of a circle at its endpoint on the circle is tangent to the circle.

You can use the converse of the tangent theorem to determine whether a line is tangent to a circle.

EXAMPLE 2

Determine whether $\overleftrightarrow{RS}$ is a tangent to circle C.

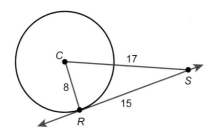

SOLUTION

Use the converse of the Pythagorean theorem to see whether $\triangle CRS$ is a right triangle.

$$c^2 = a^2 + b^2$$
$$17^2 = 8^2 + 15^2$$
$$289 = 64 + 225$$
$$289 = 289$$

$\triangle CRS$ is a right triangle with right angle CRS. So $\overline{CR} \perp \overleftrightarrow{RS}$ and $\overleftrightarrow{RS}$ is tangent to circle C. ▪

Constructing a Line Tangent to a Circle from an External Point

You can use a straightedge and compass to construct a line tangent to a circle from an external point.

Construct a line tangent to a circle from an external point.

Given   a circle and a point not on the circle

Construct   a tangent line to the circle from an external point

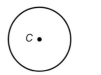

Step	Sketch
1. Construct circle C and an external point P. Draw $\overline{CP}$.	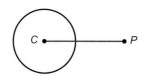
2. Construct the perpendicular bisector of $\overline{CP}$. Open the compass a width greater than one-half of CP. With the point of the compass at C, draw an arc above $\overline{CP}$ and an arc below $\overline{CP}$ as shown. Repeat the process using the compass at the same width and the compass point at P. Label the midpoint of $\overline{CP}$ as M.	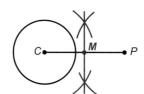
3. Set the compass so that the point is at M and width is CM. Draw arcs that intersect circle C. Label the points of intersections of the arcs and circle as A and B.	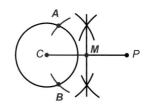
4. Draw $\overrightarrow{PA}$ and $\overrightarrow{PB}$. $\overrightarrow{PA}$ and $\overrightarrow{PB}$ are tangent to circle C.	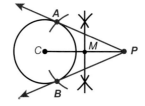

Radii and Chords

There is a relationship between the radius of a circle and a chord of that circle.

THEOREM CIRC-5 Radius and Chord Theorem

A radius that is perpendicular to a chord of a circle bisects the chord.

Given   circle A with radius $\overline{AR} \perp \overline{PQ}$

Prove $\overline{AR}$ bisects $\overline{PQ}$.

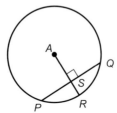

Statement	Reason	Sketch
1. circle A with radius $\overline{AR} \perp \overline{PQ}$	Given	
2. $\angle ASQ$ and $\angle ASP$ are right angles.	Definition of perpendicular lines	
3. Draw $\overline{AP}$ and $\overline{AQ}$.	Two points determine a line.	
4. $\overline{AP} \cong \overline{AQ}$	All radii of a circle are congruent.	

Statement	Reason	Sketch
5. $\overline{AS} \cong \overline{AS}$	Reflexive Property of Congruence	
6. $\triangle ASP \cong \triangle ASQ$	HL Congruence Theorem	
7. $\overline{PS} \cong \overline{QS}$	CPCTC	
8. S is the midpoint of $\overline{PQ}$.	Definition of a midpoint	
9. $\overline{AR}$ bisects $\overline{PQ}$.	Definition of a segment bisector	

Inscribed Angles and Intercepted Arcs

To find measures of inscribed angles and intercepted arcs, you need to use theorems and corollaries.

Definitions

An **inscribed angle** of a circle has its vertex on the circle and its sides are chords of the circle.

An **intercepted arc** is the arc opposite the inscribed angle.

The **endpoints of an intercepted arc** are the points where the sides of an inscribed angle meet the circle.

$\angle AED$ is an inscribed angle of the circle. $\overset{\frown}{AD}$ is the intercepted arc of $\angle AED$. $\angle AED$ intercepts $\overset{\frown}{AD}$. The endpoints of the intercepted arc $\overset{\frown}{AD}$ are point A and point D.

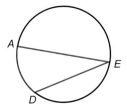

The next theorem describes how the measure of the inscribed angle relates to the measure of its intercepted arc.

Theorem CIRC-6

Inscribed Angle Theorem An angle inscribed in a circle has a measure that equals one-half the measure of its intercepted arc.

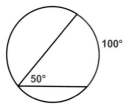

There are three cases to consider when proving the theorem.

Case 1 The center of the circle lies on a side of the inscribed angle.

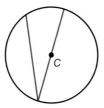

Case 2 The center of the circle lies inside the inscribed angle.

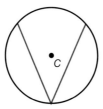

Case 3 The center of the circle lies outside the inscribed angle.

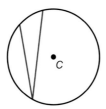

Here is the proof of Case 1.

THEOREM CIRC-6 (CASE 1)   Inscribed Angle Theorem with
Center Lying on One Side of Angle

Given   circle D with $m\angle CBA = x$

Prove $m\angle CBA = \frac{1}{2}m\overset{\frown}{AC}$

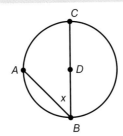

Statement	Reason	Sketch
1. circle D with $m\angle CBA = x$	Given	
2. Draw $\overline{AD}$.	Two points determine a line.	
3. $\overline{AD} \cong \overline{BD}$	All radii of a circle are congruent.	
4. $\triangle ADB$ is isosceles.	Definition of an isosceles triangle	

Statement	Reason	Sketch
5. $\angle ABD \cong \angle BAD$	Isosceles Triangle Theorem	
6. $m\angle ADC = 2x$	Exterior Angle Theorem	
7. $m\widehat{AC} = 2x$	The degree measure of a minor arc is the measure of its central angle.	
8. $\frac{1}{2}m\widehat{AC} = x$	Division Property of Equality	
9. $m\angle CBA = \frac{1}{2}m\widehat{AC}$	Substitution Property of Equality	

Recall that a semicircle measures 180°. An inscribed angle that intercepts a semicircle also measures 90°.

Corollary CIRC-1

Right-Angle Corollary An angle that is inscribed in a semicircle is a right angle.

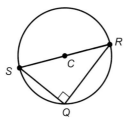

Every arc has many inscribed angles.

Corollary CIRC-2

Arc-Intercept Corollary Two inscribed angles that intercept the same arc have the same measure.

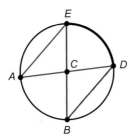

$\angle EAD$ and $\angle EBD$ both intercept $\overparen{ED}$. So $m\angle EAD = m\angle EBD$. The converse of the right-angle corollary is also true.

Corollary CIRC-3

Converse of the Right-Angle Corollary If an inscribed angle is a right angle, then the intercepted arc is a semicircle.

However, the converse of the arc-intercept corollary is not true because many different arcs are formed by inscribed angles that are congruent. For example, $m\angle B = m\angle F$, but each angle intercepts two different arcs.

$\angle B$ intercepts $\overset{\frown}{AC}$ and $\angle F$ intercepts $\overset{\frown}{EG}$.

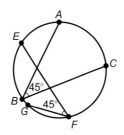

THEOREM CIRC-7 Inscribed Quadrilateral Theorem

If a quadrilateral is inscribed in a semicircle, then the opposite angles are supplementary.

Given $ABDE$ is inscribed in circle C.

Prove $\angle A$ and $\angle D$ are supplementary.
         $\angle B$ and $\angle E$ are supplementary.

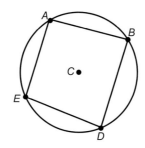

Statement	Reason	Sketch
1. $ABDE$ is inscribed in circle C.	Given	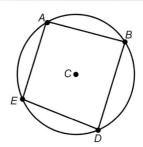

Statement	Reason	Sketch
2. Arcs $\overset{\frown}{BDE}$ and $\overset{\frown}{EAB}$ together make a circle, so $m\,\overset{\frown}{BDE} + m\,\overset{\frown}{EAB} = 360°$. Arcs $\overset{\frown}{DEA}$ and $\overset{\frown}{ABD}$ together make a circle, so $m\,\overset{\frown}{DEA} + m\,\overset{\frown}{ABD} = 360°$.	A complete rotation of a circle is 360°.	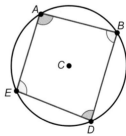
3. $m\angle A = \frac{1}{2}m\,\overset{\frown}{BDE}$ and $m\angle D = \frac{1}{2}m\,\overset{\frown}{EAB}$ $m\angle B = \frac{1}{2}m\,\overset{\frown}{DEA}$ and $m\angle E = \frac{1}{2}m\,\overset{\frown}{ABD}$	An angle inscribed in a circle has a measure that equals one-half the measure of the intercepted arc.	
4. $m\angle A + m\angle D = \frac{1}{2}m\,\overset{\frown}{BDE} + \frac{1}{2}m\,\overset{\frown}{EAB}$ $m\angle B + m\angle E = \frac{1}{2}m\,\overset{\frown}{DEA} + \frac{1}{2}m\,\overset{\frown}{ABD}$	Addition Property of Equality	
5. $m\angle A + m\angle D = \frac{1}{2}(360°)$ $m\angle B + m\angle E = \frac{1}{2}(360°)$	Substitution Property of Equality	

Statement	Reason	Sketch
6. $m\angle A + m\angle D = 180°$ $m\angle B + m\angle E = 180°$	Multiplication of real numbers	
7. $\angle A$ and $\angle D$ are supplementary. $\angle B$ and $\angle E$ are supplementary.	Definition of supplementary	

EXAMPLE

Quadrilateral $PQRS$ is inscribed in circle C. Find the measures of $\angle P$, $\angle Q$, $\angle R$, and $\angle S$.

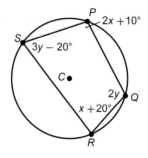

SOLUTION

If a quadrilateral is inscribed in a semicircle, then the opposite angles are supplementary.

$\angle P$ and $\angle R$ are supplementary.　　　If a quadrilateral is inscribed in a semicircle, then the opposite angles are supplementary.

$m\angle P + m\angle R = 180°$	Definition of supplementary
$(2x + 10°) + (x + 20°) = 180°$	Substitution Property of Equality
$3x + 30° = 180°$	Combine like terms.
$3x = 150°$	Subtraction Property of Equality
$x = 50°$	Division Property of Equality
$m\angle P = 2x + 10° = 2(50°) + 10° = 110°$	Substitution Property of Equality
$m\angle R = x + 20° = 50° + 20° = 70°$	Substitution Property of Equality

$\angle Q$ and $\angle S$ are supplementary.　　　If a quadrilateral is inscribed in a semicircle, then the opposite angles are supplementary.

$m\angle Q + m\angle S = 180°$	Definition of supplementary
$(2y) + (3y - 20°) = 180°$	Substitution Property of Equality
$5y - 20° = 180°$	Combine like terms.
$5y = 200°$	Subtraction Property of Equality
$y = 40°$	Division Property of Equality
$m\angle Q = 2y = 2(40°) = 80°$	Substitution Property of Equality
$m\angle S = 3y - 20° = 3(40°) - 20° = 100°$	Substitution Property of Equality ∎

Angles Formed by Secants and Tangents

When secants and tangents intersect with a circle, there are several angle relationships that are formed.

A solar eclipse occurs when the moon is between the earth and the sun at a position that causes the moon's shadow to fall on the earth's surface. Though it may seem like this would happen frequently, it is a rather rare occurrence. The moon's orbit around the earth is tilted by 5° to the earth's orbit around the sun. The tilting causes the moon's shadow to almost always miss the earth's surface. The lines in the diagram show what happens when the moon completely blocks the rays of the sun from reaching a particular spot on the earth. The lines are tangent to the circles representing the sun and moon.

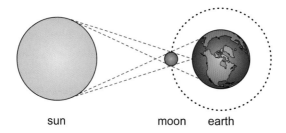

sun   moon   earth

More Angle and Arc Relationships

So far you have learned the relationships between angles and arcs for both central and inscribed angles. Now you will learn even more angle and arc relationships. They fall into three basic categories.

- The vertex is *on* the circle.

- The vertex is *outside* the circle.

- The vertex is *inside* the circle.

Vertex on the Circle

The inscribed angle theorem states that the measure of an inscribed angle is half the measure of its intercepted arc. It turns out that this theorem can be extended to include angles other than inscribed angles whose vertex is on a circle. This happens when a tangent and secant intersect.

Theorem CIRC-8

If a tangent and a secant or chord intersect on a circle at the point of tangency, then the measure of the angle formed equals one-half the measure of the intercepted arc.

$$m\angle DGB = \frac{1}{2}\ m\overset{\frown}{GB}$$
$$= \frac{1}{2}\ (130°)$$
$$= 65°$$

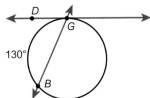

Vertex Outside the Circle

There are three ways for two lines to intersect so that the vertex is outside the circle. In each of these cases, there are two intercepted arcs. Also, in each, the measure of the angle is half the difference of the intercepted arcs. These are our next three theorems.

THEOREM CIRC-9   The measure of a secant-tangent angle with its vertex outside the circle equals one-half of the difference of the measures of the intercepted arcs.

Given $\overleftrightarrow{AC}$ is a tangent.
$\overleftrightarrow{AD}$ is a secant.

Prove $m\angle DAC = \frac{1}{2}\left(m\overset{\frown}{DB} - m\overset{\frown}{EB}\right)$

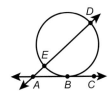

Statement	Reason	Sketch
1. $\overleftrightarrow{AC}$ is a tangent. $\overleftrightarrow{AD}$ is a secant.	Given	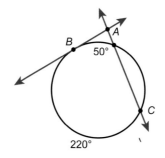
2. Draw $\overline{DB}$.	Two points determine a line.	
3. $m\angle ADB = \frac{1}{2}m\overset{\frown}{EB}$ $m\angle DBC = \frac{1}{2}m\overset{\frown}{DB}$	Inscribed Angle Theorem	
4. $m\angle ADB + m\angle DAC = m\angle DBC$	Exterior Angle Theorem	
5. $\frac{1}{2}m\overset{\frown}{EB} + m\angle DAC = \frac{1}{2}m\overset{\frown}{DB}$	Substitution Property of Equality	
6. $m\angle DAC = \frac{1}{2}m\overset{\frown}{DB} - \frac{1}{2}m\overset{\frown}{EB}$	Subtraction Property of Equality	
7. $m\angle DAC = \frac{1}{2}\left(m\overset{\frown}{DB} - m\overset{\frown}{EB}\right)$	Distributive Property	

Use the theorem to find $m\angle BAC$.

$$m\angle BAC = \frac{1}{2}(220° - 50°)$$
$$= \frac{1}{2}(170°)$$
$$= 85°$$

Theorem CIRC-10

The measure of an angle that is formed by two secants that intersect in the exterior of a circle equals one-half of the difference of the measures of the intercepted arcs.

$$m\angle SRW = \frac{1}{2}\left(m\widehat{SW} - m\widehat{PQ}\right)$$

$$= \frac{1}{2}(120° - 50°)$$

$$= \frac{1}{2}(70°)$$

$$= 35°$$

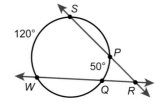

Theorem CIRC-11

The measure of a tangent-tangent angle with its vertex outside the circle equals one-half of the difference of the measures of the intercepted arcs, or the measure of the major arc minus 180°.

$$m\angle TRS = \frac{1}{2}\left(m\widehat{TQS} - m\widehat{TS}\right)$$

$$= \frac{1}{2}(238° - 122°)$$

$$= \frac{1}{2}(116°)$$

$$= 58°$$

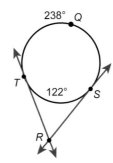

Vertex Inside the Circle

The only way for two lines to intersect inside a circle is if both lines are secants.

> ### Theorem CIRC-12
>
> The measure of an angle that is formed by two secants or chords that intersect in the interior of a circle equals one-half the sum of the measures of the arcs intercepted by the angle and its vertical angle.

$$m\angle PRS = \frac{1}{2}\left(m\widehat{PS} + m\widehat{WT}\right)$$

$$= \frac{1}{2}\left(105° + 75°\right)$$

$$= \frac{1}{2}\left(180°\right)$$

$$= 90°$$

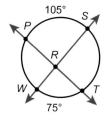

These theorems can be used to find missing arcs as well as missing angles. It just takes a little algebra.

$$m\angle QWS = \frac{1}{2}\left(m\widehat{QS} + m\widehat{RT}\right)$$

$$66° = \frac{1}{2}\left(x + 52°\right)$$

$$132° = x + 52°$$

$$80° = x$$

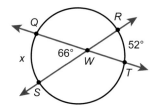

Similarity in Circles

A circle is similar to any other circle through a translation and a dilation.

Transformations with Circles

Definitions

Similar figures have the same shape but not necessarily the same size.

▶ **Remember** A **translation** is a transformation that slides a figure in a straight path without rotation or reflection.

A **dilation** is a transformation that changes the size but not the shape of a figure, either by enlarging or by shrinking it.

In a dilation, the **scale factor** is the ratio of the length of a side on the image to the length of its corresponding side on the pre-image.

EXAMPLE

Let (x, y) be points on circle C_1. Show that C_1 is similar to circle C_2 by describing a similarity transformation.

C_1: center $(-1, 4)$ and radius 1
C_2: center $(0, 0)$ and radius 2

SOLUTION

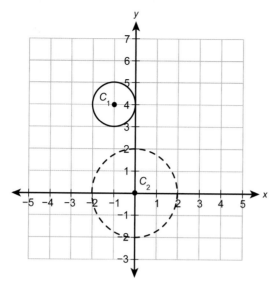

The translation of the center $(-1, 4)$ to the center $(0, 0)$ is $(x, y) \rightarrow (x + 1, y - 4)$. The dilation is with a scale factor of 2.

Radian Measure and Sector Areas

You can use properties of similarity and radian measures to derive the formula for the area of a sector.

Similarity of Arc Lengths

The three circles shown are similar by dilation. The inner circle is dilated by a scale factor of 2 to obtain the middle circle and by a scale factor of 3 to obtain the outer circle.

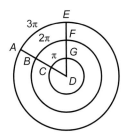

The measure of $\angle D$ is 60°. The lengths of radii $\overline{CD}$, $\overline{BD}$, and $\overline{AD}$ are 3, 6, and 9, respectively. The lengths of arcs $\overset{\frown}{CG}$, $\overset{\frown}{BF}$, and $\overset{\frown}{AE}$ are π, 2π, and 3π, respectively. Each arc length and its corresponding radius are constant for the similar circles.

$$\frac{\overset{\frown}{CG}}{\overline{CD}} = \frac{\pi}{3}$$

$$\frac{\overset{\frown}{BF}}{\overline{BD}} = \frac{2\pi}{6} = \frac{\pi}{3}$$

$$\frac{\overset{\frown}{AE}}{\overline{AD}} = \frac{3\pi}{9} = \frac{\pi}{3}$$

Finding Radian Measure

Definition
A radian is a unit of angle measure. The **radian measure** of a central angle of a circle equals the quotient of the angle's arc length and the circle's radius.

EXAMPLE 1

Find the measure of θ in radians.

SOLUTION

$$\theta = \frac{\text{arc length}}{\text{length of radius}} = \frac{10}{14} \approx 0.71$$

The measure of θ is approximately 0.71 radian. ■

Estimating Radian Measures

The protractor shows radian measures expressed as decimals and expressed in terms of π. It also shows measures in degrees for selected angles.

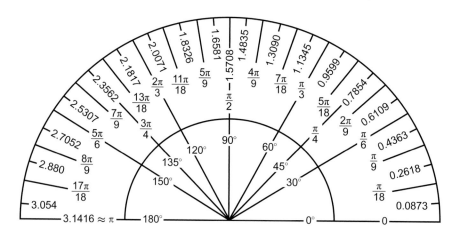

EXAMPLE 2

Is 1 radian a good estimate of the radian measure
of the angle? Why or why not?

SOLUTION

For an angle to have a measure of 1 radian, the arc length and the radius of
a circle with theta as its central angle would need to be equal. If you mark
an equal distance on the two rays of the angle and connect the points, you
will see that the arc between the endpoints is significantly smaller than the
distances that were marked on the rays. Also, the protractor indicates that
the opening of the angle would need to be larger.

No, 1 radian is not a good estimate of the radian measure of the angle. ▪

Area of Sectors

Formula for Area of a Sector

The area of a sector with a central angle measure in radians is

$$\text{area of sector} = \frac{\text{central angle in radians}}{2} \cdot (\text{radius})^2.$$

EXAMPLE 3

Find the approximate area of sector ABC, given that
$\theta \approx 1.57$ radians.

SOLUTION

$$\text{radius} = r = 100 \text{ cm}$$

$$\text{area of sector} = \frac{\text{central angle in radians}}{2} \cdot (\text{radius})^2$$

$$\approx \frac{1.57}{2} \cdot 100^2 \approx 7850$$

The approximate area of sector ABC is 7850 cm^2. ▪

Right Triangle Trigonometry

Topic List

- ▸ Tangents
- ▸ Sines and Cosines
- ▸ Special Right Triangles
- ▸ Using Special Right Triangles
- ▸ Deriving the Formula for Area of a Triangle
- ▸ The Laws of Sines and Cosines

Right triangles arise in many real-world situations. Many sails are shaped like right triangles, but triangles also help sailors figure out where they are and how to get to their destination.

Tangents

Tangent ratios can help you solve real-world problems involving lengths and angles of triangles.

Trigonometric Ratios

Definitions
A **trigonometric ratio** is the ratio of two side lengths of a right triangle.

The **hypotenuse** of a right triangle is the side opposite its right angle.

The **adjacent** side of an acute angle in a right triangle is the side that is next to the given angle but is not the hypotenuse.

The **opposite** side of an acute angle in a right triangle is across from the given angle.

For $\triangle ABC$:

- With respect to $\angle A$, a is the opposite side, and b is the adjacent side.
- With respect to $\angle B$, b is the opposite side, and a is the adjacent side.
- c is always the hypotenuse.

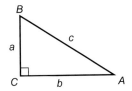

The Tangent Ratio

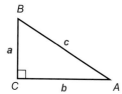

$$\tan A = \frac{\text{opposite}}{\text{adjacent}} = \frac{a}{b}$$

$$\tan B = \frac{\text{opposite}}{\text{adjacent}} = \frac{b}{a}$$

The tangent ratio in trigonometry is related to tangents to circles. Circle B has a radius of 1. $\overline{AC}$ is tangent to circle B at point C. The tangent of B is the ratio of the length of the tangent segment to the radius.

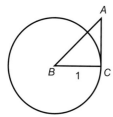

$$\tan B = \frac{\text{opposite}}{\text{adjacent}} = \frac{AC}{BC} = \frac{AC}{1} = AC$$

So the tangent of the angle is the length of the tangent segment.

Any trigonometric ratio can be expressed as either a fraction or a decimal.

EXAMPLE 1

Find the tangent of each acute angle.

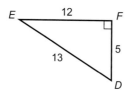

SOLUTION

$$\tan D = \frac{12}{5} = 2.4$$

$$\tan E = \frac{5}{12} \approx 0.4167 \;\blacksquare$$

You can use a calculator to find an approximation for a tangent ratio. To do so, set your calculator in degree mode and use the **tan** key.

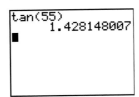

The screen shows that the tangent of a 55° angle is approximately 1.4281.

EXAMPLE 2

Find the value of x.

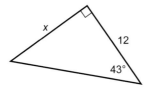

SOLUTION

To find the value of x in the diagram, set up the tangent ratio and solve for x.

$$\tan 43° = \frac{x}{12}$$

$$12(\tan 43°) = x$$

$$11.19 \approx x \;\blacksquare$$

The Inverse Tangent

Sometimes you know the lengths of the legs of a right triangle and you want to find the measure of an acute angle.

Definition
The **inverse tangent**, abbreviated $\tan^{-1}$, is the angle that has a given value as its tangent ratio.

Your calculator may have a **tan**$^{-1}$ button, or you may have to use an **INV** key.

EXAMPLE 3

Find the angle of elevation for a hill that has a 15% grade.

SOLUTION

To find the angle of elevation, draw a right triangle with a slope of $\frac{15}{100}$. Then find the inverse tangent.

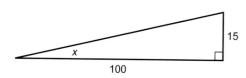

$$\tan x = \frac{15}{100}$$

$$\tan x = 0.15$$

$$x \approx 8.5°$$

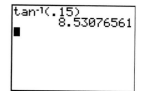

The angle of elevation is about 8.5°. ▪

Sines and Cosines

To solve problems involving indirect measurements, you need to understand sines and cosines.

The Sine and Cosine Ratios

The tangent ratio only involves the legs of a right triangle, because opposite and adjacent sides (the two legs) are never the hypotenuse. Two other trigonometric ratios do involve the hypotenuse.

Definition

The **sine of an angle**, abbreviated sin, is the ratio of the length of the leg that is opposite the angle to the length of the hypotenuse.

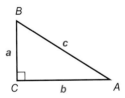

$$\sin A = \frac{\text{opposite}}{\text{hypotenuse}} = \frac{a}{c}$$

$$\sin B = \frac{\text{opposite}}{\text{hypotenuse}} = \frac{b}{c}$$

Definition

The **cosine of an angle**, abbreviated cos, is the ratio of the length of the leg that is adjacent to that angle to the length of the hypotenuse.

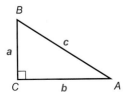

$$\cos A = \frac{\text{adjacent}}{\text{hypotenuse}} = \frac{b}{c}$$

$$\cos B = \frac{\text{adjacent}}{\text{hypotenuse}} = \frac{a}{c}$$

As with tangent, both sine and cosine can be defined as lengths of segments on a circle with a radius of 1. For circle B, where $\overline{AC}$ is a tangent segment, B, D, and A are collinear, and B, E, and C are also collinear. $\overline{DE}$ is a half-chord because $\overline{BC}$ is a perpendicular bisector of chord $\overline{DF}$.

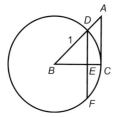

$$\sin B = \frac{\text{opposite}}{\text{hypotenuse}} = \frac{DE}{BD} = \frac{DE}{1} = DE$$

$$\cos B = \frac{\text{adjacent}}{\text{hypotenuse}} = \frac{BE}{BD} = \frac{BE}{1} = BE$$

The illustration summarizes how the ratios of sine, cosine, and tangent relate to a circle with a radius of 1 unit.

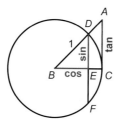

Also like the tangent ratio, the sine and cosine ratios can be expressed either as fractions or as decimals.

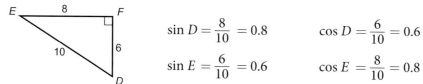

$$\sin D = \frac{8}{10} = 0.8 \qquad \cos D = \frac{6}{10} = 0.6$$

$$\sin E = \frac{6}{10} = 0.6 \qquad \cos E = \frac{8}{10} = 0.8$$

Notice that the sine of one acute angle is equal to the cosine of the other acute angle from the same triangle.

As you did for the tangent ratio, you can use your calculator to find decimal approximations for the sine and cosine of an angle. Use the **sin** and **cos** keys on your calculator. The screen shows that the sine of a 35° angle is approximately 0.5736 and the cosine is approximately 0.8192.

```
sin(35)
        .5735764364
cos(35)
        .8191520443
```

▶ **Remember** When calculating a trigonometric ratio for a given degree measure, your calculator must be set in degree mode.

EXAMPLE 1

Find the unknown side length.

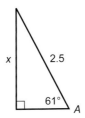

SOLUTION

$$\sin A = \frac{\text{opposite}}{\text{hypotenuse}}$$

$$\sin 61° = \frac{x}{2.5}$$

$$2.5(\sin 61°) = x$$

$$2.187 \approx x$$

EXAMPLE 2

Find the unknown side length.

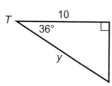

SOLUTION

$$\cos T = \frac{\text{adjacent}}{\text{hypotenuse}}$$

$$\cos 36° = \frac{10}{y}$$

$$y(\cos 36°) = 10$$

$$y = \frac{10}{\cos 36°}$$

$$y \approx 12.36 \;\blacksquare$$

You can use trigonometry to make indirect measurements.

EXAMPLE 3

Suppose a kite is at the end of a 250 ft string. If the string makes an angle of about 50° with the ground, you can approximate the height of the kite above the ground by using a trigonometric ratio to set up and solve an equation.

SOLUTION

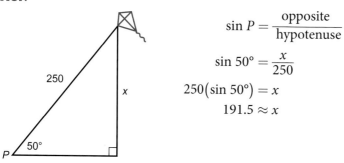

$$\sin P = \frac{\text{opposite}}{\text{hypotenuse}}$$

$$\sin 50° = \frac{x}{250}$$

$$250(\sin 50°) = x$$

$$191.5 \approx x$$

The kite is about 192 ft high. ■

The Inverse Sine and Cosine

To find the measure of an acute angle, given the length of a leg and the length of the hypotenuse, use the inverse sine and cosine: $\sin^{-1}$ and $\cos^{1}$.

EXAMPLE 4

A 16 ft ladder is leaning against a house. The top of the ladder reaches 10 ft above the ground. To find the angle that the base of the ladder makes with the ground, set up an equation and find the inverse sine.

SOLUTION

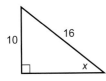

$$\sin x = \frac{10}{16}$$

$$\sin x = 0.625$$

$$x \approx 38.7°$$

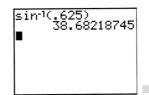

Trigonometric Identities

Definition
A **trigonometric identity** is an equation containing a trigonometric ratio that is true for all values of the variable.

▶ **Think About It** To remember that sine is **o**pposite over **h**ypotenuse, cosine is **a**djacent over **h**ypotenuse, and tangent is **o**pposite over **a**djacent, use each first letter to make the word *sohcahtoa*, pronounced "soak-a-toe-ah."

There are many trigonometric identities. You will examine two of them and show they are true.

Identity 1 $\tan x = \dfrac{\sin x}{\cos x}$

To show that this is true, substitute the ratios for sine and cosine into the equation.

$$\tan x = \frac{\dfrac{\text{opposite}}{\text{hypotenuse}}}{\dfrac{\text{adjacent}}{\text{hypotenuse}}}$$

$$\tan x = \frac{\text{opposite}}{\cancel{\text{hypotenuse}}} \cdot \frac{\cancel{\text{hypotenuse}}}{\text{adjacent}}$$

$$\tan x = \frac{\text{opposite}}{\text{adjacent}}$$

The last equation is the definition of the tangent ratio, so the original equation is true.

Identity 2 $\sin^2 x + \cos^2 x = 1$

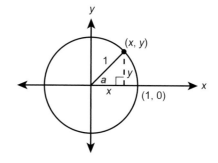

You can use a circle on the coordinate plane to show that this identity is true. Its center is located at $(0, 0)$ and it has a radius of 1. Since all radii of a circle are congruent, the hypotenuse of the triangle has a radius of 1, and you can write the sine and cosine of angle a as

$$\sin a = \frac{y}{1} = y \text{ and } \cos a = \frac{x}{1} = x.$$

The equation of a circle with its center at the origin and a radius 1 is

$$x^2 + y^2 = 1.$$

Use the commutative property of addition and substitute $\sin a$ and $\cos a$ into the equation for x and y.

$$(\sin a)^2 + (\cos a)^2 = 1$$

To make things easier to read, mathematicians usually replace $(\sin a)^2$ with $\sin^2 a$ so the identity can be written in the form

$$\sin^2 a + \cos^2 a = 1.$$

Special Right Triangles

To solve problems involving 30°, 45°, and 60° angles, you can use trigonometric ratios.

The 45°-45°-90° Triangle

Because of the measures of its angles, the 45°-45°-90° triangle is commonly used, so knowing the trigonometric ratios for a 45° angle can prove useful. First review the relationship between the legs and hypotenuse of a 45°-45°-90° triangle.

When you construct the diagonal of a square, you create two 45°-45°-90° triangles with a side length of s. You can then use the Pythagorean theorem to determine that the length of the diagonal is $\sqrt{2}$ times the length of a side.

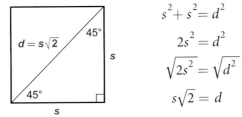

$$s^2 + s^2 = d^2$$
$$2s^2 = d^2$$
$$\sqrt{2s^2} = \sqrt{d^2}$$
$$s\sqrt{2} = d$$

Use s and $s\sqrt{2}$ to find the sine, cosine, and tangent of a 45° angle. You can use either of the 45° angles.

$$\sin 45° = \frac{\text{opposite}}{\text{hypotenuse}} = \frac{s}{s\sqrt{2}} = \frac{1}{\sqrt{2}} = \frac{\sqrt{2}}{2}$$

$$\cos 45° = \frac{\text{adjacent}}{\text{hypotenuse}} = \frac{s}{s\sqrt{2}} = \frac{1}{\sqrt{2}} = \frac{\sqrt{2}}{2}$$

$$\tan 45° = \frac{\text{opposite}}{\text{adjacent}} = \frac{s}{s} = 1$$

The 30°-60°-90° Triangle

The 30°-60°-90° triangle is also a commonly used triangle, so it is a good idea to know the trigonometric ratios for 30° and 60°.

When you construct the altitude of an equilateral triangle, you create two 30°-60°-90° triangles with a hypotenuse of s and a base (the shorter side) of $\frac{s}{2}$. Again, you can use the Pythagorean theorem to determine that the height is $\sqrt{3}$ times the length of the shorter side.

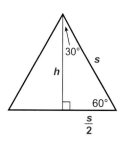

$$\left(\frac{s}{2}\right)^2 + h^2 = s^2$$

$$h^2 = s^2 - \frac{s^2}{4}$$

$$h^2 = \frac{4s^2}{4} - \frac{s^2}{4}$$

$$h^2 = \frac{3s^2}{4}$$

$$h = \frac{s\sqrt{3}}{2}$$

Use s, $\dfrac{s}{2}$, and $\dfrac{s\sqrt{3}}{2}$ to find the sine, cosine, and tangent of a 30° and 60° angle.

$$\sin 30° = \frac{\text{opposite}}{\text{hypotenuse}} = \frac{\frac{s}{2}}{s} = \frac{s}{2s} = \frac{1}{2}$$

$$\sin 60° = \frac{\text{opposite}}{\text{hypotenuse}} = \frac{\frac{s\sqrt{3}}{2}}{s} = \frac{s\sqrt{3}}{2s} = \frac{\sqrt{3}}{2}$$

$$\cos 30° = \frac{\text{adjacent}}{\text{hypotenuse}} = \frac{\frac{s\sqrt{3}}{2}}{s} = \frac{s\sqrt{3}}{2s} = \frac{\sqrt{3}}{2}$$

$$\cos 60° = \frac{\text{adjacent}}{\text{hypotenuse}} = \frac{\frac{s}{2}}{s} = \frac{s}{2s} = \frac{1}{2}$$

$$\tan 30° = \frac{\text{opposite}}{\text{adjacent}} = \frac{\frac{s}{2}}{\frac{s\sqrt{3}}{2}} = \frac{2s}{2s\sqrt{3}} = \frac{1}{\sqrt{3}} = \frac{\sqrt{3}}{3}$$

$$\tan 60° = \frac{\text{opposite}}{\text{adjacent}} = \frac{\frac{s\sqrt{3}}{2}}{\frac{s}{2}} = \frac{2s\sqrt{3}}{2s} = \sqrt{3}$$

Using Trigonometric Ratios to Solve Problems

EXAMPLE 1

A construction worker stands on a rooftop 65 ft above the ground. She throws down a rope for another worker to anchor to the ground at a 30° angle. To the nearest foot, how far away from the base of the building should the rope be anchored to make the correct angle?

SOLUTION

Use the tangent of a 30° angle to set up and solve a proportion.

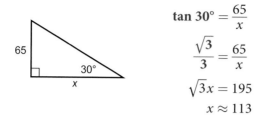

$$\tan 30° = \frac{65}{x}$$

$$\frac{\sqrt{3}}{3} = \frac{65}{x}$$

$$\sqrt{3}x = 195$$

$$x \approx 113$$

The rope should be anchored 113 ft from the base of the building. ▪

EXAMPLE 2

A display screen is shaped like a square with a diagonal length of 14 cm. To the nearest tenth of a centimeter, find the length and width of the screen.

SOLUTION

Use the sine (or cosine) of a 45° angle to set up and solve a proportion.

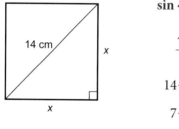

$$\sin 45° = \frac{x}{14}$$

$$\frac{\sqrt{2}}{2} = \frac{x}{14}$$

$$14\sqrt{2} = 2x$$

$$7\sqrt{2} = x$$

$$9.9 \approx x$$

The screen has a length and width of about 9.9 cm. ▪

Using Special Right Triangles

You can use special right triangles to determine the surface area of regular pyramids.

Right Triangles in a Pyramid

A pyramid is a polyhedron in which the base is a polygon and the lateral faces are triangles with a common vertex. The height of a pyramid is the perpendicular distance between the vertex and the base. The intersection of two lateral faces is a lateral edge. The intersection of the base and a lateral face is a base edge. The altitude of a lateral face is called the slant height of the pyramid. A regular pyramid is a pyramid in which the base is a regular polygon and the lateral edges are all equal in length. The lateral faces of a regular pyramid are congruent isosceles triangles.

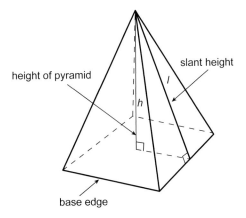

height of pyramid

slant height

l

h

base edge

Definition

The **lateral surface area** of a pyramid is the area of the lateral faces. The total surface area is the lateral surface area and the area of the base.

EXAMPLE 1

Find the total surface area of a regular tetrahedron with a side length of 8 cm.

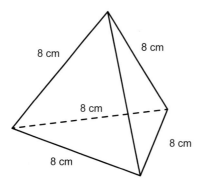

▶ **Think About It** A regular tetrahedron is a triangular pyramid with a base and lateral faces that are equilateral triangles.

SOLUTION

To find the surface area, you need the area of each face.

Step 1 The base of the equilateral triangle is 8 cm. The right triangle formed is a 30°-60°-90° triangle with a shorter leg length of 4 cm and hypotenuse 8 cm, so the longer leg length has the relationship $x\sqrt{3}$ where x is the length of the shorter leg.

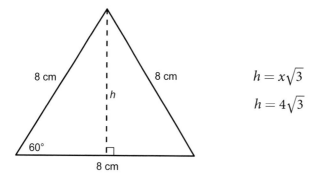

$$h = x\sqrt{3}$$
$$h = 4\sqrt{3}$$

Step 2 Use the height to find the area of one face.

$$A = \frac{1}{2} bh$$
$$A = \frac{1}{2}(8)\left(4\sqrt{3}\right)$$
$$A = 16\sqrt{3}$$

▶ **Remember** The area of a triangle is given by $A = \frac{1}{2} \text{base} \times \text{height}$.

Step 3 The pyramid has four sides. Multiply by 4 to find the total surface area.

$$SA = 4\left(16\sqrt{3}\right) = 64\sqrt{3}$$

The total surface area of a regular tetrahedron with a side length of 8 cm is 64 $\sqrt{3}$ cm^2. ▪

Formula for Lateral Area of a Regular Pyramid

The lateral area of a regular pyramid equals one-half the perimeter, P, of the base times the slant height, l.

lateral area $= \frac{1}{2} Pl$

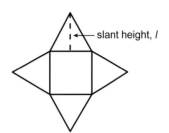

slant height, l

EXAMPLE 2

Find the total area of a square pyramid if a lateral edge and a base edge form a 60° angle, and a diagonal of the base is 8 ft.

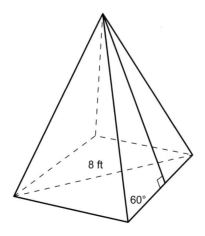

8 ft

60°

SOLUTION

To find the total surface area, find the area of the base and the lateral area.

Step 1 Use what you know about a 45°-45°-90° triangle to find the length

of the base, b. The length of the legs are $\dfrac{x\sqrt{2}}{2}$ where x is the length of the hypotenuse.

$$b = \dfrac{x\sqrt{2}}{2}$$
$$b = 4\sqrt{2}$$

▶ **Remember** The diagonal of a square forms two 45°-45°-90° right triangles.

Step 2 Find the area of the base.

$$A = b^2 = \left(4\sqrt{2}\right)^2 = 32 \text{ ft}^2$$

Step 3 Find the perimeter of the base.

$$P = 4b = 4\left(4\sqrt{2}\right) = 16\sqrt{2} \text{ ft}$$

▶ **Remember** For a square with side length s:
area $= s^2$
perimeter $= 4s$

Step 4 The length of the shorter leg is half the length of the side of the square. To find the slant height, l, use the relationship $x\sqrt{3}$ where x is the length of the shorter leg.

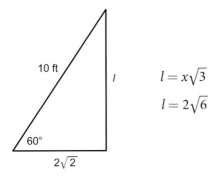

$$l = x\sqrt{3}$$
$$l = 2\sqrt{6}$$

Step 5 Use the formula to find the lateral area.

$$\text{lateral area} = \frac{1}{2}Pl$$
$$= \frac{1}{2}\left(16\sqrt{2}\right)\left(2\sqrt{6}\right)$$
$$= 16\sqrt{12}$$
$$= 32\sqrt{3} \text{ ft}^2$$

Step 6 Add to find the total surface area.

$$\text{total surface area} = \text{lateral area} + \text{base area}$$
$$= 32\sqrt{3} + 32 \text{ ft}^2$$

The total surface area is $32\sqrt{3} + 32 \text{ ft}^2$. ▪

Deriving the Formula for Area of a Triangle

Trigonometry can be used to find the areas of triangles when certain information is given.

How can you use the sine function to find the area of a nonright triangle?

Given $\triangle ABC$, draw perpendicular segment h from B to $\overline{AC}$. The length of h is the height of $\triangle ABC$.

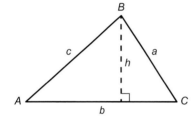

$$\sin C = \frac{h}{a}$$

$$h = a \sin C$$

Determine the area of $\triangle ABC$.

$$A = \frac{1}{2}\,bh$$

$$A = \frac{1}{2}b(a \sin C)$$

$$A = \frac{1}{2}\,ab \sin C$$

Formula for the Area of a Triangle Using Trigonometry

The area of $\triangle ABC$ is

$$A = \frac{1}{2}\, ab\, \sin C.$$

EXAMPLE

Mary is making a pin of the math club's triangular logo. The pin has one side of 4 cm and one side of 3 cm with an included angle of 30°. What is the area of the pin?

SOLUTION

Draw and label the triangle.

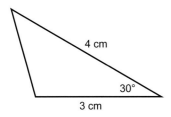

$A = \frac{1}{2}\, ab\, \sin C$

$A = \frac{1}{2}(4)(3)\sin 30°$

$A = \frac{1}{2}(4)(3)\frac{1}{2}$

$A = 3$

The area of the pin is 3 cm^2. ▪

The Laws of Sines and Cosines

The Pythagorean theorem is an invaluable tool, but it has its limitations. It is only true for right triangles.

There are many situations that involve triangles that are not right triangles. For example, imagine that two boats leave a dock at the same time and head in different directions. At any point in time, the two boats and dock make up the vertices of a triangle. The new formulas you will learn will allow you to find side and angle measures for any type of triangle, not just a right triangle.

The Law of Sines

So far you have used trigonometric ratios only to solve right triangles. You can also use trigonometry to solve triangles that are not right. One way is to use the law of sines. You will prove it before you state it.

Consider $\triangle ABC$. It is not a right triangle, but drawing the altitude $\overline{CD}$ creates two right triangles: $\triangle ADC$ and $\triangle BDC$.

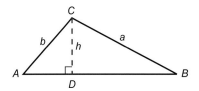

First find the sine of $\angle A$: $\qquad \sin A = \dfrac{h}{b}$

and solve for h: $\qquad\qquad h = b \sin A$

Then find the sine of $\angle B$: $\qquad \sin B = \dfrac{h}{a}$

and solve for h: $\qquad\qquad h = a \sin B$

Now you have two expressions equal to h. By substitution,

$$b \sin A = a \sin B.$$

Finally, divide both sides by ab.

$$\frac{\sin A}{a} = \frac{\sin B}{b}$$

By drawing different altitudes, you can show that $\frac{\sin A}{a} = \frac{\sin B}{b} = \frac{\sin C}{c}$.
This is the law of sines.

The Law of Sines

For any $\triangle ABC$, where a, b, and c are the
measures of the opposite sides of
A, B, and C, respectively,

$$\frac{\sin A}{a} = \frac{\sin B}{b} = \frac{\sin C}{c}.$$

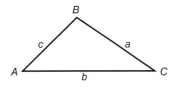

Using the law of sines, you can find a missing triangle measure in the
following two cases.

- You are given two angles and any side (ASA or AAS).

- You are given two sides and the nonincluded angle (SSA).

When you use the law of sines, you set up and solve a proportion using two
of the three ratios. To find the length of side a, set up a proportion using the
ratios with A and B.

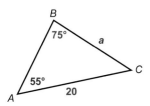

$$\frac{\sin A}{a} = \frac{\sin B}{b}$$

$$\frac{\sin 55°}{a} = \frac{\sin 75°}{20}$$

$$a(\sin 75°) = 20(\sin 55°)$$

$$a = \frac{20(\sin 55°)}{\sin 75°}$$

$$a \approx 17$$

You can also use the law of sines to find angle measures of triangles. To find the measure of $\angle E$, set up a proportion and use the inverse sine.

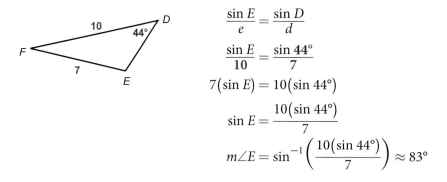

$$\frac{\sin E}{e} = \frac{\sin D}{d}$$

$$\frac{\sin E}{10} = \frac{\sin 44°}{7}$$

$$7(\sin E) = 10(\sin 44°)$$

$$\sin E = \frac{10(\sin 44°)}{7}$$

$$m\angle E = \sin^{-1}\left(\frac{10(\sin 44°)}{7}\right) \approx 83°$$

The Law of Cosines

The law of sines can only be used for certain angle and side combinations. When you cannot use the law of sines, you may be able to use the law of cosines. You will prove the law before you state it.

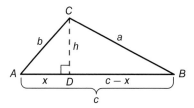

$\triangle ABC$ has altitude $\overline{CD}$ creating two right triangles: $\triangle ADC$ and $\triangle BDC$. Let $AD = x$ and $BD = c - x$.

First find the cosine of angle A: $\qquad \cos A = \dfrac{x}{b}$

and solve for x: $\qquad x = b \cos A$

Use the Pythagorean theorem
for $\triangle ADC$: $\qquad b^2 = h^2 + x^2$
and solve for h^2: $\qquad h^2 = b^2 - x^2$

Then use the Pythagorean theorem
in $\triangle BDC$: $\qquad a^2 = h^2 + (c - x)^2$

and square the binomial: $\qquad a^2 = h^2 + c^2 - 2cx + x^2$

Now substitute for h^2: $\qquad a^2 = b^2 - x^2 + c^2 - 2cx + x^2$

combine like terms: $\qquad a^2 = b^2 + c^2 - 2cx$

substitute for x: $\qquad a^2 = b^2 + c^2 - 2c(b \cos A)$

and rearrange factors: $\qquad a^2 = b^2 + c^2 - 2bc \cos A$

You can draw different altitudes and follow similar reasoning for each.

The Law of Cosines

For any $\triangle ABC$, where a, b, and c are the
measures of the opposite sides of
A, B, and C, respectively,

$a^2 = b^2 + c^2 - 2bc \cos A$
$b^2 = a^2 + c^2 - 2ac \cos B$
$c^2 = a^2 + b^2 - 2ab \cos C.$

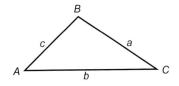

Use the law of cosines to find a missing triangle measure in the following
two cases.

- You are given two sides and the included angle (SAS).

- You are given three sides (SSS).

When you use the law of cosines to find a missing side, choose the formula that has that side on the left side of the equation. To find the length of side b, choose the formula with b^2 on the left side.

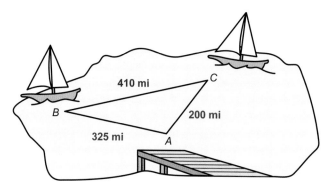

$$b^2 = a^2 + c^2 - 2ac \cos B$$

$$b^2 = 4^2 + 10^2 - 2(4)(10)\cos 34°$$

$$b^2 = 116 - 80 \cos 34°$$

$$b^2 \approx 49.6770$$

$$b \approx 7.05$$

If you know the lengths of three sides of a triangle, you can use the law of cosines to find the measure of any angle of the triangle.

Two ships leave a dock at the same time and head in different directions without changing course. After a few hours, one ship is 200 mi from the dock and the other is 325 mi from the dock. They are 410 mi from each other. What angle is formed by the paths of the two ships at the dock?

In the diagram, $\angle A$ is the missing angle, so use the formula that has A on the right side. The figure isolates $\cos A$ and then uses the inverse cosine.

$$a^2 = b^2 + c^2 - 2bc \cos A$$

$$410^2 = 200^2 + 325^2 - 2(200)(325)\cos A$$

$$168{,}100 = 145{,}625 - 130{,}000 \cos A$$

$$22{,}475 = -130{,}000 \cos A$$

$$-\frac{22{,}475}{130{,}000} = \cos A$$

$$m\angle A \approx 100°$$

If you want to **solve the triangle**, which means to find all missing measures, you can now use the law of sines to find another angle, and then subtract the sum of the two known measures from 180° to find the last angle measure.

Conic Sections

Topic List

▸ Introduction to Conic Sections

▸ Circles

▸ Parabolas

▸ Deriving Conic Equations

Cassegrain antennae have a parabolic shape that allows them to focus incoming light or sound at a single receiving point. Their reflective properties make parabolas (and other conics) perfect for use in antennae that communicate with satellites or listen to outer space.

Introduction to Conic Sections

As the name suggests, a conic section is a cross section of a cone.

Identifying Conic Sections

Definitions

A **conic section** (or **conic**) is a two-dimensional graph that can be formed by the intersection of a plane with a double-napped cone.

A **double-napped** cone is formed as follows:
One line, called the **generating line**, intersects and revolves around another line, called the axis. The axis is stationary, and the two lines cannot be perpendicular. The point where the lines intersect is the **vertex** of the cone.

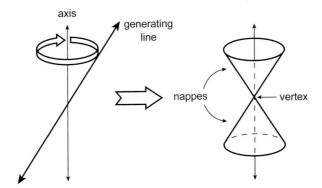

Note: The double-napped cone is a surface without any bases. If a circular base were added to one nappe, then the resulting figure would be the familiar cone that you study in geometry.

There are four important types of conic sections.

Circle	Ellipse
A **circle** is a conic section formed when a plane intersects only one nappe, perpendicular to the axis.	An **ellipse** is a conic section formed when a plane intersects only one nappe, not parallel to the generating line. A circle can be considered a special kind of ellipse.

Parabola	Hyperbola
A **parabola** is a conic section formed when a plane intersects only one nappe, parallel to the generating line.	A **hyperbola** is a conic section formed when a plane intersects both nappes.

Definition

A **degenerate conic section** is formed when a plane intersects the vertex of the double-napped cone.

There are three types of degenerate conic sections.

Point	Line	Pair of intersecting lines
The plane intersects only the vertex. This figure is a **degenerate ellipse**.	The plane contains the generating line. This figure is a **degenerate parabola**.	The plane intersects both nappes through the vertex. This figure is a **degenerate hyperbola**.

▶ **Think About It** In mathematics, degenerate cases are cases that are simpler than normal cases. Points and lines are degenerate conic sections because they are simpler than the other conic sections.

EXAMPLE 1

Identify the conic that is formed by the intersection of the plane and the cone.

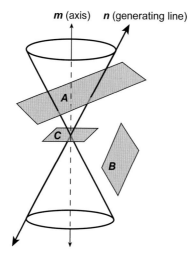

m (axis)   **n** (generating line)

A Plane A intersects line m, is not perpendicular to m, and is not parallel to n.

SOLUTION

The conic is an ellipse.

B Plane B is parallel to line n.

SOLUTION

The conic is a parabola.

C Plane C is perpendicular to line m and at the center of the cone.

SOLUTION

The conic is a degenerate ellipse (a point). ■

▶ **Remember** A line extends without end in one dimension. A plane extends without end in two dimensions.

Using Tools of Analytic Geometry: Distance Formula

Definition

Analytic geometry (also called **coordinate geometry**) is the study of geometry using the tools of algebra. You'll use the tools of analytic geometry to study conic sections.

The distance formula is an important tool in analytic geometry. The distance formula is based on the Pythagorean theorem. To find an expression for the distance d from A to B, form right $\triangle ABC$ and use the Pythagorean theorem.

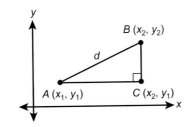

$$(AB)^2 = (AC)^2 + (BC)^2$$
$$d^2 = (x_2 - x_1)^2 + (y_2 - y_1)^2$$
$$d = \sqrt{(x_2 - x_1)^2 + (y_2 - y_1)^2}$$

▶ **Remember** The distance d between two points (x_1, y_1) and (x_2, y_2) is

$$d = \sqrt{(x_2 - x_1)^2 + (y_2 - y_1)^2}.$$

EXAMPLE 2

Find the length of $\overline{AB}$.

SOLUTION

Let $A(1, 4)$ be (x_1, y_1) and $B(6, 2)$ be (x_2, y_2).

$$AB = \sqrt{(x_2 - x_1)^2 + (y_2 - y_1)^2}$$

$$= \sqrt{(6 - 1)^2 + (2 - 4)^2}$$

$$= \sqrt{5^2 + (-2)^2}$$

$$= \sqrt{25 + 4}$$

$$= \sqrt{29} \ \blacksquare$$

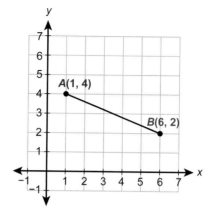

▶ **Remember** The length of $\overline{AB}$ is denoted AB.

Using Tools of Analytic Geometry: Midpoint Formula

The midpoint formula, another useful tool in analytic geometry, helps you determine the coordinates of the midpoint of a segment.

▶ **Remember** The coordinates of the midpoint M of the segment with endpoints (x_1, y_1) and (x_2, y_2) are

$$M = \left(\frac{x_1 + x_2}{2}, \frac{y_1 + y_2}{2} \right).$$

EXAMPLE 3

Solve.

A Find the coordinates of M, the midpoint of $\overline{AB}$ in Example 2.

SOLUTION

$$\left(\frac{x_1 + x_2}{2}, \frac{y_1 + y_2}{2}\right) = \left(\frac{1 + 6}{2}, \frac{4 + 2}{2}\right)$$

The coordinates of M are $(3.5, 3)$.

> ▶ **Think About It** You can use the distance formula to verify that M is the midpoint. Show that $AM = MB$.
>
> $$AM = \sqrt{(3.5 - 1)^2 + (3 - 4)^2}$$
> $$= \sqrt{7.25}$$
>
> $$MB = \sqrt{(6 - 3.5)^2 + (2 - 3)^2}$$
> $$= \sqrt{7.25}$$

B A line segment $\overline{CD}$ has one endpoint D at $(2, 4)$ and a midpoint M at $(0, 2.5)$. Find the coordinates of the other endpoint C.

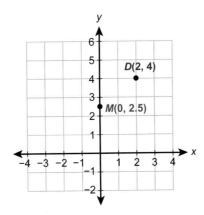

SOLUTION

$$\left(\frac{x+2}{2}, \frac{y+4}{2} \right) = (0, 2.5)$$

Substitute the coordinates of the given endpoint $(2, 4)$ and the midpoint $(0, 2.5)$ into the formula.

$$\frac{x+2}{2} = 0 \qquad \frac{y+4}{2} = 2.5$$

Set each expression equal to its corresponding coordinate, and then solve for x and y.

$$x + 2 = 0 \qquad y + 4 = 5$$

$$x = -2 \qquad y = 1$$

The coordinates of C are $(-2, 1)$. ■

Circles

The circle is the simplest and most familiar conic section.

Deriving an Equation of a Circle from the Definition

Definitions

A **circle** is the set of all points in a plane that are a fixed distance r (the **radius**) from a given point (the **center**).

In a coordinate plane, a circle is a set of points (x, y). For any circle, r has the same value no matter where (x, y) is on the circle.

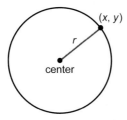

▶ **Think About It** The word *radius* can mean either a line segment from the center to the circle, or the length of such a line segment.

EXAMPLE 1

Derive an equation of the circle with the given center and radius.

A center $= (0, 0)$, $r = 6$

SOLUTION

For any point (x, y) on the circle, the distance from the center $(0, 0)$ is 6.

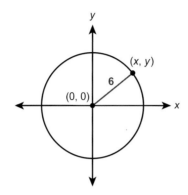

$$\sqrt{(x_2 - x_1)^2 + (y_2 - y_1)^2} = d \qquad \text{Distance Formula}$$

$$\sqrt{(x - 0)^2 + (y - 0)^2} = 6 \qquad \text{The distance between } (0, 0) \text{ and any point } (x, y) \text{ on the circle is 6.}$$

$$(x - 0)^2 + (y - 0)^2 = 6^2 \qquad \text{Square each side.}$$

$$x^2 + y^2 = 36 \qquad \text{Simplify.}$$

B center $= (2, 5)$, $r = 3$

SOLUTION

For any point (x, y) on the circle, the distance from the center $(2, 5)$ is 3.

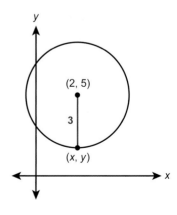

$$\sqrt{(x_2 - x_1)^2 + (y_2 - y_1)^2} = d \qquad \text{Distance Formula}$$

$$\sqrt{(x - 2)^2 + (y - 5)^2} = 3 \qquad \text{The distance between } (2, 5) \text{ and any point } (x, y) \text{ on the circle is 3.}$$

$$(x - 2)^2 + (y - 5)^2 = 9 \qquad \text{Square each side.} \quad \blacksquare$$

Writing an Equation of a Circle, Given Its Graph

Equation of a Circle

The equation of the circle, in graphing form, with center (h, k) and radius r, is

$$(x - h)^2 + (y - k)^2 = r^2.$$

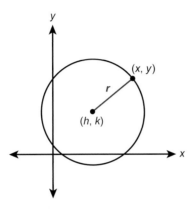

EXAMPLE 2

Write the equation in graphing form of the circle shown.

SOLUTION

The center is $(-3, 6)$, so $h = -3$ and $k = 6$.

To find the radius, calculate the distance between the center $(-3, 6)$ and the point $(0, 2)$ on the circle.

$$r = \sqrt{(0 - (-3))^2 + (2 - 6)^2} = \sqrt{9 + 16} = \sqrt{25} = 5$$

Substitute h, k, and r into the equation in graphing form.

$$(x - h)^2 + (y - k)^2 = r^2$$
$$(x - (-3))^2 + (y - 6)^2 = 5^2$$
$$(x + 3)^2 + (y - 6)^2 = 25 \ \blacksquare$$

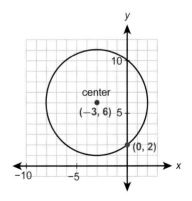

Finding the Center, Radius, and Diameter of a Circle, Given Its Equation in Graphing Form

EXAMPLE 3

Find the center, radius, and diameter of the circle with equation $(x + 1)^2 + (y + 3)^2 = 16$.

SOLUTION

Rewrite the equation as $\left(x - (-1)\right)^2 + \left(y - (-3)\right)^2 = 4^2$ to identify h, k, and r.

The circle is in graphing form with $h = -1$, $k = -3$, and $r = 4$.

The center of the circle (h, k) is $(-1, -3)$.

The radius r is 4, so the diameter is $4 \cdot 2 = 8$. ▪

Graphing a Circle, Given Its Equation in Graphing Form

EXAMPLE 4

Graph the circle with equation $(x - 4)^2 + (y + 1)^2 = 4$.

SOLUTION

The equation is in graphing form with $h = 4$, $k = -1$, and $r = 2$.

Step 1 Plot the center (h, k) at $(4, -1)$.

Step 2 The radius is 2, so every point on the circle is 2 units from the center. Count 2 units left, right, up, and down from the center to find four points on the circle: $(2, -1)$, $(4, 1)$, $(6, -1)$, and $(4, -3)$.

Step 3 Draw the circle through the four points.

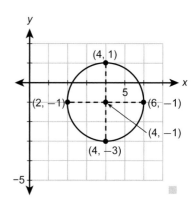

Finding the Equation of a Circle, Given Three Points

EXAMPLE 5

Find the equation of the circle that contains $A(-3, 6)$, $B(3, 4)$, and $C(5, 0)$.

SOLUTION

You need the center and radius. To find the center, find the point of intersection of the perpendicular bisectors of two chords of the circle.

Step 1 Identify two chords, say $\overline{AB}$ and $\overline{BC}$. Find the slope of each chord. Then find the slope of each perpendicular bisector by using the opposite reciprocal.

Chord	Slope of chord	Slope of perpendicular bisector
$\overline{AB}$	$\dfrac{4-6}{3-(-3)} = \dfrac{-2}{6} = -\dfrac{1}{3}$	3
$\overline{BC}$	$\dfrac{0-4}{5-3} = \dfrac{-4}{2} = -2$	$\dfrac{1}{2}$

Step 2 Find the midpoint of each chord.

midpoint of $\overline{AB}$: $\left(\dfrac{-3+3}{2}, \dfrac{6+4}{2}\right) = \left(\dfrac{0}{2}, \dfrac{10}{2}\right) = (0, 5)$

midpoint of $\overline{BC}$: $\left(\dfrac{3+5}{2}, \dfrac{4+0}{2}\right) = \left(\dfrac{8}{2}, \dfrac{4}{2}\right) = (4, 2)$

Step 3 Find the equation of each perpendicular bisector. Use the point-slope form $y - y_1 = m(x - x_1)$. Use the slopes from Step 1 and the midpoints from Step 2.

perpendicular bisector of $\overline{AB}$: $y - 5 = 3(x - 0)$, or $y = 3x + 5$

perpendicular bisector of $\overline{BC}$: $y - 2 = \frac{1}{2}(x - 4)$, or $y = \frac{1}{2}x$

Step 4 Solve the system of linear equations.

$y = 3x + 5$ Perpendicular bisector of $\overline{AB}$

$\frac{1}{2}x = 3x + 5$ Substitute $\frac{1}{2}x$ for y.

$x = -2$ Solve for x.

Substitute and solve for y.

$$y = \frac{1}{2} \cdot (-2) = -1$$

The solution to the system is $(-2, -1)$. The solution to the system is the center of the circle, so $(h, k) = (-2, -1)$.

Step 5 Calculate the radius. Use the center $(-2, -1)$ and any point on the circle, say $A(-3, 6)$.

$$r = \sqrt{(-3 - (-2))^2 + (6 - (-1))^2} = \sqrt{1 + 49} = \sqrt{50}$$

Step 6 Use the center and radius to write the equation in graphing form.

$$(x - h)^2 + (y - k)^2 = r^2$$
$$(x - (-2))^2 + (y - (-1))^2 = (\sqrt{50})^2$$
$$(x + 2)^2 + (y + 1)^2 = 50 \ \blacksquare$$

Parabolas

The graph of a quadratic function is a parabola that opens upward or downward. Parabolas can also open left and right (these graphs do not represent functions).

Deriving an Equation of a Parabola from the Definition

Definitions

A **parabola** is the set of all points in a plane that are equidistant from a fixed line (the **directrix**) and a fixed point (the **focus**).

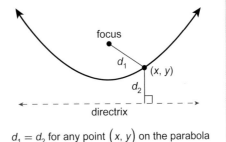

$d_1 = d_2$ for any point (x, y) on the parabola

The standard equation of a parabola can be derived by using the definition. The distance from a point to a line is the length of the line segment from the point perpendicular to the line. The distance from (x, y) to the horizontal directrix is the vertical distance from (x, y) to $(x, -3)$.

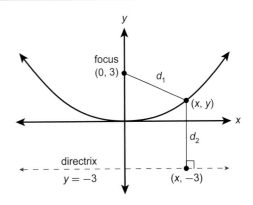

$$d_1 = d_2$$

$$\sqrt{(x-0)^2 + (y-3)^2} = \sqrt{(x-x)^2 + (y+3)^2} \qquad \text{Distance Formula}$$

$$\sqrt{x^2 + y^2 - 6y + 9} = \sqrt{y^2 + 6y + 9} \qquad \text{Expand binomials.}$$

$$x^2 + y^2 - 6y + 9 = y^2 + 6y + 9 \qquad \text{Square each side.}$$

$$x^2 = 12y \qquad \text{Simplify.}$$

Writing an Equation of a Parabola, Given Its Graph

There are many equivalent ways to write the equation $x^2 = 12y$. You could write it in the general form of a second-degree equation: $x^2 - 12y = 0$. Or, because the parabola represents a function, you could also write it in the standard form of a quadratic function: $y = \frac{1}{12}x^2$.

Definitions

Every parabola has a single **vertex** that lies halfway between the focus and directrix. The **axis of symmetry** is the line that passes through the focus and vertex, perpendicular to the directrix.

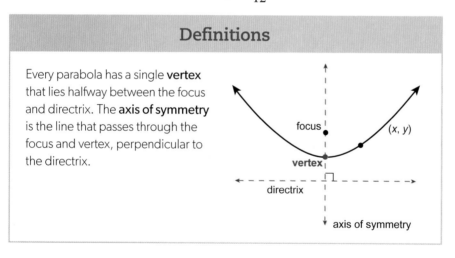

The axis of symmetry separates the graph into two halves that are reflection images of each other.

In the diagrams, V is the vertex with coordinates (h, k), F is the focus, and f is the directed distance from V to F (positive for right or up; negative for left or down).

Graphs of Parabolas

Parabola with horizontal axis of symmetry:

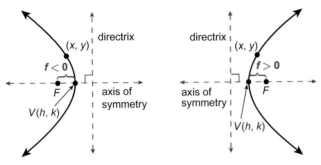

Equation in graphing form:
$$x - h = a(y - k)^2$$

Parabola with vertical axis of symmetry:

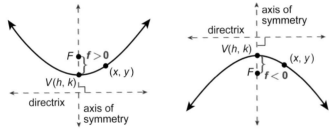

Equation in graphing form:
$$y - k = a(x - h)^2$$

Properties of Parabolas

If the directed distance from vertex to focus (the focal distance) is represented by f, then the directed distance from vertex to directrix is $-f$, and $a = \dfrac{1}{4f}$, or $f = \dfrac{1}{4a}$.

- $f \neq 0$ and $a \neq 0$.
- $f > 0$ and $a > 0$ if the parabola opens right or up.
- $f < 0$ and $a < 0$ if the parabola opens left or down.

EXAMPLE 1

Write the equation in graphing form of the parabola shown.

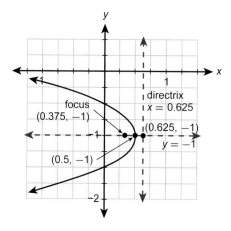

SOLUTION

The axis of symmetry has the equation $y = -1$, and it intersects the directrix at $(0.625, -1)$.

The vertex (h, k) is halfway between the focus and directrix, so it is the midpoint of the segment from $(0.375, -1)$ to $(0.625, -1)$.

$$(h, k) = \left(\frac{0.375 + 0.625}{2}, \frac{-1 + (-1)}{2} \right) = \left(\frac{1}{2}, \frac{-2}{2} \right) = (0.5, -1)$$

The focus is 0.125 unit left of the vertex, so $f = -0.125$. Find a.

$$a = \frac{1}{4f} = \frac{1}{4(-0.125)} = -2$$

Substitute h, k, and a into the equation in graphing form for a horizontal parabola.

$$x - h = a(y - k)^2$$
$$x - 0.5 = -2(y + 1)^2$$

Graphing a Parabola, Given Its Equation in Graphing Form

EXAMPLE 2

Graph the parabola with equation $x - 3 = 2(y - 4)^2$.

> ▶ **Think About It** In the study of conic sections, $x - h = a(y - k)^2$ and $y - k = a(x - h)^2$ are called equations in graphing form of parabolas. Equations of the form $y - k = a(x - h)^2$ represent functions and can be rewritten in the form $y = ax^2 + bx + c$, which is called standard form in the study of quadratic functions. (Try it. You should find that $b = -2ah$ and $c = ah^2 + k$.)

SOLUTION

Use the same techniques that you learned to graph the vertex form of a quadratic function.

The equation is in the graphing form $x - h = a(y - k)^2$, so the parabola has a horizontal axis of symmetry. Since the value of a is positive, the parabola opens to the right.

Step 1 Plot the vertex $(3, 4)$ and sketch the axis of symmetry $y = 4$.

Step 2 Find and plot two more solutions to the equation $x - 3 = 2(y - 4)^2$, such as $(5, 5)$ and $(8, 5.58)$.

Step 3 Reflect the points you found in Step 2 across the axis of symmetry to find two points on the other side: $(5, 3)$ and $(8, 3.58)$.

Step 4 Draw a smooth curve through all the points.

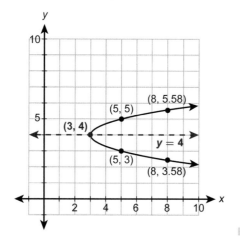

▶ **Think About It** The focus, directrix, and axis of symmetry are not really part of the graph, but they provide important information. If you identify them in a problem, it is useful to include them in the graph.

Identifying the Vertex, Focal Length, Focus, and Directrix of a Parabola, Given Its Equation

EXAMPLE 3

The equation of a parabola is $y - 4 = 0.125(x + 3)^2$.

A Identify the coordinates of the vertex.

SOLUTION
The equation is in the graphing form $y - k = a(x - h)^2$, with $h = -3$, $k = 4$, and $a = 0.125$. So the vertex (h, k) is at $(-3, 4)$.

B Identify the focal length and the coordinates of the focus.

SOLUTION

The distance from the vertex to the focus is

$$f = \frac{1}{4a} = \frac{1}{4(0.1254)} = \frac{1}{0.5} = 2.$$

Because $f = 2$, the focus is 2 units above the vertex at $F(-3, 6)$.

C Identify the equation of the directrix.

SOLUTION

Because $-f = -2$, the directrix is 2 units below the vertex and passes through $(-3, 2)$. The axis of symmetry is vertical, so the directrix is horizontal. The equation of the directrix is $y = 2$.

D Graph the parabola. Label the vertex, focus, axis of symmetry, directrix, and two other points on the curve.

SOLUTION

The value of a is positive, so the parabola opens upward.

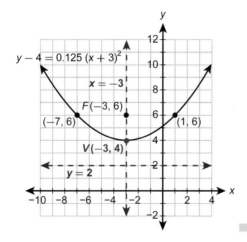

Deriving Conic Equations

The distance formula is used to derive equations of conic sections.

Circles and the Distance Formula

The general equation for a circle can be derived using the distance formula.

▶ **Remember** If (x_1, y_1) and (x_2, y_2) are points on the coordinate plane, then the distance between the points is

$$d = \sqrt{(x_2 - x_1)^2 + (y_2 - y_1)^2}.$$

By definition, a circle is a set of fixed points that are equidistant from the center. If a circle has a center at (h, k) and a radius of r, then the distance from the center to any point (x, y) on the circle is equal to r.

$$d = \sqrt{(x_2 - x_1)^2 + (y_2 - y_1)^2}$$

$$r = \sqrt{(x - h)^2 + (y - k)^2}$$

$$r^2 = \left(\sqrt{(x - h)^2 + (y - k)^2}\right)^2$$

$$r^2 = (x - h)^2 + (y - k)^2$$

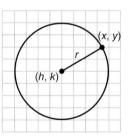

Completing the Square and the Circle Equation

EXAMPLE 1

Complete the square to find the center and radius of the circle represented by the equation $x^2 + y^2 + 2x + 6y - 15 = 0$.

SOLUTION

$$x^2 + y^2 + 2x + 6y - 15 = 0$$
$$x^2 + y^2 + 2x + 6y = 15$$
$$\left(x^2 + 2x + \blacksquare\right) + \left(y^2 + 6y + \blacksquare\right) = 15$$
$$\left(x^2 + 2x + 1\right) + \left(y^2 + 6y + 9\right) = 15 + 1 + 9$$
$$\left(x^2 + 2x + 1\right) + \left(y^2 + 6y + 9\right) = 25$$
$$\left(x + 1\right)^2 + \left(y + 3\right)^2 = 5^2$$

The center is at $(-1, -3)$, and the radius is 5. ■

EXAMPLE 2

Complete the square to find the center and radius of the circle represented by the equation $x^2 + y^2 + 10y - 11 = 0$.

SOLUTION

$$x^2 + y^2 + 10y - 11 = 0$$
$$x^2 + y^2 + 10y = 11$$
$$\left(x^2\right) + \left(y^2 + 10y + \blacksquare\right) = 11$$
$$\left(x^2\right) + \left(y^2 + 10y + 25\right) = 11 + 25$$
$$\left(x^2\right) + \left(y^2 + 10y + 25\right) = 36$$
$$\left(x - 0\right)^2 + \left(y + 5\right)^2 = 6^2$$

The center is at $(0, -5)$, and the radius is 6. ■

Modeling with Geometry

Topic List

▸ Geometry in Space

▸ Geometry on Earth

▸ Manufacturing: Design and Optimization

▸ Density in Two Dimensions

▸ Density in Three Dimensions

▸ Fermi Problems

How does a ship that weighs 47,000 tons stay afloat? It's all about density. Massive vessels like the *Zenith* are marvels of engineering that rely on geometric models to determine their capacity, speed, and cost.

Geometry in Space

Two- and three-dimensional shapes result from cross sections and rotations of figures.

Identifying Cross Sections

When a three-dimensional figure is sliced by a plane, the cross section is usually a two-dimensional figure. These cross sections are often shapes you are already familiar with: circles, squares, rectangles, triangles, and other commonly known figures.

EXAMPLE 1

A cylinder is sliced so that the cross section is perpendicular to the cylinder's central axis. What is the shape of the cross section?

▶ **Remember** The central axis of a right cylinder is the line that contains the centers of both circular bases.

SOLUTION
Slice the cylinder so that the cross section is perpendicular to the central axis of the cylinder.

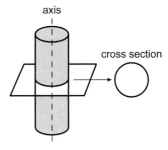

The cross section is a circle. ▪

EXAMPLE 2

What are the shape and area of any cross section that is parallel to the front face of the prism?

> ▶ **Remember** Every rectangular prism has six faces, each in the shape of a rectangle or a square.

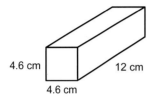

SOLUTION

The front face is a square with side lengths of 4.6 cm. Any cross section parallel to this face is congruent to it, so it has the same area.

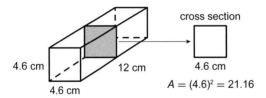

The cross section is a square with area 21.16 cm². ▪

Rotating Two-Dimensional Objects

When a two-dimensional object is rotated about an axis, the shape it traces out is a three-dimensional object. The shape of the three-dimensional object depends on the two-dimensional figure from which it is generated, as well as the placement of the axis.

EXAMPLE 3

Describe the object generated when the rectangle is rotated about the axis.

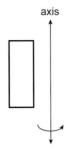

SOLUTION

A three-dimensional object is generated when the rectangle makes one full revolution about the axis. Throughout the entire rotation, the rectangle stays the same distance from the axis, creating a hollow region in the generated object.

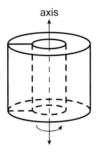

A hollow cylinder, also called a shell, is generated when the rectangle is rotated about the axis. ▨

Geometry on Earth

Two- and three-dimensional figures can be used to model real-world situations.

Determining Distance to the Horizon

When a person is above much of the surrounding surface, such as a passenger on a jet or a hiker on a tall mountain, that person can see a great distance to earth's horizon. In fact, the higher the viewpoint, the greater the distance to the horizon.

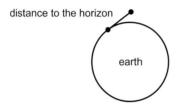

distance to the horizon

earth

▶ **Think About It** Earth's shape is very close to the shape of a sphere. However, you can use a perfect sphere as a model for the earth to estimate distance to the horizon.

The earth's radius, right triangles, and the Pythagorean theorem can help you estimate the distance from an object to the horizon.

EXAMPLE 1

A pilot is flying an airplane 2.8 mi above the earth's surface. From the pilot's viewpoint, what is the distance to the horizon, rounded to the nearest mile?

▶ **Think About It** The radius of the earth is about 3959 mi, or 6371 km.

SOLUTION

Start by drawing and labeling a diagram. Use d to represent distance to the horizon.

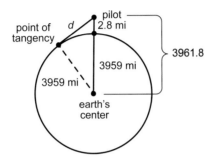

The point at the center of the circle represents the earth's center. The point above the earth's surface represents the pilot.

Notice that the line segment representing the distance d to the horizon is tangent to the earth's surface. It is perpendicular to the radius drawn to the point of tangency, and it forms a right triangle.

The distance from the earth's center to the pilot is $3959 + 2.8 = 3961.8$ mi. This length is the hypotenuse of the right triangle.

Use the Pythagorean theorem to find d.

$$(3959)^2 + d^2 = (3961.8)^2$$
$$15{,}673{,}681 + d^2 = 15{,}695{,}859.24$$
$$d^2 = 22{,}178.24$$
$$d = \sqrt{22{,}178.24} \approx 148.9$$

From the pilot's viewpoint, the distance to the horizon is about 149 mi. ■

Estimating Volume with Three-Dimensional Figures

You can use ideal three-dimensional figures, such as cubes, spheres, and prisms, to model and solve problems. For example, you can use a cylinder to model a log to estimate its volume.

EXAMPLE 2

A fish tank is in the shape of a rectangular prism with dimensions 42 in. × 16 in. × 20 in. The tank is 90% filled with water. A 10 in. long log, roughly in the shape of a cylinder with a 2 in. radius, is to be placed in the tank. Will any water spill out of the tank?

SOLUTION
Start by finding the volume of the entire tank and the volume of water in the tank.

$$\text{volume of tank} = 42 \cdot 16 \cdot 20 = 13{,}440 \text{ in}^3$$
$$\text{volume of water} = 0.9 \cdot 13{,}440 = 12{,}096 \text{ in}^3$$

Use the formula for the volume of a cylinder, $V = \pi r^2 h$, to estimate the volume of the log. Use $\pi \approx 3.14$.

$$\text{volume of log} = \pi r^2 h \approx 3.14 \cdot 2^2 \cdot 10 \approx 126 \text{ in}^3$$

Add the volume of the water in the tank and the volume of the log. Compare this volume with the total volume of the tank.

$$\text{volume of water and log} = 12{,}096 + 126 = 12{,}222 \text{ in}^3$$

The combined volume of the water and the log is less than the total volume of the tank, so water will not spill out of the tank. ▪

Manufacturing: Design and Optimization

Concepts from geometry are frequently used to help solve problems involving design and manufacturing.

Using Ratios in Typography

Web designers often choose a scale for the different font sizes they will use on a website, which is done to make the website more visually pleasing. Designers start by choosing a base font size, such as 16-point font, which is then represented by 1 on the scale that they choose.

Designers can choose any scale that they feel will enhance the appearance of the website, and there are many different scale factors that designers can choose. For example, these font sizes are for a scale factor of 1.2.

1.44   website text sizes

1.2   website text sizes

1   website text sizes

0.833   website text sizes

0.694   website text sizes

Notice how each scale size is 1.2 times the size of the next smaller font size.

▶ **Think About It** Scales for font sizes form a geometric sequence.

EXAMPLE 1

What is the scale size for the largest font shown?

? **website text sizes**

2.25 website text sizes

1.5 website text sizes

1 website text sizes

> ▶ **Think About It** Many font size scales have names. Some scales are named after musical scales, such as major second, perfect fourth, and minor third.

SOLUTION

Start by finding the scale factor. Use the two smallest fonts.

$$\frac{1.5}{1} = 1.5$$

Multiply the previous font size, 2.25, by the scale factor.

$$2.25 \bullet 1.5 = 3.375$$

So the scale size for the largest font is 3.375. ▪

Manufacturing and Optimization

Finding an optimal design for a product is important when it comes to manufacturing. For example, when boxes are manufactured from a flat piece of cardboard, it might be desirable to create a box that has the greatest volume possible.

EXAMPLE 2

A box without a top is to be made from a rectangular piece of cardboard, with dimensions 10 in. × 14 in., by cutting out square corners with side length x. Use technology to estimate the value of x that gives the greatest volume, to the nearest tenth.

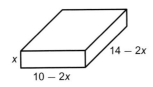

SOLUTION

Step 1 Write an equation for the volume V of the box in terms of x. When the box is folded, you can see that the length is $14 - 2x$, the width is $10 - 2x$, and the height is x.

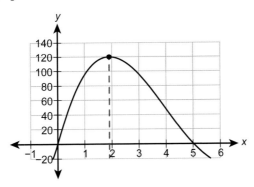

$$V = lwh = (14 - 2x) \cdot (10 - 2x) \cdot x$$

Step 2 Use technology to graph the equation found in Step 1.

The shortest side of the piece of cardboard is 10 in., so x can't be greater than 5 in. View the graph from $x = 0$ to $x = 5$.

The graph shows that the volume of the box is maximized when $x \approx 1.9$ in. ▪

Density in Two Dimensions

Population density is a measure of the number of organisms that make up a population in a defined area.

Calculating Population Density

Population density is the number of organisms per unit area. For people, the area is usually given in square miles, square kilometers, or acres and may include or exclude inhabitable areas such as bodies of water, deserts, or high mountains. Human population density is often reported for a city, county, state, country, and other territories.

EXAMPLE 1

The population of a major city is 637,479. The land area of the city is 48.5 mi^2. What is the population density of the city?

SOLUTION
Divide the population by the land area.

$$\text{population density} = 637{,}479 \div 48.5 \approx 13{,}144$$

The population density of the city is 13,144 people/mi^2. ▪

Applying Population Density to Science

Population density is often used in scientific research to evaluate the number of animals, plants, or other organisms found in a specific region.

EXAMPLE 2

A biologist is researching the number of deer near a small water source. She estimates that there are 16 deer within a $\frac{1}{4}$ mi radius of the water source, 25 deer within a $\frac{1}{2}$ mi radius of the water source, and 30 deer within a $\frac{3}{4}$ mi radius of the water source. Calculate the population density of deer based on the distance in miles from the water source.

SOLUTION

To find the population density for the deer, divide the estimated number of deer by the area of the region where the deer are located.

Number of deer	Radius distance from water source (mi)	Area of location (mi^2)	Population density (deer/mi^2)
16	$\frac{1}{4}$	$\pi r^2 = \pi \cdot \left(\frac{1}{4}\right)^2 \approx 0.20$	$16 \div 0.20 = 80$
25	$\frac{1}{2}$	$\pi r^2 = \pi \cdot \left(\frac{1}{2}\right)^2 \approx 0.79$	$25 \div 0.79 \approx 32$
30	$\frac{3}{4}$	$\pi r^2 = \pi \cdot \left(\frac{3}{4}\right)^2 \approx 1.71$	$30 \div 1.77 \approx 17$

Density in Three Dimensions

Density is the ratio of the mass of an object to its volume.

Calculating Density

The mass of an object is normally measured with a scale, and its volume may be measured directly based on the geometric shape of the object or by the displacement caused when the object is placed in a liquid.

Density Formula
density = mass ÷ volume

EXAMPLE 1

An aluminum ball has a 1.68 cm radius and a 54 g mass. What is the density of aluminum?

SOLUTION
Divide the mass of the aluminum ball by the volume of the ball to find the density. Begin by finding the volume of the ball.

$$\text{volume of sphere} = \frac{4}{3}\pi r^3 = \frac{4}{3}\pi \left(1.68 \text{ cm}\right)^3 \approx 20 \text{ cm}^3$$

Calculate the density.

$$\text{density} = \text{mass} \div \text{volume}$$
$$= 54 \div 20$$
$$\approx 2.7$$

The density of aluminum is approximately 2.7 g/cm^3. ▪

EXAMPLE 2

Water's density is 1 g/cm^3. A cylindrical container with radius 40 cm and height 220 cm is half filled with water. What is the mass of the water in the container?

SOLUTION

Find the volume of the cylindrical container.

$$\text{volume of cylinder} = \pi r^2 h$$
$$= \pi \cdot 40^2 \cdot 220$$
$$\approx 1{,}110{,}000$$

Determine the volume of water in the container.

$$\text{volume of water} = \text{volume of cylinder} \div 2$$
$$= 1{,}110{,}000 \div 2$$
$$\approx 555{,}000 \text{ cm}^3$$

Find the mass of the water.

$$\text{mass} = \text{density} \cdot \text{volume}$$
$$= 1 \text{ g/cm}^3 \cdot 555{,}000 \text{ cm}^3$$
$$= 555{,}000 \text{ g}$$

The mass of the water is 555,000 g. ▨

Fermi Problems

Large quantities can be estimated by rounding values to the nearest number that is a product of a counting number less than 10 and a power of 10.

A **Fermi estimate** is an estimate of a very large number using the Fermi process. This process involves being able to estimate quantities, and then rounding the estimates to the nearest number that is a product of a counting number less than 10 and a power of 10.

EXAMPLE

Use the Fermi process to estimate the number of tennis balls needed to fill an empty bedroom.

SOLUTION

Step 1 Estimate the volume of a typical bedroom to the nearest power of 10.

Bedrooms come in many sizes. However, many bedroom volumes measured in the same units will round to the same power of 10. Suppose that a typical bedroom is 12 ft in width, 10 ft in length, and 10 ft in height.

$$V = lwh$$
$$= 10 \cdot 12 \cdot 10$$
$$= 1200$$
$$\approx 10^3$$

To the nearest power of 10, many bedrooms have a volume of about 10^3 ft^3.

▶ **Think About It** Solving Fermi problems requires the estimated quantities to have compatible units.

Step 2 Estimate the volume of a tennis ball to the nearest power of 10.

Any reasonable estimate of the volume of a tennis ball (using the same units) will round to the same power of 10. Suppose that a tennis ball has a radius of a little more than 1 in., or about 0.1 ft. Use the formula for the volume of a sphere to estimate the tennis ball's volume in cubic feet to the nearest power of 10.

$$\text{volume of sphere} = \frac{4}{3}\pi r^3$$

$$= \frac{4}{3} \cdot 3 \cdot 0.1^3$$

$$\approx 0.004$$

The volume of a tennis ball is about $0.004 = 4 \times 10^{-3}$ ft^3.

Step 3 Divide to find the Fermi estimate.

$$\text{number of tennis balls} = \frac{\text{volume of bedroom}}{\text{volume of tennis ball}}$$

$$= \frac{10^3 \text{ ft}^3}{4 \times 10^{-3} \text{ ft}^3}$$

$$= 0.25 \times 10^6 = 2.5 \times 10^5$$

According to the Fermi estimate, it takes about 2.5×10^5 tennis balls to fill an empty bedroom. ▨

Pronunciation Guide

The tables provide sample words to explain the sounds associated with specific letters and letter combinations used in the respellings in this book. For example, *a* represents the short "a" sound in *cat*, while *ay* represents the long "a" sound in *day*.

Letter combinations are used to approximate certain more complex sounds. For example, in the respelling of *trapezoid*—TRA-puh-zoyd—the letters *uh* represent the vowel sound you hear in *shut* and *other*.

VOWELS	
a	short a: **a**pple, c**a**t
ay	long a: c**a**ne, d**ay**
e, eh	short e: h**e**n, b**e**d
ee	long e: f**ee**d, t**ea**m
i, ih	short i: l**i**p, act**i**ve
iy	long i: tr**y**, m**i**ght
ah	short o: h**o**t, f**a**ther
oh	long o: h**o**me, thr**ow**
uh	short u: sh**u**t, **o**ther
yoo	long u: **u**nion, c**u**te

LETTER COMBINATIONS	
ch	**ch**in, an**ci**ent
sh	**sh**ow, mi**ss**ion
zh	vi**si**on, a**z**ure
th	**th**in, heal**th**
th	**th**en, hea**th**er
ur	b**ir**d, f**ur**ther, w**or**d
us	b**us**, cr**us**t
or	c**our**t, f**or**mal
ehr	**er**ror, c**are**
oo	c**oo**l, tr**ue**, r**u**le
ow	n**ow**, **ou**t
ou	l**oo**k, p**u**ll, w**ou**ld
oy	c**oi**n, t**oy**
aw	s**aw**, m**au**l, f**a**ll
ng	so**ng**, fi**ng**er
air	**A**ristotle, b**a**rrister
ahr	c**ar**t, m**ar**tyr

CONSONANTS	
b	**b**utter, **b**a**b**y
d	**d**og, cra**d**le
f	**f**un, **ph**one
g	**g**rade, an**g**le
h	**h**at, a**h**ead
j	**j**u**dg**e, **g**orge
k	**k**ite, **c**ar, bla**ck**
l	**l**ily, mi**l**e
m	**m**o**m**, ca**m**el
n	**n**ext, ca**nd**id
p	**p**rice, co**pp**er
r	**r**ubber, f**r**ee
s	**s**mall, **c**ircle, ha**ss**le
t	**t**on, po**tt**ery
v	**v**ase, vi**v**id
w	**w**all, a**w**ay
y	**y**ellow, ka**y**ak
z	**z**ebra, ha**z**e

Glossary

absolute value function   a function whose rule contains an absolute value expression

accuracy   how close a measure is to its true value

acute angles   angles that measure less than 90°

addition counting principle   if there are m ways of doing one thing and n ways of doing another thing, then there are $m + n$ ways of doing one thing or the other

adjacent angles   angles that share a common side, have the same vertex, and do not share any interior common points

adjacent side of acute angle in a right triangle the side next to the given angle in a right triangle but is not the hypotenuse

alternate exterior angles   angles outside the two lines that are not the transversal and are on diagonal opposite sides of the transversal

altitude of a pyramid   a perpendicular line segment that joins the vertex to the plane of the base; An altitude may lie inside, on, or outside a pyramid.

altitude of a triangle   a perpendicular segment from a vertex of the triangle to a line containing the base opposite the vertex

amplitude of a sinusoidal function   one-half the distance between the maximum value and the minimum value; the height of a sinusoidal function above the midline

analytic geometry   the study of geometry using the tools of algebra; also called coordinate geometry

angle   a figure formed by two rays, called sides, that share the same endpoint

angle bisector   a line or line segment or ray that divides an angle into two congruent angles

angle of depression of an object   the downward angle that the object makes with the horizontal

angle of elevation of an object   the upward angle that the object makes with the horizontal

annulus   the region between two concentric circles

arc   the set of points on a circle between two points on the circle

arc length   a part of the circumference of a circle; It can be found by writing the part as a fraction over 360° and multiplying by the circumference.

arccosine (arccos) function $y = \arccos x$ if and only if $\cos y = x$ where $-1 \leq x \leq 1$ and $0 \leq y \leq \pi$

arcsine (arcsin) function $y = \arcsin x$ if and only if $\sin y = x$ where $-1 \leq x \leq 1$ and $-\frac{\pi}{2} \leq y \leq \frac{\pi}{2}$

area   the number of square units contained in the interior of a figure

argument   a set of statements, called premises, which are needed to reach a conclusion; Both the premise and the conclusion are considered to be part of the argument.

arithmetic sequence   a sequence in which the difference between consecutive terms is a constant

association   the relationship between two variables

asymptote   a line that a graph of a given function approaches without touching

average rate of change in a quantity   the ratio of the change in a quantity to the change in time

axis of a cylinder   the line connecting the centers of the bases

axis of a double-napped cone   the line about which a generating line revolves to produce a double-napped cone

axis of symmetry   a line drawn through a figure so that one side is a reflection of the image on the opposite side; also called a line of symmetry

base   a number raised to an exponent; For example, in 5^2, 5 is the base.

base edges of pyramid   edges that form the base of a pyramid; A base edge is formed when a lateral face and the base meet.

bell-shaped distribution   a type of symmetric distribution of data sets that is nearly bell-shaped, where the mean and median are nearly equal

bi–   prefix that means "two"

biased sample   a sample that is not representative of its population

binomial   a polynomial with two terms

bivariate data   data that show the relationship between paired variables

boundary line   a line that divides the coordinate plane into two half-planes

bounded closed interval   an interval that includes both endpoints

bounded half-open interval   an interval that includes one and only one endpoint

bounded interval   the set of all real numbers between two numbers, called endpoints; The endpoints may or may not be included.

bounded open interval   an interval that does not include either endpoint

box-and-whisker plot   a diagram that shows the distribution or spread of data with the minimum, the maximum, and the three quartiles of the data; The box extends from Q_1 to Q_3. The median is on the vertical line in the box. The whiskers extend from the first quartile to the minimum and from the third quartile to the maximum.

ceiling function   another name for the least integer function

center of a circle   the point inside a circle that is an equal distance from every point on the circle

center of a polygon   the point inside a polygon that is equidistant from each vertex

center of a sphere   the point inside a sphere from which all points on the surface of the sphere are an equal distance

center of dilation   the point where the lines connecting each point on the pre-image with its corresponding point on the image intersect

central angle of a circle   an angle that has its vertex at the center of a circle and its sides as radii of the circle

central angle of a polygon   an angle formed by line segments drawn from the center to two consecutive vertices

central limit theorem   when several random samples of size n are taken from a population and n is sufficiently large, then the means of the samples will have a distribution that is approximately normal

centroid   the point where all three medians of a triangle intersect

chord   a segment that connects any two points on a circle

circle   the set of all points in a plane that are a fixed distance r (the radius) from a given point (the center)

circle (as a conic section)   a conic section formed when a plane intersects only one nappe, perpendicular to the axis

circle graph   a graph that uses sectors of a circle to display and compare data that can be broken down into separate categories

circumcenter   the point where the perpendicular bisectors on each side of a triangle intersect

circumscribed circle   for a given triangle, the circle that contains each vertex of the triangle; The circumcenter of the triangle is the center of the circumscribed circle.

classes   equal-sized groups used to separate and categorize data; also called intervals

closed half-plane   a half-plane in a nonstrict inequality where the boundary line is a solid line

closed set a set such that, under an operation, the result of the operation on any two elements of the set is also an element of the set

coefficient the nonvariable factor of a term

coefficient of determination the square of the correlation coefficient; written r^2

coincident system a system with infinitely many solutions

collinear points that lie on the same line

common difference the difference between a term and the previous term; the constant difference d in an arithmetic sequence such that $d = a_n - a_{n-1}$

common factor a factor shared by two or more numbers

common logarithm a logarithm with base 10; Common logarithms, such as $\log_{10} x$, are usually written without the base, as $\log x$.

common logarithmic function with base 10 $f(x) = \log x$ when x is a positive real number; The domain is $x > 0$ and the vertical asymptote is $x = 0$.

common ratio of a geometric sequence the ratio of a term to the previous term; the constant r in a geometric sequence such that $r = \dfrac{a_n}{a_{n-1}}$

complementary angles angles whose measures sum to 90°

completing the square the process of transforming an expression of the form $x^2 + bx$ into a perfect square trinomial by adding the term $\left(\dfrac{b}{2}\right)^2$ to it

complex conjugates two complex numbers of the form $a + bi$ and $a - bi$

complex numbers numbers of the form $a + bi$ where a is the real part and b is the imaginary part and a and b are real numbers; denoted $\mathbb{C}$

complex plane the plane on which every complex number can be graphed; The horizontal axis is the real axis and the vertical axis is the imaginary axis.

compound event an event that consists of two or more simple events

compound inequality a pair of inequalities joined by the word *and* or the word *or*; a type of compound statement

computer algebra system (CAS) a computer program that performs algebraic manipulations such as simplifying algebraic expressions and solving equations

conclusion of a conditional statement the part of a conditional statement that includes the words following *then*

conclusion of an argument the end part of an argument that follows the premises

conditional probability the probability of an event given that another event has already happened; The conditional probability that event B occurs after event A has already occurred can be represented as $P(B \mid A)$, which is read as "the probability of B given A."

conditional statement a statement that has two parts; The first part begins with the word *if* and the second part begins with the word *then*.

cone a solid with a circular base, a vertex, and a curved surface

confidence interval an interval estimate that is likely to contain a population parameter being estimated

confidence level the percent chance that a population parameter falls inside the confidence interval

congruent line segments line segments that have equal length

congruent polygons polygons that are the same size and shape

conic section a two-dimensional graph that can be formed by the intersection of a plane with a double-napped cone

conjecture a statement that is thought to be true but is yet to be proven

conjugate binomials two binomials with the same terms but opposite signs; for example, $(a + b)$ and $(a - b)$

conjugate pair a pair of expressions of the form $a + bi$ and $a - bi$

conjunction   a compound statement that uses the word *and*

consistent dependent system of equations a system with infinitely many solutions

consistent independent system of equations a system with exactly one solution

consistent system of equations   a system with exactly one solution or infinitely many solutions

constant   a term that has no variables

constant function   a function is constant within an interval if the value of $f(x)$ remains the same

constraint   a necessary condition in a problem, often written in the form of an inequality

continuous function   a function with a connected graph

continuous random variable   a variable whose outcomes are both random and continuous

contraction   a dilation for which the absolute value of the scale factor is between 0 and 1

contradiction (equation)   an equation that is true for no values of the variable; A contradiction has no solutions, represented by the null set: $\{\ \}$ or $\varnothing$.

contradiction (statement)   a statement that is logically at odds with a previous statement that was assumed to be true

converse   a conditional statement that switches the hypothesis and the conclusion of the original conditional statement

conversion factor   a fraction that is used to convert measures and rates and that has a numerator and denominator of the same quantity written in different units

coordinate   the number on a number line that gives the location of a point

coordinate plane   a plane in which the coordinates of any point are the point's distances from two intersecting perpendicular lines called axes (the x-axis and y-axis)

coplanar   points that lie on the same plane

corollary   a proposition that follows directly from a postulate or theorem and can be easily proven

correlation coefficient   written as r, describes the strength and direction of the association between two variables; Values for r range from 1 (perfect positive correlation) to 0 (no correlation) to -1 (perfect negative correlation).

corresponding angles of figures   the angles that lie in the same position or match up when a transversal intersects two lines

corresponding sides of figures   the sides that lie in the same position or match up when a transversal intersects two lines

cosine function $\cos x = a$ is a trigonometric function of x when x is a radian measure of the angle that intercepts the unit circle at (a, b)

cosine of an angle   the ratio of the length of the leg that is adjacent to that angle to the length of the hypotenuse; abbreviated cos

coterminal angles   angles in standard position that have the same terminal side but have different amounts of rotation; Their angles differ by a multiple of 360°, or 2π radians.

counterexample   an example that shows that a statement is false

critical *z*-scores z-scores for the upper limit and lower limit of the confidence interval

cylinder   a solid with two parallel, congruent, circular bases joined by a curved surface

decreasing function   a function is decreasing within an interval if the value of $f(x)$ decreases as the value of x increases

deductive reasoning   a type of reasoning that uses previously proven or accepted properties to reach conclusions

degenerate conic section   a conic section formed when a plane intersects the vertex of the double-napped cone

degree of a monomial   the sum of the exponents of the variable factors

degree of a polynomial   the degree of the monomial with the greatest degree

density   the ratio of the mass of an object to its volume; density = mass ÷ volume

dependent events   events in which knowing one outcome has an effect on the probability of the other event(s)

dependent variable   the output variable of a function

descriptive statistics   statistics that are used to numerically summarize or represent a set of data

deviation   in a data set, the difference between a data value x_i and the mean $\overline{x}$ of the data set; $x_i - \overline{x}$

diagonals   line segments with endpoints on nonconsecutive vertices

diameter   a line segment that connects two points on a circle and contains the center of the circle; also the length of any diameter of a given circle

dilation   a transformation that changes the size but not the shape of a figure, either by enlarging it or shrinking it

dimensional analysis   the process of multiplying by conversion factors and dividing out common units

directed line segment   a segment between two points A and B with a specified direction from A to B or from B to A and a standard distance between the two points

directrix   one of two references in the definition of a parabola; The distance from any point on the parabola to the directrix (a line) is equal to the distance from that same point to the parabola's focus (a point).

discrete function   a function with a graph that is disconnected

discriminant   the radicand $b^2 - 4ac$ in the quadratic formula

disjunction   a compound statement that uses the word *or*

dividend   the number being divided by the divisor

divisor   the number that divides the dividend

domain   the set of all allowable inputs for a relation or function

double-napped cone   cone formed by the generating line that intersects and revolves around another line called the axis; The axis is stationary and the two lines cannot be perpendicular.

element   a member of a set

ellipse   a conic section formed when a plane intersects only one nappe, not parallel to the generating line

end behavior   how a function behaves when the domain values increase or decrease without bound

endpoints of an interval   the minimum and maximum real numbers on a bounded interval

endpoints of an intercepted arc   the points where the sides of an inscribed angle meet the circle

equal complex numbers   complex numbers with real parts that are equal and with imaginary parts that are equal; $a + bi = c + di$ if and only if $a = c$ and $b = d$

equation   a number sentence that indicates that two expressions have the same value

equiangular polygon   a polygon with all angles congruent

equilateral triangle   a triangle that has three congruent sides

equivalent equations   equations with the same solution or solutions

equivalent fractions   fractions that have the same value

equivalent inequalities   inequalities with the same solutions

even function   a function in which $f(-x) = f(x)$; The graph of an even function is symmetric about the y-axis.

event   any particular subset of a sample space

expanded form of a sum   a representation of a sum as every term added or subtracted to create the sum

expansion a dilation for which the absolute value of the scale factor is greater than 1

experiment any process that results in one or more results

explanatory variable the variable graphed along the horizontal axis in a scatter plot; the independent variable in a statistical analysis

exponent in a power, a number used to indicate the number of factors of the base that should be multiplied; For example, in 5^2, 2 is the exponent.

exponential equation an equation with variable expressions as exponents

exponential function an equation of the form $f(x) = b^x + k$ where $b > 0$ and $b \neq 1$

expression a number, a variable, or a combination of numbers, variables, and operations

exterior angle of a triangle an angle formed by one side of the triangle and another side of the triangle when it is extended

extremes the exterior variables of a proportion

factor one of two or more quantities that are multiplied together

factor of a number a number that divides into the given number without a remainder

factorial of a positive integer _n_ the product of all the positive integers less than or equal to _n_; written _n_!

family of functions a group of functions with the same fundamental characteristics

feasible region the set of all ordered pairs that satisfy the constraints of an optimization problem and are possible solutions to the problem

Fermi estimate an estimate of a very large number using the Fermi process; This process involves being able to estimate quantities and then round the estimates to the nearest number that is a product of a counting number less than 10 and a power of 10.

finite set a set that has a number of elements that can be described with a whole number

first quartile, Q$_1$ the median of the lower subset of a data set

five-number summary the minimum, the maximum, and the three quartiles of a data set

floor function another name for the greatest integer function

flowchart proof a graphical representation of the logical flow of a proof; In a flowchart proof, statements and conclusions are connected with arrows.

focus for a parabola one of two references in the definition of a parabola; The distance from any point on the parabola to the focus (a point) is equal to the distance from that same point to the parabola's directrix (a line).

FOIL a mnemonic used for a method to perform the distributive property when multiplying binomials; first-outer-inner-last

frequency distribution a table or graph that describes the number of times a value or interval of values occurs in a data set

frequency of a sinusoidal function the number of periods per unit; A function's frequency is the reciprocal of its period.

frequency table a table that describes the number of times a value or interval of values occurs in a data set

function a relation in which each member of the domain is assigned to exactly one member of the range

function composition a mapping in which each element of the range of one function is the domain of another function; If _f_ and _g_ are functions of _x_, the composition of the _f_ with _g_ is denoted by _fg_ and is defined as $f(g)$. The domain of $f(g(x))$ is the set of the domain values of _g_ with range values that are in the domain of _f_.

function notation a function equation written so that the dependent variable is replaced with $f(x)$; for example, $f(x) = 2x + 4$

generating line of a double-napped cone the line that revolves about another line, called the axis, to produce a double-napped cone

geometric sequence a sequence in which the ratio between consecutive terms is a constant

geometric series   a series that results from adding the terms of a geometric sequence

graph of an inequality   a display of all possible solutions of the inequality

greatest integer function   a function that assigns the greatest integer less than or equal to each real number in an interval; denoted by $f(x) = \lfloor x \rfloor$ or $f(x) = \text{int}(x)$; also called the floor function

half-life   the length of time it takes for one-half of a radioactive substance to decay

half-plane   a plane that has been divided in half by a boundary line

height   the length of the altitude

histogram   a bar graph that displays the frequency of data values that occur within certain intervals; The height of each bar gives the frequency in the respective interval.

horizontal asymptote   the line $y = b$ for the graph of the function f if $f(x)$ approaches b as x approaches ∞ or $-\infty$

horizontal line test   a test to determine whether a function f is invertible; If a horizontal line intersects a function more than once, then the function is not invertible. If every horizontal line intersects a function only once, then the function is invertible.

hyperbola   a conic section formed when a plane intersects both nappes

hypotenuse   the side opposite the right angle of a right triangle

hypothesis   the part of a conditional statement that includes the words following *if*

identity   an equation that is true for all values of the variable; It has infinitely many solutions and is often represented as $\{x \mid x \in \mathbb{R}\}$.

image   a figure after transformation

imaginary axis   the vertical axis of a complex plane along which the imaginary part of a complex number is graphed

imaginary number   any number that can be written in the form ai where a is any real number and i is the imaginary unit

imaginary unit i where $i^2 = -1$ and $i = \sqrt{-1}$

improper fraction   a fraction in which the numerator is greater than or equal to the denominator

incenter of a triangle   the point where the angle bisectors drawn through each vertex intersect

included angle of a triangle   an angle formed by two sides of a triangle

included side of a triangle   a side of a triangle that lies between two specific angles

inconsistent system of equations   a system with no solutions

increasing function   a function is increasing within an interval if the value of $f(x)$ increases as the value of x increases

independent events   two events in which knowing one outcome has no effect on the probability of the other event

independent variable   the input variable of a function

index in sigma notation   the variable i in sigma notation $\sum\limits_{i=0}^{3} a_i$; the variable that takes on all integer values from the lower limit to the upper limit of the summation

index of a radical n in a radical expression $\sqrt[n]{b}$; The index is always greater than 1.

inductive reasoning   a type of reasoning that starts with observation and moves from a specific observation to a general conclusion

inequality   a statement formed by placing one of the inequality symbols $<, >, \leq, \geq,$ or $\neq$ between two expressions

inferential statistics   statistics used to draw conclusions or make predictions by taking the information gained from the sample and generalizing it to the population it came from

infinite set   a set with a boundless number of elements

initial side of angle   the ray from which the rotation of an angle starts

inscribed angle   an angle that has its vertex on a circle and its sides as chords of the circle

inscribed circle   for a given triangle, a circle in the interior of the triangle that touches each side of the triangle at a single point; The incenter is the center of the inscribed circle.

integers   all the natural numbers, their opposites, and zero; denoted $\mathbb{Z} = \{\ldots, -2, -1, 0, 1, 2, \ldots\}$

intercepted arc   the arc opposite an inscribed angle

interior angles of a triangle   the three angles inside the triangle

interquartile range (IQR)   the difference between the third and first quartiles of a data set; $IQR = Q_3 - Q_1$

interval estimate   a range of values that contains the point estimate and is likely to contain the population parameter

inverse functions   two functions f and g that "undo" each other; If you start with a value x, apply f, and then apply g, the result is the original value x: $(f \circ g)(x) = x$ and $(g \circ f)(x) = x$. The inverse of a function f is denoted by f^{-1} ("f inverse"). For every pair of inverse functions, if $f^{-1} = g$, then $g^{-1} = f$.

inverse of a function   a relationship that interchanges the members of the ordered pairs of the original function; denoted by f^{-1}; The domain of the inverse function is the range of the original function. The range of the inverse function is the domain of the original function.

inverse of a relation   a relationship that switches the x- and y-values of the ordered pairs of the original relation; The domain of the inverse relation is the range of the original relation. The range of the inverse relation is the domain of the original relation. The graph of the inverse of a relation is its reflection over the line $y = x$.

inverse tangent   the angle that has a given value as its tangent ratio; abbreviated $\tan^{-1}$

invertible function   a function f whose inverse is also a function

irrational number   a real number that cannot be written in the form $\frac{a}{b}$ for any integers a and b

isometric transformation   any transformation that results in an image that is congruent to the pre-image; also called an isometry

isosceles triangle   a triangle that has at least two congruent sides

iterative rule   a rule that can be used to find the nth term of a sequence without calculating previous terms of the sequence

lateral edges of a pyramid   the edges of a pyramid that do not form the base; A lateral edge is formed when two lateral faces meet.

lateral side of an angle   the ray from which the rotation of an angle starts

lateral surface   the curved surface of a cylinder

law of detachment   an argument that has two true premises and a valid conclusion; The premises and conclusion have the following form:

> premise — If a, then b.
> premise — a is true.
> conclusion — Therefore, b is true.

law of syllogism   a logical argument that always contains two premises and a conclusion; The premises and conclusion have the following form:

> premise — If a, then b.
> premise — If b, then c.
> conclusion — Therefore, if a, then c.

leading coefficient of a polynomial in simplified form   the coefficient of the first term

leaf   the digits on the right side of a stem-and-leaf plot

least common denominator (LCD)   the least common multiple of two or more denominators

least integer function   a function that assigns the least integer greater than or equal to each real number in an interval; denoted by $f(x) = \lceil x \rceil$; also called the ceiling function

least squares regression line   the line that makes the sum of the squares of the vertical distances from each data point to the line as small as possible

length of a line segment   the distance between the endpoints of a line segment

like radicals   two or more square root expressions that have the same radicand

like terms   terms that contain the same variable factors taken to the same powers

line   a collection of points arranged in a straight path

line of best fit   a least squares regression equation

line of symmetry   a line over which you can flip a given figure, leaving the figure unchanged; A line of symmetry divides a figure into two congruent (mirror-image) halves.

line segment   a part of a line that consists of any two points on the line and all the points in between those two points

line symmetry   a characteristic of a figure in which there is at least one line such that when the figure is folded over the line, the two halves are mirror images that match up perfectly; also called reflection symmetry

linear equation   an equation whose graph in a coordinate plane is a line

linear inequality   an inequality that has terms with degree zero or one and an inequality symbol to relate two variables

linear pair of angles   two angles that have a common side and the same vertex with their other sides point in opposite directions

linear programming   the process of maximizing or minimizing a linear function subject to a set of conditions, called constraints, that are linear inequalities

logarithm   the exponent to which a base would have to be raised to result in a given value; The logarithm of a with base b, $\log_b a$, where $b > 0$, $b \neq 1$, and $a > 0$, is defined as $\log_b a = x$ if and only if $b^x = a$.

logistic growth function   a function of the form $f(x) = \dfrac{C}{1 + Ae^{-Bx}}$ where A, B, and C are all positive constants

lower limit   in sigma notation, the starting value for the index n; In $\sum\limits_{n=1}^{n} a_n$, the lower limit is 1.

major arcs   arcs larger than a semicircle

margin of error   the greatest likely difference between the point estimate and the parameter

marginal frequency   the ratio of the total for a particular column or row to the overall total in a two-way table

mean   the statistical average of a data set

means of a proportion   the middle variables of a proportion

median of a data set   the middle value when the values are ordered; If the data set has an even number of values, the median is the mean of the two middle values.

median of a triangle   a segment from the vertex of a triangle to the midpoint of its opposite side

midline of a sinusoidal function   the horizontal line that is halfway between the maximum and the minimum; The equation of the midline of a sinusoidal function is $y = \dfrac{\text{maximum} + \text{minimum}}{2}$.

midpoint   a point that divides a line segment into two congruent parts

minor arcs   arcs smaller than a semicircle

mixed number   a number consisting of both a whole number and a fraction or the opposite of such a number

mode   the value that occurs most frequently

model parameter   a value that is held constant for a specific model

model variable   a variable that takes on different values for a particular model

modified box-and-whisker plot a box-and-whisker plot in which outliers are shown with dots and the whiskers extend to the least and greatest values in the data set that are not outliers

monomial a number, a variable, or the product of a number and one or more variables

multiplication counting principle if a task can be broken into two stages and there are m ways of doing the first stage and n ways of doing the second stage, then there are $m \bullet n$ ways of doing one thing and the other

multiplicity for a root a of $p(x) = 0$, the number of times the factor $x - a$ occurs in the factorization of any polynomial $p(x)$

nappe one of two equal pieces of a cone where the cone is divided at the vertex by a plane perpendicular to the axis

natural logarithm a logarithm with a base e; Natural logarithms, such as $\log_e x$, are often written using the notation $\ln x$.

natural logarithmic function with base e $g(x) = \ln x$ where x is a positive real number; The domain is $x > 0$, and the vertical asymptote is $x = 0$.

natural numbers the set of numbers $\mathbb{N} = \{1, 2, 3, \dots\}$; also called counting numbers or positive integers

nearest integer function a function that assigns the nearest integer to each real number in an interval; denoted by $\text{nint}(x)$; also called the round function

negative association when comparing two data sets, as the data from one set increase, the data from the second set decrease; In a scatter plot, the data points decrease from left to right.

noncollinear points that do not lie on the same line

nonstrict inequality an inequality that uses $\leq$ or $\geq$

normal distribution a bell-shaped distribution, centered on the mean

nth root of b a when $a^n = b$, a and b are both real numbers, and n is a positive integer

number line a line with equally spaced intervals that are labeled with numbers

numerical expression an expression that consists of numbers, operations, and sometimes grouping symbols

objective function a linear function that models a quantity that is to be optimized in a linear programming problem

oblique cone a cone with an axis that is not an altitude

oblique cylinder a cylinder with an axis that is not an altitude

obtuse angles angles that measure greater than 90° and less than 180°

odd function a function in which $f(-x) = -f(x)$; The graph of an odd function is symmetric about the origin.

one-to-one function a function in which every element of the domain corresponds to exactly one element on the range

open half-plane a half plane in a strict inequality where the boundary line is dashed

open sentence an equation or inequality containing one or more variables

opposite side of an acute angle in a right triangle the side across from the given angle

ordered pair a pair of numbers on a coordinate plane, in which the first number is the x-coordinate the second is the y-coordinate

origin the intersection of the x- and y-axes

outcomes the results of an experiment

outlier a value far away from most other values in a data set

parabola a symmetric curve that is the graph of a quadratic function

parabola (conic section) a conic section formed when a plane intersects only one nappe, parallel to the generating line

parabola (locus of points) the set of all points in a plane that are equidistant from a fixed line (the directrix) and a fixed point (the focus)

paragraph proof a proof in the form of a paragraph

parallel lines coplanar lines that never intersect

parallelogram a quadrilateral with two pairs of parallel sides

parameter a measurement that describes a population

parent function the most basic function in a family of functions

partition a directed line segment to divide a directed line segment into segments based on a given ratio

percentile rank the percentage of data that falls below a particular value

perfect square a rational number with a square root that is also rational

perimeter the distance around a figure

period the length of each interval in a periodic function

period of a sinusoidal graph the interval over which a sinusoidal graph repeats itself

periodic function a function that repeats itself in regular intervals

perpendicular bisector a line, line segment, or ray that passes through the midpoint of a line segment and forms a right angle with the segment

perpendicular lines lines that meet at right angles

piecewise function a function defined using different rules for different intervals of the domain

plane a flat surface that has infinite length and width but no thickness

point references a location in space; It has no length, width, or depth.

point estimates statistics, such as $\hat{p}$ and $\hat{x}$, that are used to estimate population parameters

point of tangency a point where a circle and one of its tangents intersect

point-slope form of a linear equation an equation of the form $y - y_1 = m(x - x_1)$ where m is the slope and (x_1, y_1) is a point on the corresponding line

polygon a closed figure in a plane formed by three or more line segments, such that each line segment intersects exactly two other line segments at their endpoints only

polynomial a monomial or the sum of monomials

polynomial in x a polynomial of the form $a_n x^n + a_{n-1} x^{n-1} + \ldots + a_2 x^2 + a_1 x + a_0$ where the exponents are all whole numbers, the coefficients are all real numbers, and $a_n \neq 0$

population an entire set of members that you want to know something about

positive association when comparing two data sets, if the data from one set increase, the data from the second set also increase; In a scatter plot, data points increase from left to right.

postulates mathematical statements that are accepted as true without proof

power a number that is, or could be, represented by a base with an exponent

power function any function that can be written in the form $f(x) = ax^2 + b$ when n is a positive integer, a is any nonzero real number, and b is any real number

practical domain and range of a function the sets of all realistic inputs and outputs for a particular situation

pre-image the original figure before a transformation

premises statements that are presumed to be true in the course of a logical argument

prime polynomial a polynomial that cannot be factored

principal of a loan the amount of money actually borrowed

principal square root another name for a positive square root; indicated by the radical sign $\sqrt{}$

probability distribution table a frequency table where each frequency is replaced by the probability of the outcome

probability of an event a measure of the likelihood that an event will occur; Probability is always a number between 0 and 1 (inclusive) that can be written as a fraction, a decimal, or a percent.

product of the functions f and g
$(fg)(x) = f(x) \cdot g(x)$

proof a clear, logical structure of reasoning that begins from accepted ideas and proceeds through logic to reach a conclusion

proper fraction a fraction in which the numerator is less than the denominator

proportion an equation that states that two ratios are equal; often written as $a : b = c : d$ or $\frac{a}{b} = \frac{c}{d}$

pyramid a polyhedron with a polygonal base and lateral faces; The faces are triangles that meet at a common vertex.

Pythagorean identity for any angle θ, $\sin^2 \theta + \cos^2 \theta = 1$

quadrantal angles angles in standard position that have their terminal sides along the horizontal or vertical axis

quadrants the sections of a coordinate plane; The first quadrant is between the positive horizontal axis and the positive vertical axis. The second, third, and fourth quadrants are located counterclockwise from the first quadrant, respectively.

quadratic formula a formula for finding the solutions of a quadratic equation in the form
$ax^2 + bx + c = 0$ where $a \neq 0$; $x = \dfrac{-b \pm \sqrt{b^2 - 4ac}}{2a}$

quadratic function a second-degree polynomial function

quadrilateral a four-sided polygon

quotient the number of times the divisor goes into the dividend evenly

quotient of the functions f and g $\dfrac{f}{g}(x) = \dfrac{f(x)}{g(x)}$, $g(x) \neq 0$

radian measure of a central angle of a circle the quotient of the angle's arc length and the circle's radius

radian measure of an angle the length of the arc on a unit circle subtended (intercepted) by the angle

radical equation an equation that contains at least one radical expression with a variable in the radicand

radical expression an expression that contains a radical sign $\sqrt{}$

radical function a function of the form $f(x) = a\sqrt{x - h} + k$ where n is an integer greater than 1

radicand the expression under a radical sign; For example, in the expression $\sqrt[n]{b}$, b is the radicand.

radius a line segment that connects the center of a circle to a point on the circle; also the length of all radii of a given circle

range of a data set the difference between its greatest value (maximum) and its least value (minimum)

range of a relation the set of possible outputs

rational expression a ratio with a numerator and a denominator that are polynomials and with a denominator that is nonzero

rational function any function that can be written as the quotient of two polynomials

rational number any number that can be expressed as a ratio $\frac{a}{b}$, where a and b are integers and $b \neq 0$; denoted $\mathbb{Q}$

raw score an original data value

ray part of a line that starts at an endpoint and extends infinitely in one direction

real axis the horizontal axis of a complex plane along which the real part of a complex number is graphed

real numbers the set of numbers that can be written as decimals; the combined set of the rational and irrational numbers; denoted $\mathbb{R}$

reciprocal power function a function that has the power of x in the denominator of a rational function; The functions $f(x) = \frac{1}{x}$, $g(x) = \frac{1}{x^2}$, and $h(x) = \frac{1}{x^3}$ are reciprocal power functions.

rectangle a parallelogram with four right angles

recursive rule a rule for generating terms of a sequence that depends on one or more previous terms of the sequence

reference angle for an acute angle x, the positive acute angle made by the terminal side of x and the horizontal axis

reflection an isometric transformation that flips a figure across a line or line segment, creating a mirror image of the figure

reflection symmetry when a figure that has at least one axis of symmetry; The figure can be folded along the axis of symmetry so that both halves match up.

regression line a line drawn through the points of a scatter plot to summarize the straight line pattern that the points fit

regular hexagon a six-sided polygon with congruent sides and congruent angles

regular polygon a polygon that is both equiangular and equilateral

regular pyramid a pyramid whose base is a regular polygon and whose lateral faces are congruent isosceles triangles

relation a mapping from one set, called the domain, to another set, called the range

relative frequency the ratio of the value of a subtotal to the value of the total

relative maximum point of a function a point that has a greater function value than all the points on the function that are close to it

relative minimum point a point that has a value that is less than all the points on the function that are close to it

remainder the amount left over after evenly dividing a dividend by a divisor

remote interior angles the angles that are inside the triangle and are not adjacent to a given exterior angle

repeating decimal a decimal that does not end but shows a repeating of digits (not made up of all zeros) that goes on forever after the decimal point

residual the difference between an observed value and the predicted value from a model; residual (e) = observed (y) − predicted $(\hat{y})$; the vertical distance between a point on the scatter plot and the point on the linear model directly above or below the point

residual plot a graph that shows the residual for each value of the explanatory variable

response variable the variable graphed along the vertical axis in a scatter plot; the independent variable(s) in a statistical analysis

rhombus a parallelogram with four congruent sides

right angle an angle that measures exactly 90°

right cone a cone with an axis that is also an altitude

right cylinder a cylinder with an axis that is also an altitude

rigid motion motion that relocates a figure while preserving its shape and size

roots of a polynomial the solutions to a polynomial equation in which one side of the equation is a factored polynomial and the other side of the equation is equal to zero

rotation an isometric transformation that turns a figure a certain number of degrees, called the angle of rotation, around a central point, called the center of rotation

rotation symmetry when a figure can be rotated around its center less than one full turn so that the rotated figure looks exactly like the original figure

round function another name for the nearest integer function

same-side interior angles angles in between the two lines that are not the transversal and are on the same side of the transversal

sample   a subset of a population

sample space   the set of all possible outcomes of an experiment

scale factor _t_ of a dilation   the ratio of the length of any side of on an image to the length of its corresponding side on the pre-image

scalene triangle   a triangle that has no congruent sides

scatter plot   a graph that displays a set of bivariate data

secant   a line that intersects a circle in two points

second quartile, Q$_2$ the median of the entire data set that separates the ordered data set into a lower subset and an upper subset

sector   a region whose boundaries are two radii and part of the circle

segment bisector   a line, line segment, or ray that passes through the midpoint of a line segment

semicircle   an arc with endpoints that are also the endpoints of a diameter

sequence   a function whose domain is the set of natural numbers

series   the sum of consecutive terms of a sequence

set   a collection of objects

sides   the line segments that form a polygon

sigma notation   a way to write a sum as sum as

$\sum_{i=1}^{n} a_i = a_1 + a_2 + a_3 + \ldots + a_n$; $\sum_{i=1}^{n} a_i$, read as "the sum from 1 to _n_ of a_i," where _i_ is the index, _n_ is the upper limit, and 1 is the lower limit; The right side of the equation is the expanded form of the sum.

similar figures   figures that are the same shape but are not necessarily the same size; The symbol $\sim$ means "is similar to."

similar solids   solids that have the same shape and all the corresponding dimensions are proportional

similar triangles   two triangles with congruent corresponding angles and proportional corresponding side lengths

simple event   a single outcome of an experiment; a single element of a sample space

simplified form of a polynomial   a polynomial that has no like terms, every term is in simplest form, and its terms are in order of decreasing degree with respect to a variable

simplified radical form of a square root expression   a square root expression in which the radicand is not a fraction, there are no radicals in the denominator, and no factor is a perfect square other than 1

sine of an angle   the ratio of the length of the leg opposite the angle to the length of the hypotenuse; abbreviated sin

sine function $\sin x = b$ is a trigonometric function of _x_ when _x_ is a radian measure of the angle that intercepts the unit circle at (a, b)

sinusoidal function   a function that has the equation $f(x) = A \sin Bx + C$ or $f(x) = A \cos Bx + C$ where $A \neq 0$ and $B \neq 0$

skewed distribution   one side has lower frequencies than the other side

slope   a number that describes the steepness of a line; the ratio of the vertical change, or rise, to the horizontal change, or run, between any two points on a line

slope of a line   the ratio of the vertical change, or rise, to the horizontal change, or run, between any two points on the line

slope-intercept form of a linear equation   an equation of the form $y = mx + b$ where _m_ is the slope and _b_ is the _y_-intercept of the corresponding line

solution   a value for the variable that makes the equation or open sentence a true statement

solve   to find all the solutions for an equation

sphere   the set of all points in space that are a given distance from a point called the center

square   a parallelogram with four congruent sides and four right angles

square root   a factor of a number that, when multiplied by itself, results in the number

standard deviation a measure of spread of a data set; the standard deviation $s = \sqrt{\dfrac{\Sigma(x - \overline{x})^2}{n - 1}}$ where x is a data value, $\overline{x}$ is the mean of the data set, and n is the number of data values in the set

standard form of a linear equation an equation of the form $Ax + By = C$ where A, B, and C are integers, and A and B are both nonzero

standard form of a polynomial the form of a polynomial in which every term is simplified and its terms are listed by decreasing degree

standard normal curve a probability distribution where the mean is 0, the standard deviation is 1, and the total area under the curve is 1

standard position of an angle an angle on coordinate plane that has its vertex is at the origin and its initial side along the positive horizontal axis

statement a sentence that is either true or false

statistic a measurement that describes a sample

stem leftmost digit of data values in a stem-and-leaf plot

stem-and-leaf plot a data display that lists the last digits (leaves) of the data values to the right of the earlier digits (stems)

step function a function defined using a rule that produces a constant value for each designated interval of the domain

straight angles angles that measure exactly 180°; A straight angle is a line.

strength of association how closely the data points on a scatter plot fit a straight line pattern

strict inequality inequality that uses $<$ or $>$

substitute to replace

sum of the functions f and g
$(f + g)(x) = f(x) + g(x)$

supplementary angles angles with measures that sum to 180°

system of equations a group of two or more equations in the same variables

system of linear equations two or more linear equations with the same variables

system of linear inequalities a set of two or more linear inequalities using the same variables

tangent function $\tan x = \dfrac{\sin x}{\cos x}$; a trigonometric function of x in which x is the radian measure of the angle that intercepts the unit circle at (a, b); The value of x may not result in the cosine being zero.

tangent of an angle the ratio of the length of the leg opposite the angle to the length of the leg adjacent to the angle; abbreviated tan

tangent to a circle a line in the plane of the circle that intersects the circle in exactly one point

terminal side of angle the ray at which the rotation of an angle stops

terms the parts of an expression that are added or subtracted

terms of a sequence the values of a function whose domain is the set of natural numbers; the range of a sequence

theorem a mathematical statement that has been proven to be true

theoretical domain and range of a function the sets of all allowable inputs and outputs

third quartile, Q_3 the median of the upper subset

transformation a one-to-one mapping between two sets of points

translate (a figure) the sliding of a figure in a straight path without rotating or reflecting it

translation a transformation that slides a figure in a straight path without rotation or reflection

transversal a line that intersects two or more lines in a plane

trapezoid a quadrilateral with exactly one pair of parallel sides

triangle a three-sided polygon

trigonometric functions of angle θ $\sin \theta = \dfrac{b}{r}$, $\cos \theta = \dfrac{a}{r}$, $\tan \theta = \dfrac{b}{a}$ $(a \neq 0)$ where (a, b) is a point other than the origin on the terminal side of an angle θ in standard position, and r is the distance $\sqrt{a^2 + b^2}$ from the point to the origin

trigonometric identity an equation containing a trigonometric ratio that is true for all values of the variable

trigonometric ratio the ratio of two sides of a right triangle

trinomial a polynomial with three terms

two-column proof a proof shown in two columns; The first column sows the steps and the second column shows the justification for each step.

two-way table a table that shows data from one sample group as it relates to two different categories

unbounded interval the set of all real numbers on one side of a number, called an endpoint; The endpoint may or may not be included.

uniform distribution a type of symmetric distribution of data sets where all intervals have the same frequency

uniform probability distribution the probability distribution resulting when all values of a random variable X are equally likely to occur

unit circle circle with a radius of one unit

upper limit in sigma notation $\displaystyle\sum_{i=1}^{n} a_i$, the variable n, which indicates the maximum value for the index i

valid argument an argument in which, if the premises are all true, then the conclusion must also be true

variable a symbol that represents a value

variable expression a combination of variables, numbers, and operations

variance a measure of variability of a set relative to its mean; For a data set with values $x_1, x_2, \ldots, x_n$, the variance is $s^2 = \dfrac{\displaystyle\sum_{i=1}^{n}\left(x_i - \overline{x}\right)^2}{n-1}$ where each difference $x_i - \overline{x}$ is called a deviation and s is called the standard deviation

vertex form of a quadratic function $f(x) = a(x - h)^2 + k$ where $a \neq 0$

vertex of a double-napped cone the point where the axis and the generating line of a double-napped cone intersect

vertex of a parabola the highest or lowest point on a parabola that opens down or up

vertex of a polygon a point where the sides of a polygon meet

vertex of a pyramid the common vertex where the triangular faces of a pyramid meet

vertex of an angle the common endpoint of two rays that form an angle

vertex points corner points of the feasible region

vertical angles nonadjacent angles formed by intersecting lines; Vertical angles are congruent.

vertical asymptote the line $x = a$ of the graph of the function f if $f(x)$ approaches ∞ or $-\infty$ as x approaches a, either from the left or the right

vertical line test a test used to determine whether a graphed relation is a function; If the graph is a function, then there is no vertical line that passes through the graph more than once.

volume the measure of the space inside (or the space occupied by) a three-dimensional figure; expressed in cubed units

volume of rectangular prism the product of the rectangular prism's length, width, and height

whole number a number in the set $\{0, 1, 2, 3, \ldots\}$

x-coordinate the first number in an ordered pair

x-intercept the x-coordinate of a point where a graph intersects the x-axis

y-coordinate the second number in an ordered pair

y-intercept the y-coordinate of a point where a graph intersects the y-axis

zeros of a polynomial function f(x) the roots (solutions) of the equation $f(x) = 0$

z-score the number of standard deviations that a data value is from the mean

Symbols

$\mid$	such that	a_n	nth element of a sequence
$\in$	is an element of	π	pi
$\varnothing$ or $\{\ \}$	null or empty set	σ	standard deviation of a population
$\subset$	is a proper subset of	S_n	the sum of the first n terms of a series
$\subseteq$	is a subset of	$\sum\limits_{i=1}^{n} a_i$	the sum from 1 to n of a_i
$\cap$	intersection	$n!$	factorial of a nonnegative integer n
$\cup$	union	$\bar{x}$	sample mean
$-a$	the opposite of a	$\approx$	is approximately equal to
∞	infinity	$=$	is equal to
$\sqrt{}$	radical sign; the principal square root	$\neq$	is not equal to
$\sqrt[n]{x}$	nth root of x	$<$	is less than
i	imaginary unit	$>$	is greater than
$\mathbb{N}$	the set of natural numbers	$\leq$	is less than or equal to
$\mathbb{Z}$	the set of integers	$\geq$	is greater than or equal to
$\mathbb{Q}$	the set of rational numbers	$f(x)$	f is a function of x
$\mathbb{R}$	the set of real numbers	$\lfloor x \rfloor$	greatest integer function; floor function
$\mathbb{I}$	the set of irrational numbers		
$\mathbb{W}$	the set of whole numbers	$\lceil x \rceil$	least integer function; ceiling function
$\mathbb{C}$	the set of complex numbers	$\text{nint}(x)$	nearest integer function; round function
e	base of the natural logarithm		
$\ln x$	logarithm with base e; natural logarithm	$f \circ g$	the composition of function f with function g
$\log x$	logarithm with base 10	f^{-1}	inverse of a function f
$\log_b a$	log base b of a	$|x|$	absolute value of x
		$\{\ldots\}$	description or list of all elements in a set; roster notation

$\{x \mid \text{condition}\}$	the set of all x that satisfy the given condition; set-builder notation	$\perp$	is perpendicular to
		$\therefore$	therefore
$P(A)$	the probability of event A	$\angle$	angle
$P(A \mid B)$	the conditional probability of A given B	$\triangle$	triangle
ϕ	phi; the golden ratio	$\overleftrightarrow{AB}$	line AB
$\prime$	prime	$\overline{AB}$	line segment AB
$^\circ$	degree	$\overrightarrow{AB}$	ray AB
		$m\angle CAB$	measure of angle CAB
$\dots$	continues	$\overset{\frown}{AB}$	arc AB
$\sim$	is similar to	$m\overset{\frown}{AB}$	measure of arc AB
$\cong$	is congruent to		
$\parallel$	is parallel to		

Properties

Real Number Properties

Let a, b, and c be any real numbers.

Addition Property of Equality	If $a = b$, then $a + c = b + c$ and $c + a = c + b$.
Addition Property: Addends with Like Signs	For all $a > 0$ and $b > 0$, $a + b = |a| + |b|$. For all $a < 0$ and $b < 0$, $a + b = -|a| + |b|$.
Addition Property: Addends with Unlike Signs	For all $a > 0$ and $b < 0$, If $|a| > |b|$, then $a + b = |a| - |b|$. If $|a| < |b|$, then $a + b = -|b| - |a|$.
Subtraction Property of Equality	If $a = b$, then $a - c = b - c$.
Substitution Property of Equality	If $a = b$, then a may be replaced with b in any expression or equation.
Multiplication Property of Equality	If $a = b$, then $c \cdot a = c \cdot b$ and $a \cdot c = b \cdot c$.
Division Property of Equality	If $a = b$ and $c \neq 0$, then $\dfrac{a}{c} = \dfrac{b}{c}$.
Distributive Property	$a(b + c) = ab + ac$

	Addition	Multiplication
Commutative Properties	$a + b = b + a$	$a \cdot b = b \cdot a$
Associative Properties	$(a + b) + c = a + (b + c)$	$(a \cdot b) \cdot c = a \cdot (b \cdot c)$
Inverse Properties	$a + (-a) = 0$ and $(-a) + a = 0$	$a \cdot \dfrac{1}{a} = 1$ and $\dfrac{1}{a} \cdot a = 1$, $a \neq 0$
Identity Properties	$a + 0 = a$ and $0 + a = a$	$a \cdot 1 = a$ and $1 \cdot a = a$

Absolute Value Equations

If $|x| = a$ for some positive number a, then $x = a$ or $x = -a$.

Properties of Exponents

Let a and b be nonzero real numbers. Let m and n be integers.

If n is a positive integer, then $a^n = a \cdot a \cdot a \cdot \ldots \cdot a$ (n factors).

Zero Exponent Property	$a^0 = 1, a \neq 0$
Negative Exponent Property	$a^{-m} = \dfrac{1}{a^m}, a \neq 0$
Product of Powers Property	$a^m \cdot a^n = a^{m+n}$

Square Root Properties

For nonnegative values of m, n, and p, if $m < n < p$, then $\sqrt{m} < \sqrt{n} < \sqrt{p}$.

Product Property	For real numbers a and b, $\sqrt{ab} = \sqrt{a} \cdot \sqrt{b}$ and $\sqrt{a} \cdot \sqrt{b} = \sqrt{ab}$.
Quotient Property	For real numbers a and b with $b \neq 0$, $\sqrt{\dfrac{a}{b}} = \dfrac{\sqrt{a}}{\sqrt{b}}$.

Reciprocal Properties

Reciprocal Property of Multiplication	For any nonzero real number a, $a \cdot \dfrac{1}{a} = 1$.

For all nonzero real numbers a and b, the reciprocal of $\dfrac{a}{b}$ is $\dfrac{b}{a}$.

For any nonzero real number a, $\dfrac{1}{-a} = \dfrac{-1}{a} = -\dfrac{1}{a}$.

For all nonzero real numbers a and b, $\dfrac{1}{ab} = \dfrac{1}{a} \cdot \dfrac{1}{b}$.

Division Properties

For any real number a and nonzero real number b, $a \div b = a \cdot \dfrac{1}{b}$.

For all real numbers a and b and nonzero real number c, $a + \dfrac{b}{c} = \dfrac{a}{c} + \dfrac{b}{c}$.

For all $a > 0$ and $b > 0$, $a \div b > 0$.

For all $a < 0$ and $b < 0$, $a \div b > 0$.

For all $a < 0$ and $b > 0$, $a \div b < 0$.

Properties of Order

Comparison Property of Order	If $a > b$, then $b < a$. If $a < b$, then $b > a$.
Transitive Property of Order	If $a > b$ and $b > c$, then $a > c$. If $a < b$ and $b < c$, then $a < c$.
Addition Property of Order	If $a > b$, then $a + c > b + c$. If $a < b$, then $a + c < b + c$.
Subtraction Property of Order	If $a > b$, then $a - c > b - c$. If $a < b$, then $a - c < b - c$.
Multiplication Property of Order, Positive Multiplier	If $a > b$ and $c > 0$, then $ca > cb$ and $ac > bc$. If $a < b$ and $c > 0$, then $ca < cb$ and $ac < bc$.
Multiplication Property of Order, Negative Multiplier	If $a > b$ and $c < 0$, then $ca < cb$ and $ac < bc$. If $a < b$ and $c < 0$, then $ca > cb$ and $ac > bc$.
Division Property of Order, Positive Multiplier	If $a > b$ and $c > 0$, then $\dfrac{a}{c} > \dfrac{b}{c}$. If $a < b$ and $c > 0$, then $\dfrac{a}{c} < \dfrac{b}{c}$.
Division Property of Order, Negative Multiplier	If $a > b$ and $c < 0$, then $\dfrac{a}{c} < \dfrac{b}{c}$. If $a < b$ and $c < 0$, then $\dfrac{a}{c} > \dfrac{b}{c}$.

Comparison Property of Rational Numbers

For nonzero integers a and c and positive integers b and d,

$\dfrac{a}{b} > \dfrac{c}{d}$ if, and only if, $ad > bc$.

$\dfrac{a}{b} < \dfrac{c}{d}$ if, and only if, $ad < bc$.

Properties of Proportions

Let a, b, c, and d be real numbers.

Means-Extremes Product Property	$\dfrac{a}{b} = \dfrac{c}{d}$ if, and only if, $ad = bc$, given that b and d are not 0.
Reciprocal Property	If $\dfrac{a}{b} = \dfrac{c}{d}$, then $\dfrac{b}{a} = \dfrac{d}{c}$, given that a, b, c, and d are all nonzero.

Formulary

Real, Imaginary, and Complex Numbers

RATIONAL EXPONENTS

$$x^{\frac{a}{b}} = \sqrt[b]{x^a}$$

POWERS OF i

$$i = \sqrt{-1}$$
$$i^2 = -1$$
$$i^3 = -i$$
$$i^4 = 1$$

ADDING COMPLEX NUMBERS

For any real a, b, c, and d, if $w = a + bi$ and $z = c + di$, then $w + z = (a + c) + (b + d)i$.

Factoring Patterns

PERFECT SQUARE TRINOMIAL PATTERNS

$$a^2 + 2ab + b^2 = (a + b)^2$$

DIFFERENCE OF SQUARES PATTERNS

$$a^2 - b^2 = (a + b)(a - b)$$

$$a^3 + b^3 = (a + b)(a^2 - ab + b^2)$$

DIFFERENCE OF CUBES

$$a^3 - b^3 = (a - b)(a^2 + ab + b^2)$$

Plane Geometry

CIRCLE

circumference $C = \pi d = 2\pi r$

area $A = \pi r^2$

length of an arc with degree measure m $L = \left(\frac{m}{360°}\right)2\pi r$

equation with center (h, k) on a coordinate plane $(x - h)^2 + (y - k)^2 = r^2$

PARALLELOGRAM

area $A = bh$

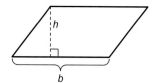

REGULAR POLYGON WITH n SIDES

sum of interior angles $I = (n - 2)180°$

interior angle of regular polygon $i = \dfrac{(n - 2)180°}{n}$

perimeter of regular polygon $P = ns$

area of regular polygon $A = \dfrac{1}{2}aP$

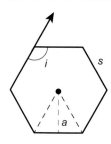

RECTANGLE

area $A = lw$

perimeter $P = 2l + 2w$

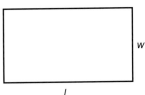

TRAPEZOID

length of midsegment $\text{length} = \dfrac{b_1 + b_2}{2}$

area $A = \dfrac{1}{2}h(b_1 + b_2)$

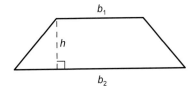

TRIANGLE: GENERAL

sum of interior angles $m\angle A + m\angle B + m\angle C = 180°$

area $A = \dfrac{1}{2}bh$

length of midsegment $\text{length} = \dfrac{1}{2}$ length of parallel side

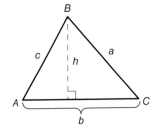

TRIANGLE: RIGHT

Pythagorean theorem $a^2 + b^2 = c^2$

Solid Geometry

CONE

volume $V = \frac{1}{3}Bh = \frac{1}{3}\pi r^2 h$

surface area $S = L + B = \pi r l + \pi r^2$

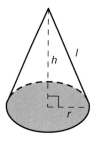

CYLINDER

volume $V = Bh = \pi r^2 h$

surface area $S = L + 2B$

$\ S = 2\pi r h + 2\pi r^2$

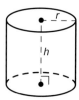

PRISM: CUBE

volume $V = s^3$

surface area $S = 6s^2$

PRISM: GENERAL

volume $V = Bh$

surface area $S = 2B + L$

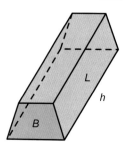

PRISM: RIGHT RECTANGULAR

volume $V = lwh$

surface area $S = 2lw + 2lh + 2wh$

length of diagonal $d = \sqrt{l^2 + w^2 + h^2}$

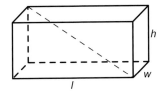

PYRAMID

volume $V = \frac{1}{3}Bh$

surface area $S = \frac{1}{2}lP + B$

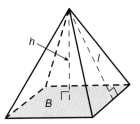

SPHERE

volume $V = \frac{4}{3}\pi r^3$

surface area $S = 4\pi r^2$

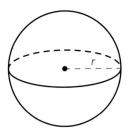

Coordinate Geometry

LINE AND SEGMENT

slope $m = \dfrac{\text{rise}}{\text{run}} = \dfrac{y_2 - y_1}{x_2 - x_1}$

coordinates of midpoint $M = \left(\dfrac{x_1 + x_2}{2}, \dfrac{y_1 + y_2}{2} \right)$

distance $d = \sqrt{(x_2 - x_1)^2 + (y_2 - y_1)^2}$

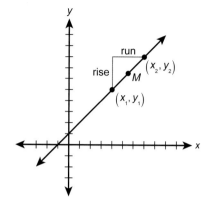

LINEAR EQUATION FORMS

standard $Ax + By = C$

slope-intercept $y = mx + b$

point-slope $y - y_1 = m(x - x_1)$

CIRCLE

equation in graphing form $(x - h)^2 + (y - k)^2 = r^2$

center (h, k) and radius r

PARABOLA GRAPHING FORMS

vertical axis of symmetry
$y - k = a(x - h)^2$ (axis of symmetry $x = h$)

horizontal axis of symmetry
$x - h = a(y - k)^2$ (axis of symmetry $y = k$)

vertex (h, k)

focal distance $f = \dfrac{1}{4a}$

eccentricity $e = 1$

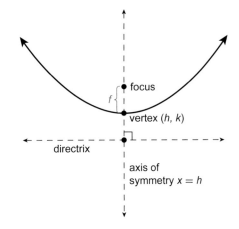

THREE-DIMENSIONAL SPACE

distance between points $\quad d = \sqrt{(x_2 - x_1)^2 + (y_2 - y_1)^2 + (z_2 - z_1)^2}$

coordinates of midpoint $\quad \left(\dfrac{x_1 + x_2}{2}, \dfrac{y_1 + y_2}{2}, \dfrac{z_1 + z_2}{2} \right)$

general equation of a line $\quad Ax + By + Cz = D$

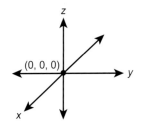

FUNCTIONS

average rate of change $\quad \dfrac{f(b) - f(a)}{b - a}$

axis of symmetry for $f(x) = ax^2 + bx + c \quad x = -\dfrac{b}{2a}$

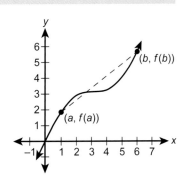

Solving Equations

completing the square   Given the equation $ax^2 + bx = c$, add $\left(\dfrac{b}{2a}\right)^2$ to both sides.

discriminant   Given the equation $ax^2 + bx + c = 0$, the discriminant is $b^2 - 4ac$.

quadratic formula   The solutions of the equation $ax^2 + bx + c = 0$, where $a \neq 0$,

are $x = \dfrac{-b \pm \sqrt{b^2 - 4ac}}{2a}$.

$$x^a \bullet x^b = x^{a+b}$$
$$\frac{x^a}{x^b} = x^{a-b}$$
$$x^0 = 1$$
$$x^1 = x$$

For any $a > 0$ and $b > 0$, $b \neq 1$: $\log_b a = x$ if and only if $b^x = a$.

$$\log mn = \log m + \log n$$
$$\log\left(\frac{m}{n}\right) = \log m - \log n$$
$$\log m^a = a \log m$$

Counting and Probability

$$n! = n \bullet (n-1) \bullet (n-2) \bullet \ldots \bullet 1 \ (n \text{ factors})$$
$$0! = 1$$

SIMPLE THEORETICAL PROBABILITY

$$P(E) = \frac{\text{number of outcomes in event } E}{\text{total number of outcomes in sample space } S} = \frac{n(E)}{n(S)}$$

PROBABILITY OF DEPENDENT EVENTS

$$P(A \text{ and } B) = P(A) \bullet P(B|A)$$

PROBABILITY OF INDEPENDENT EVENTS

$$P(A \text{ and } B) = P(A) \bullet P(B)$$

PROBABILITY OF MUTUALLY EXCLUSIVE EVENTS

$$P(A \text{ or } B) = P(A) + P(B)$$

PROBABILITY OF COMPLEMENTARY EVENTS

$$P(A) = 1 - P(B)$$

EXPERIMENTAL PROBABILITY OF EVENT E

$$P(E) = \frac{\text{number of times event } E \text{ has occurred}}{n}$$

Statistics

MEAN

For a data set with n elements, the mean is

$$\bar{x} = \frac{x_1 + x_1 + \ldots + x_n}{n}.$$

MEDIAN

Arrange the values in order from least to greatest. For an

Odd number of values, use the middle value.

Even number of values, use the average of the middle two values.

MODE

The mode is the value that occurs most often in a set of data. If no one value occurs most often, then there is no mode for the set.

STANDARD DEVIATION

To find the standard deviation s of a data set with n values, where x is the data value and $\bar{x}$ is the mean, use the formula

$$s = \sqrt{\frac{\Sigma(x - \bar{x})^2}{n - 1}}.$$

z-SCORE

If x is a raw data value from a normally distributed data set with mean μ and standard deviation σ, then

$$z = \frac{x - \mu}{\sigma}$$

is the number of standard deviations x is from the mean.

SAMPLING STANDARD DEVIATION

If random samples of size n are taken from a distribution with poplation standard deviation σ, then the sampling distribution will have standard deviation approximately equal to

$$\frac{\sigma}{\sqrt{n}}.$$

STANDARD DEVIATION OF A SAMPLING DISTRIBUTION OF A PROPORTION

If a sample of size n is drawn from a population with proportion p, then the sampling distribution of the proportion will have standard deviation approximately equal to

$$\sqrt{\frac{p(1 - p)}{n}}.$$

Sequences and Series

SEQUENCES: ARITHMETIC

common difference of an arithmetic sequence $d = a_n - a_{n-1}$

iterative rule for an arithmetic sequence $a_n = a_1 + (n-1)d$

recursive rule for an arithmetic sequence $a_n = a_{n-1} + d$

SEQUENCES: GEOMETRIC

common ratio of a geometric sequence $r = \dfrac{a_n}{a_{n-1}}$

iterative rule for a geometric sequence $a_n = a_1 \cdot r^{n-1}$

recursive rule for a geometric sequence $a_n = r \cdot a_{n-1}$

GENERAL FORMULA FOR THE SUM OF A SERIES

sigma notation   The sum of the first n terms of a sequence can be written as

$$S_n = \sum_{i=0}^{n} a_i = a_1 + a_2 + a_3 + \ldots + a_n$$

where i is the index, 1 is the lower limit, and n is the upper limit.

arithmetic series   The nth partial sum of an arithmetic series a with common difference d is

$$S_n = \frac{n}{2}(a_1 + a_2) \text{ or } S_n = \frac{n}{2}\left(2a_1 + (n-1)d\right).$$

geometric series   The nth partial sum of a geometric series a with common ratio r is

$$S_n = \frac{a_1(1 - r^n)}{1 - r}, \text{ or } S_n = \frac{a_1 - a_n r}{1 - r} \text{ where } r \neq 1.$$

Exponential Growth and Decay

EXPONENTIAL DECAY FORMULA

If a quantity is decaying exponentially from initial amount b and with decay rate r, then the amount y remaining after t time periods is

$$y = b(1 - r)^t.$$

EXPONENTIAL GROWTH FORMULA

If a quantity is growing exponentially from the initial amount b where r is the fixed percent expressed as a decimal, then the total amount y after t time periods is

$$y = b(1 + r)^t.$$

COMPOUND INTEREST FORMULA

The total amount A of an investment with initial principal P, earning compound interest at an annual interest rate r and compounded n times per year for t years, is

$$A = P\left(1 + \frac{r}{n}\right)^{nt}.$$

HALF-LIFE FORMULA

The amount y of a radioactive substance after t time periods, where b is the initial amount and h is the half-life, is

$$y = b\left(\frac{1}{2}\right)^{\frac{t}{h}}.$$

Trigonometry

RIGHT TRIANGLE RATIOS

tangent: $\tan A = \dfrac{\text{opposite}}{\text{adjacent}} = \dfrac{a}{b}$

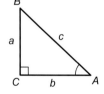

cosine: $\cos A = \dfrac{\text{adjacent}}{\text{hypotenuse}} = \dfrac{b}{c}$

sine: $\sin A = \dfrac{\text{opposite}}{\text{hypotenuse}} = \dfrac{a}{c}$

SPECIAL RIGHT TRIANGLES

Angle measure	Sine	Cosine	Tangent
30°	$\dfrac{1}{2}$	$\dfrac{\sqrt{3}}{2}$	$\dfrac{\sqrt{3}}{3}$
45°	$\dfrac{\sqrt{2}}{2}$	$\dfrac{\sqrt{2}}{2}$	1
60°	$\dfrac{\sqrt{3}}{2}$	$\dfrac{1}{2}$	$\sqrt{3}$

UNIT CIRCLE ON THE COORDINATE PLANE

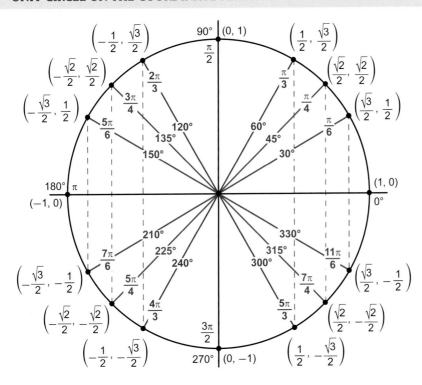

TRIGONOMETRIC IDENTITIES

$$\sin^2 x + \cos^2 x = 1$$

$$\tan x = \frac{\sin x}{\cos x}$$

$$\sin x = \cos(90° - x)$$

$$\cos x = \sin(90° - x)$$

General Applications

DISTANCE

For uniform motion, where d is distance, r is rate, and t is time,

$$d = rt.$$

PROJECTILE MOTION

The height of an object, in meters, after t seconds, with initial vertical velocity v_0 and initial height h_0, is given by

$$h(t) = -4.9t^2 + v_0 t + h_0.$$

The height of an object, in feet, after t seconds, with initial vertical velocity v_0 and initial height h_0, is given by

$$h(t) = -16t^2 + v_0 t + h_0.$$

SIMPLE INTEREST

The amount of simple interest I earned, where P is the principal (amount borrowed, deposited, or invested), r is the annual interest rate, and t is the time in years, is given by

$$I = Prt.$$

TEMPERATURE CONVERSION

$$F = \frac{9}{5}C + 32$$

where F is degrees Fahrenheit and C is degrees Celsius.

Postulates and Theorems

Euclid's Postulates

POSTULATE EUC-1

Any two points can be connected with a line segment.

POSTULATE EUC-2

Any line segment can be extended indefinitely in two directions to make a line.

POSTULATE EUC-3

Given any line segment, a circle can be drawn that has the segment as its radius and one endpoint as its center.

POSTULATE EUC-4

All right angles are equivalent to each other.

POSTULATE EUC-5

Given any straight line and a point not on the line, there is exactly one line through the point that is parallel to the line.

General

POSTULATE GEN-1

Two points determine a line.

POSTULATE GEN-2

Three noncollinear points determine a plane.

Measurement

Ruler Postulate   The points on a line can be numbered so that positive number differences measure distances.

Segment Addition Postulate   If B is between A and C, then $AB + BC = AC$. Also, if $AB + BC = AC$ and A, B, and C are collinear, then B is between A and C.

Segment Congruence Postulate   If two segments have the same length as measured by a fair ruler, then the segments are congruent ($\cong$). Also, if two segments are congruent, then they have the same length as measured by a fair ruler.

Angle Addition Postulate   If point D lies in the interior of $\angle ABC$, then $m\angle ABD + m\angle DBC = m\angle ABC$.

Angle Congruence Postulate   If two angles have the same measure as measured by a protractor, then the angles are congruent. Also, if two angles are congruent, then they have the same measure as measured by a protractor.

Linear Pair Postulate   If two angles form a linear pair, then they are supplementary angles.

Vertical Angles Theorem   If two angles form a pair of vertical angles, then they are congruent.

Parallels

POSTULATE PAR-1

Corresponding Angles Postulate   If two parallel lines are intersected by a transversal, then corresponding angles are congruent.

POSTULATE PAR-2

Converse of the Corresponding Angles Postulate   If two coplanar lines are intersected by a transversal and the corresponding angles are congruent, then the lines are parallel.

THEOREM PAR-1

Alternate Interior Angles Theorem   If two parallel lines are intersected by a transversal, then the alternate interior angles are congruent.

THEOREM PAR-2

Alternate Exterior Angles Theorem   If two parallel lines are intersected by a transversal, then the alternate exterior angles are congruent.

THEOREM PAR-3

Same-Side Interior Angles Theorem   If two parallel lines are intersected by a transversal, then the same-side interior angles are supplementary.

THEOREM PAR-4

Converse of the Alternate Interior Angles Theorem   If two coplanar lines are intersected by a transversal and the alternate interior angles are congruent, then the lines are parallel.

THEOREM PAR-5

Converse of the Alternate Exterior Angles Theorem   If two coplanar lines are intersected by a transversal and the alternate exterior angles are congruent, then the lines are parallel.

THEOREM PAR-6

Converse of the Same-Side Interior Angles Theorem   If two coplanar lines are intersected by a transversal and the same-side interior angles are supplementary, then the lines are parallel.

Lines

Parallel Postulate   Given a line and a point not on the line, there is one and only one line that contains the given point and is parallel to the given line.

If two coplanar lines are perpendicular to ($\perp$) the same line, then the two lines are parallel.

If two coplanar lines are parallel to the same line, then the two lines are parallel.

Coordinate

Parallel Lines Theorem   Two coplanar nonvertical lines are parallel if and only if they have the same slope. Any two vertical lines are parallel.

Perpendicular Lines Theorem   Two coplanar nonvertical lines are perpendicular if and only if the product of their slopes equals -1. Any vertical line is perpendicular to any horizontal line.

Congruence

Polygon Congruence Postulate   Two polygons are congruent if and only if there is a correspondence between their sides and angles so that all pairs of corresponding angles are congruent and all pairs of corresponding sides are congruent.

Side-Side-Side (SSS) Congruence Postulate   If the three sides of one triangle are congruent to the three sides of another triangle, then the two triangles are congruent.

POSTULATE CONG-3

Side-Angle-Side (SAS) Congruence Postulate   If two sides and the included angle in one triangle are congruent to two sides and the included angle in another triangle, then the two triangles are congruent.

POSTULATE CONG-4

Angle-Side-Angle (ASA) Congruence Postulate   If two angles and the included side in one triangle are congruent to two angles and the included side in another triangle, then the two triangles are congruent.

THEOREM CONG-1

Hypotenuse-Leg (HL) Congruence Theorem   If the hypotenuse and a leg of one right triangle are congruent to the hypotenuse and corresponding leg of another right triangle, then the two triangles are congruent.

Triangles

THEOREM TRI-1

Triangle Sum Theorem   The sum of the measures of the interior angles of a triangle is 180°.

THEOREM TRI-2

Exterior Angle Theorem   The measure of an exterior angle of a triangle is equal to the sum of the measures of the remote interior angles.

THEOREM TRI-3

Isosceles Triangle Theorem   If two sides of a triangle are congruent, then the angles opposite those sides are congruent.

THEOREM TRI-4

Converse of the Isosceles Triangle Theorem   If two angles of a triangle are congruent, then the sides opposite those angles are congruent.

Quadrilaterals

THEOREM QUAD-1

In a parallelogram, the opposite sides are congruent.

THEOREM QUAD-2

In a rectangle, the diagonals are congruent.

THEOREM QUAD-3

If two pairs of opposite sides of a quadrilateral are congruent, then the quadrilateral is a parallelogram.

THEOREM QUAD-4

If two opposite sides of a quadrilateral are parallel and congruent, then the quadrilateral is a parallelogram.

THEOREM QUAD-5

If the diagonals of a quadrilateral bisect each other, then the quadrilateral is a parallelogram.

THEOREM QUAD-6

If the diagonals of a parallelogram are congruent, then the parallelogram is a rectangle.

THEOREM QUAD-7

If the diagonals of a parallelogram are perpendicular, then the parallelogram is a rhombus.

THEOREM QUAD-8

If two adjacent sides of a parallelogram are congruent, then the parallelogram is a rhombus.

THEOREM QUAD-9

If the diagonals of a parallelogram bisect the angles of the parallelogram, then the parallelogram is a rhombus.

THEOREM QUAD-10

If one angle of a parallelogram is a right angle, then the parallelogram is a rectangle.

Right Triangles

THEOREM RIGHT-1

Pythagorean Theorem   For all right triangles, the square of the length of the hypotenuse c equals the sum of the squares of the lengths of the legs a and b.

$$c^2 = a^2 + b^2$$

THEOREM RIGHT-2

Converse of the Pythagorean Theorem   If the square of the length of the longest side of a triangle equals the sum of the squares of the lengths of the other two sides, then the triangle is a right triangle.

THEOREM RIGHT-3

45°-45°-90° Triangle Theorem   In any 45°-45°-90° triangle, the length of the hypotenuse is $\sqrt{2}$ times the length of a leg.

THEOREM RIGHT-4

30°-60°-90° Triangle Theorem   In any 30°-60°-90° triangle, the length of the hypotenuse is 2 times the length of the shorter leg, and the length of the longer leg is $\sqrt{3}$ times the length of the shorter leg.

Similarity

POSTULATE SIM-1

Polygon Similarity Postulate   Two polygons are similar if and only if there is a correspondence between their angles and their sides so that all corresponding angles are congruent and all corresponding sides are proportional.

POSTULATE SIM-2

Angle-Angle (AA) Similarity Postulate   If two angles of a triangle are congruent to two angles of another triangle, then the triangles are similar.

COROLLARY SIM-1

Two-Transversal Proportionality Corollary   Three or more parallel lines divide two intersecting transversals proportionally.

THEOREM SIM-1

Side-Side-Side (SSS) Similarity Theorem   If the three sides of a triangle are proportional to the three sides of another triangle, then the triangles are similar.

THEOREM SIM-2

Side-Angle-Side (SAS) Similarity Theorem   If two sides of a triangle are proportional to two sides of another triangle and if their included angles are congruent, then the triangles are similar.

THEOREM SIM-3

Triangle Proportionality Theorem   A line parallel to one side of a triangle divides the other two sides proportionally.

THEOREM SIM-4

Angle Bisector Theorem   An angle bisector of an angle of a triangle divides the opposite side in two segments that are proportional to the other two sides of the triangle.

Circles

COROLLARY CIRC-1

Right-Angle Corollary An angle that is inscribed in a semicircle is a right angle.

COROLLARY CIRC-2

Arc-Intercept Corollary Two inscribed angles that intercept the same arc have the same measure.

COROLLARY CIRC-3

Converse of the Right-Angle Corollary If an inscribed angle is a right angle, then the intercepted arc is a semicircle.

THEOREM CIRC-1

Chords and Arcs Theorem In a circle or in congruent circles, the arcs of congruent chords are congruent.

THEOREM CIRC-2

Converse of the Chords and Arcs Theorem In a circle or in congruent circles, the chords of congruent arcs are congruent.

THEOREM CIRC-3

Tangent Theorem A line that is tangent to a circle is perpendicular to a radius of the circle at the point of tangency.

THEOREM CIRC-4

Converse of the Tangent Theorem A line that is perpendicular to a radius of a circle at its endpoint on the circle is tangent to the circle.

THEOREM CIRC-5

Radius and Chord Theorem   A radius that is perpendicular to a chord of a circle bisects the chord.

THEOREM CIRC-6

Inscribed Angle Theorem   An angle inscribed in a circle has a measure that equals one-half the measure of its intercepted arc.

THEOREM CIRC-7

Inscribed Quadrilateral Theorem   If a quadrilateral is inscribed in a semicircle, then the opposite angles are supplementary.

THEOREM CIRC-8

If a tangent and a secant or chord intersect on a circle at the point of tangency, then the measure of the angle formed equals one-half the measure of the intercepted arc.

THEOREM CIRC-9

The measure of a secant-tangent angle with its vertex outside the circle equals one-half of the difference of the measures of the intercepted arcs.

THEOREM CIRC-10

The measure of an angle that is formed by two secants that intersect in the exterior of a circle equals one-half of the difference of the measures of the intercepted arcs.

THEOREM CIRC-11

The measure of a tangent-tangent angle with its vertex outside the circle equals one-half of the difference of the measures of the intercepted arcs, or the measure of the major arc minus 180°.

THEOREM CIRC-12

The measure of an angle that is formed by two secants or chords that intersect in the interior of a circle equals one-half the sum of the measures of the arcs intercepted by the angle and its vertical angle.

Illustrations Credits

All illustrations © K12 Inc. unless otherwise noted

Front cover Abstract ladybug. © Dobrynina Elena/Shutterstock

Back cover Yellow and pink watercolor. © Dobrynina Elena/Shutterstock

K¹² Summit Curriculum Computer monitor. © antpkr/Shutterstock; Tablet and phone. © Radu Bercan/Shutterstock

Basic Tools, Transformations, Reasoning, and Proof Nationale-Nederlanden, Prague. © tichr/Shutterstock

Congruence and Constructions Delta Solar sculpture. © Dtfoxfoto/Dreamstime

Analytic Geometry *Curiosity* Mars Rover. NASA

Line and Triangle Relationships Double helix spiral staircase. © Baloncici/Dreamstime

Similarity Model trains. © Oleksiy Mark/Shutterstock

Similar Triangle Relationships Navajo Bridge, Arizona. © Michael Zysman/Shutterstock

Area and Volume Bubbles. © Calek/Shutterstock

Circles Ferris wheel. © iStock/Thinkstock

Right Triangle Trigonometry Racing sailboats. © imagIN.gr photography/Shutterstock

Conic Sections Cassegrain antennae. © Josemaria Toscano/Shutterstock

Modeling with Geometry Cruise ship. © Yuriy Chertok/Shutterstock